IN THE
DRAGONS'
DEN

IN THE DRAGONS' DEN

Paul Abbandonato

The publishers wish to acknowledge
the support of the Books Council of Wales.

Cover design: Sion Ilar

ISBN: 978-1-912631-59-9

Published and printed in Wales
on paper from well-maintained forests by
Y Lolfa Cyf., Talybont, Ceredigion SY24 5HE
website www.ylolfa.com
e-mail ylolfa@ylolfa.com
tel 01970 832 304

Contents

Introduction

A football story like no other – from the best seat in the house

'HOW MANY VOLUMES are you going to write, Paul?'

The immediate reaction of the Wales Youth guru who brought through Gareth Bale when I told him of my plans to put pen to paper for a book on my 30-plus years of covering Welsh football.

Brian Flynn's comment was only semi tongue-in-cheek. The beautiful game is littered with extraordinary stories. Leicester City winning the Premier League, Greece the Euros, Wimbledon's Crazy Gang shocking Liverpool's Culture Club in the FA Cup final, a whole array of controversies, bust-ups and even Eric Cantona kung-fu kicks which almost defy logic. However, for sheer drama, longevity, shock, awe, excitement and moments that genuinely stretch credulity, you will struggle to match the truly exhilarating highs and utterly demoralising lows that have happened to the Wales team over the past three decades.

It really has been quite the most amazing rollercoaster ride, with so much happening I could indeed pen a number of volumes as Flynnie suggests. As it is, I've tried to cram it all into this action-packed one, the sub-title of which says everything: 'The scarcely believable stories from 30 years at the sharp end of Welsh football.' Scarcely believable, but very true tales.

We toyed with 'You Couldn't Write It' as the main title, a

play on my role as a journalist, because the stories swing from such extremes even the most visionary of Hollywood script-writers would struggle to make it up. Eventually we settled upon *In The Dragons' Den*, given the uniquely privileged position I have been afforded, witnessing events close-up over that period of time, travelling with the team, creating a bond with players, managers, coaches and top FA of Wales movers and shakers. I'm truly grateful that so many have taken time out to help offer even greater insights for this book, which enables me to take you right inside the dressing room and up into the decision-making corridors of power. It adds up to a remarkable and at times tantalising tale, a football story simply like no other.

Welsh football certainly didn't begin with the Euro 2016 magic carpet ride. There was a very long, and at times excruciatingly painful journey to get there first.

As first a chief soccer writer, and then head of sport of Wales' mainstream newspapers and *Wales Online*, I've been fortunate enough to have a ringside seat during the greatest era in the history of Welsh sport. We've had everything – and then a little bit more on top. Six Nations Grand Slams for Warren Gatland's rugby side; Cardiff City and Swansea City – lower division clubs when I first started reporting – soaring into the Premier League and contesting major Wembley finals; Wrexham and Hollywood. The UEFA Champions League final – between Cristiano Ronaldo's Real Madrid, no less, and Italian aristocrats Juventus – came to the Millennium Stadium. So too FA Cup finals, huge play-off games and the 2012 Olympics.

For a wonderful little period Wales appeared to eclipse even Las Vegas as the boxing capital of the world with a plethora of champions, led by the incomparable Joe Calzaghe, bursting on to the scene. There seemed to be a world title fight staged in Cardiff every couple of months. Even the sport's biggest big prize, world heavyweight title showdowns involving Lennox

Lewis, Frank Bruno and Anthony Joshua, were staged in the Welsh capital. We've witnessed unforgettable Ashes contests at Sophia Gardens, golf's Ryder Cup at the Celtic Manor in Newport, Colin Jackson's domination in athletics, Geraint Thomas winning the Tour de France. The list goes on... and on.

I feel honoured to have reported on everything above during this halcyon period, but nothing, and I do mean nothing, eclipses the eye-popping tales, the rise, fall and dramatic rise again, that we have seen with Welsh football. Some of the stories over those 30 years seem unfathomable. Yet what appears fanciful and far-fetched really did happen.

Gary Speed, a hugely popular young manager bringing an entire nation together after troubled times, transforming the national team, offering a beautiful glimpse into a golden future. Suddenly, all the joy, optimism and hope he created disappeared amid the shock of him taking his own life at the age of 42 with the world apparently at his feet.

Ryan Giggs, another rookie manager doing a brilliant job in creating a hugely exciting team, giving fans reason to smile and look ahead with confidence once more. Suddenly implosion. Those same unfortunate Welsh football bosses were left to pick up the devastating pieces once again.

Yes, Sven-Göran Eriksson, Glenn Hoddle and Sam Allardyce each left the England manager's job under strange circumstances, but it was hardly the same as events surrounding Giggs and Speed, was it?

As superb players, those two had been part of Welsh teams who for many years were the biggest underachievers in world football. While Scotland, Northern Ireland and the Republic of Ireland qualified for World Cups or European Championships, Wales' sides containing a much greater array of stellar names failed time and again, sometimes in the most heartbreaking of fashions at the final hurdle.

Whenever one of those magazine articles is produced about

'The greatest players never to appear at a World Cup', the name of George Best is invariably at number one – but also making the list are the likes of Giggs, Ian Rush, Mark Hughes and Neville Southall. Many others, Speed, Craig Bellamy and Kevin Ratcliffe among them, would have graced that global stage too.

The qualifying hoodoo lasted almost 60 agonising years. Of course, typical of Wales, once they did actually manage to break the decades' old jinx they absolutely wowed not just a nation, but also an entire continent with a Gareth Bale-inspired march all the way to the semi-finals of Euro 2016.

No half-measures with Welsh football. Suddenly they metamorphosed from the team punching most below their weight in the world game to perhaps the biggest over-achievers. From being 117th in the FIFA rankings, below those football forces of Haiti, Mozambique and Guatemala, something Speed once told me he was 'embarrassed about for everybody' and vowed to put right, Wales stormed up to an all-time high of eighth position, ahead of England, Spain, Italy and the Netherlands.

Success-starved Welsh fans, now christened by Bale as 'The Red Wall', were at last able to joyfully join in the jamboree, travelling in their thousands to France for those Euros, enchanting the locals, having the greatest summer they have known after those decades of hurt and envy at watching supporters from the other home countries regularly take part in tournaments. Why them, not us? The bad times we had endured made the good times feel even more special.

I ended up having a Twitter spat with Piers Morgan who was openly scornful that Wales held an open-top bus parade when they didn't even reach the Euro final, let alone win the competition. In defence of the team and supporters I penned an article headlined '200,000 reasons why Piers is wrong'. That is how many lined the streets of Cardiff to celebrate the homecoming. This was little old Wales' equivalent of England winning the 1966 World Cup. When you've waited that long just to qualify...

'Good article,' Piers finally relented, before insisting, 'But you're still wrong!'

Ah well. Guess sometimes you just can't win with Piers. In any case, by then, unlike him, I had become familiar with the extraordinary boom-or-bust nature of the Wales football team. Years earlier they had gone from among the worst watched countries in Europe, with barely 5,000 witnessing a 0–2 Euro defeat to Switzerland at Wrexham's Racecourse Ground, to the best supported as a move to Cardiff's newly built Millennium Stadium saw them regularly pull in record 74,000 crowds. This dramatic turnaround happened in the space of just a few months, yet another example of when things have gone right for Wales they have gone very right; when it's been wrong, it's often bordered on disastrous.

Which other country can you name where the manager challenges his star centre-forward to a fight in front of bewildered team-mates at training? It happened with Bobby Gould and John Hartson though, part of the astounding tales from that particular era which are covered in great detail in this book.

What about the story of Gareth Bale? For many the greatest sportsman Wales has ever produced, talisman, captain, inspiration and top scorer for his country – yet just a year and a bit before making his senior international bow under John Toshack he had been deemed not good enough to be picked for Wales Schools at under-16 level. Seems mind-boggling today, but it is another true story we detail, part of the early struggles a young Bale was having to even make the grade as a professional footballer, let alone one who turned out to be so darned good.

For 30 years Giggs and Bale hogged the bulk of the Wales headlines, for me the greatest two British footballers of their generation. Yes, of course, supporters of Wayne Rooney, Steven

Gerrard, Alan Shearer, David Beckham might beg to differ, but I will sum it up thus – if England had had the brilliance of either Giggs or Bale available to them, they might well have won the World Cup. That is how special those two exceptional talents were in their pomp. Welsh fans were wonderfully privileged to watch them produce some truly dazzling displays in the red No. 11 shirt.

Vincent Peter Jones wasn't in that class as a footballer, of course, but how many other players who have captained their country in a World Cup qualifier go on to make a name for themselves as a Hollywood superstar? *Mean Machine, Snatch* and *X-Men: The Last Stand* are just a few of the blockbusters Vinnie starred in after hanging up his Wales boots.

Again, even Vinnie's own film-makers might have struggled to come up with the plot which saw this out-and-out Cockney tough guy controversially chosen to captain Wales after, supposedly, winning a dressing room vote, try to fire up his team in Wimbledon Crazy Gang spirit by declaring, 'We've gotta give it some' to the Netherlands – then trudge off after a 7–1 thumping which really could have been 20-plus had Neville Southall not produced his greatest game in goal for his country! More like *Gone in 60 Seconds* for Vinnie's World Cup dreams than *Lock, Stock and Two Smoking Wales Barrels*, but I guess things didn't turn out too bad for this particular adopted Welshman.

Giggs, Bale, Big Nev, Speed, Rush, Hughes, John Toshack, even Vinnie – some of the biggest names in world football have been a key part of this quite mind-blowing story which has been three decades in the making and can be told properly for the first time now.

By virtue of my job, I have been fortunate to personally get to know and build working relationships with leading dressing room figures and boardroom powerbrokers over that period of time. Some are happy to be quoted in fresh interviews for this book, others have spoken with anonymity, which I respect – but each and every one of them told me how much they enjoyed our chats, reminiscing about those incredible times. That's the passion, and drama, of Welsh football for you, I guess.

I suppose I have also been lucky enough to transcend two very different eras of sports journalism; the modern, digitally-driven instant online and 24-hour TV approach, but also the generation when newspapers, rather than internet and social media, were king.

Back then, and we're not talking that long ago really, you could sit down with a manager in his office, cup of coffee or bottle of beer in hand, fag sometimes in his, and indulge in a proper chat about the game just gone, or the one coming up. Elements would be on the record, other disclosures would be off the record. You were trusted to keep those confidences, but in doing so were given a proper inside track on the manager's thought process so you were able to write in an informed manner.

It would also be nothing for a tiny handful of us scribes to pop along to Wales training, wait until everyone was finished, and say 'Hey Rushie' or 'Hey Sparky' (the great Mark Hughes' nickname), 'Any chance of a quick word please?' Invariably the players would oblige, standing informally on the side of the pitch to talk to us, their desire to promote Welsh football coming through loud and clear. Or we'd chat over a cup of coffee at the team hotel. Sometimes they might whisper, 'Perhaps you'd better not quote me on that', which we didn't of course, but once more it gave a proper inkling into the real dressing room mindset as we penned our articles for the newspapers.

Flying abroad with the team also opened up opportunities. One good way to relieve boredom while waiting to board the plane at airports, wait for our luggage to arrive at the other end, or indeed during the flight itself, was to sit down with a player or manager and conduct the interview that way. That is how we and the team operated. There was a mutual trust and understanding of how to help one another.

It was certainly a much less structured approach than we have today, where top-table media conferences are stage-managed by press officers (once dubbed 'suppress officers' by Fleet Street legend Peter Jackson of the *Daily Mail*). They are often streamed live on TV or the internet, meaning managers and players are invariably wary about what they actually say. There is no switching between on and off the record in those circumstances. It's obviously not possible. I'm not necessarily arguing the old way was the best – there are certainly bigger online audiences these days – but let's just say the character, and shall we call it 'real' views of individuals came across in a more private setting and you were able to foster the kind of rapports which have certainly held me in good stead in enabling me to write this book.

That doesn't mean it was all jolly-jolly, lovey-dovey before, mind. Anything but. There is probably not a Wales manager I didn't have a run-in with at some point. That goes with the territory, particularly when you're prepared to voice opinions and constructively criticise when necessary if results are going wrong. I even had the great Sir Alex Ferguson on the phone one day, calling our offices to rebut my criticism of Ryan Giggs' constant withdrawals from Wales matches. The thing is though, rarely were grudges held. The co-operation was too important for that. The following day the row would be forgotten, manager, player or official having let off steam, got matters off their chest – and invariably then going out of their way to help by giving you a good old scoop. That was the beauty of having those one-to-ones, I guess, as opposed to the more formal press conference structure of today where it's all-in.

These many highly-placed contacts built up over 30 years in the job have helped offer compelling insight into what really happened behind the scenes during an awe-inspiring period covering the emergence of Giggs as a 17-year-old teen sensation under Terry Yorath in the early 1990s, through the

Bobby Gould, Mark Hughes, John Toshack, Gary Speed, Chris Coleman and Giggs managerial eras, and right to the modern day under Craig Bellamy. I initially planned to write chapters on Cardiff, Swansea, Wrexham, Newport and the League of Wales as well, but quickly came to realise there is already way too much brilliant subject material that needs to be crammed in as it is. Perhaps the club scene is a project for another day.

Mind, maybe I had better keep secret the name of a manager I was told was getting the sack after I was summoned one lunchtime to meet a chairman and vice-chairman in their boardroom. This was major news so, after patiently listening to the reasons for the shock dismissal, I stood up and went to make a telephone call to my office.

'Where are you going,' they asked?

'I've just got time to get this into our final edition,' I said, evening newspapers having different print slots up until around 2pm back then.

'You can't do that,' they replied, a look of sheer panic coming across their faces. 'We haven't even told him yet!'

I felt like responding 'Well you'd better hurry up and do so then', but opted to remain polite! They did tell him though. He was gone within the hour. I certainly hope he found out before our last edition hit the streets.

Sports journalists can often be given that kind of inside track. This book details many of those truly mad, but also very real, behind-the-scenes stories from an astonishing Welsh football tale of trauma, trials, tribulations, triumphs and terrific achievements – as told from the very best seat in the house. At the time, so centrally involved as part of my job, I just went with the flow. Story after story. Good and bad. It's only now, when I look back and package all the tales together for this book, that I realise this really is a quite unique and utterly compelling football story.

I hope you enjoy.

15

1

A scriptwriter couldn't make it up

November 2020 – the bombshell phone call

It was a normal Monday, a quiet start to the week, when the telephone call came that was to shake Welsh football to its core.

For the second time in just a few years.

As Football Association of Wales chief executive Jonathan Ford glanced down at his mobile, an unknown number flashed up. When he answered, Ryan Giggs was on the other end of the line.

'Oh, I just called you,' said Ford, having left a voicemail on Giggs' normal number half an hour earlier asking for his regular weekly catch-up with the Wales manager.

'I need to speak to you too,' Giggs responded.

Then came the bombshell as Giggs explained the arrest by police which was to eventually see him appear in court accused of attacking and controlling his girlfriend Kate Greville and assaulting her sister Emma. Giggs always protested his innocence. In time, almost three years down the line, not guilty verdicts were formally brought in by a judge. In the interim, Giggs' employers were placed in a truly impossible position. Innocent until proven guilty, but clearly unable to carry on as manager of Wales at the same time. This was another of those many unique complications that could only happen to Welsh football, it seems.

As Giggs started to tell Ford of what had occurred at his palatial home on the outskirts of Manchester in late autumn 2020, the magnitude of the situation quickly began to dawn on the FAW boss. 'Oh heck, was my initial reaction,' reflects Ford today as he speaks about the situation for the first time for this book. 'The difficult thing, I quickly realised and explained to Ryan, was the fact that the police had been called.'

Wales, under their go-ahead young manager, were flying at the time. The exciting new-look team Giggs had put together had lost just once in 11 matches, qualified splendidly for the finals of the European Championships and were about to join the elite of France, Spain, Italy and Germany with promotion to the top table of the UEFA Nations League. The future really did look rosy under a rookie boss doing so much to promote the Wales brand and who appeared destined to land a big club job one day. Manchester United perhaps, given the Old Trafford hierarchy have hardly nailed that position properly post Sir Alex Ferguson.

Suddenly, having been given a glimpse into those golden days ahead, it all came crashing down, hope turning to despair. Again.

This wasn't the first time Ford had been rocked by an autumn telephone call about his highly-rated young manager. Nine years earlier, Cheshire Constabulary were on the line to tell him Gary Speed had taken his own life. Speed, like Giggs, was another progressive boss and hugely respected former captain of his country handed his first real managerial chance by Wales who, too, appeared destined for bigger things. The two of them each boasted a 50 per cent winning record – the best ratio of any manager in Wales' history, comfortably clear of the likes of Chris Coleman, John Toshack, Mark Hughes and Terry Yorath. They each achieved the feat by creating a dynamic team built around younger players who very much had the best years in front of them for their country. Things could only continue on a steep upward curve, it appeared, only for the scarcely believable double dose of jolting news to change everything.

Ford had spotted the managerial potential in the two Welsh legends. He was the driving force behind their appointments, confident Giggs and Speed were the perfect ambassadors to sell the Wales dream. On each occasion, he was left to pick up the devastating pieces.

The telephone call Ford received from Giggs, of course, was nowhere near as grave as the one taken earlier from Cheshire Police, but it was pretty bad nonetheless. Because of who he was, this news about Giggs was bound to reach the newspapers. Wales needed to go into crisis mode for the second time in nine years about their manager.

'We knew this would be big, so we convened a board meeting to ensure quick decisions could be made. A group of us, including HR, went up to Ryan's house to see him in person,' recounts Ford. 'Ryan talked us through it all. We could see in his body language how upset he was. Drinks and sandwiches were out, but it was almost like he was too nervous to eat himself. I suppose he was talking to his boss, must have had an inkling that his job might be in jeopardy.

'Ryan was pretty candid as he explained events. Maybe he dampened down one or two bits, I'm not sure. But his barrister was also at the house and he came into the room and told us the exact same story. So I guess Ryan had been as honest with us as he could be. In the circumstances, he handled himself pretty well, but he was clearly gutted. How on earth have I found myself in a position like this, that kind of thing. I suppose that's what we felt about it, too.

'Ryan realised straightaway that, while the police were investigating, it would be a difficult situation for us to navigate. It was just such a shame his career was thrown away with a matter like this. I honestly believe he would have gone on to achieve major things as manager of Wales – and then afterwards at the top of the club game, too.'

Suddenly everything started to move with incredible haste. Within 24 hours of the arrest, news of the alleged altercation at Giggs' house duly broke late at night on *The Sun* newspaper's website. Coincidentally, Giggs was due in Cardiff the following lunchtime to name his squad for the next batch of three back-to-back Wales internationals, looking to carry on the impressive winning run under him.

However, given the gravitas of the accusations and knowing the workings of the FAW hierarchy, I realised this was probably an untenable situation and spent much of that Tuesday morning frantically ringing around my highly placed contacts at the top of Welsh football to find out if Giggs could even carry on in the job. This was a very fast-moving story, some of my calls went straight to answerphone because senior figures were involved in high-level meetings at the time, legal advice being taken all the while.

By late morning it was confirmed to me that Giggs would not be in the dugout for the upcoming matches with the USA, Republic of Ireland and Finland. Thus, shortly before midday, *Wales Online* were able to splash with the headline: 'Ryan Giggs to stand down from Wales' three matches this month after assault allegations.' We explained he was being given what was being dubbed 'special leave', pending a full FAW review into the matter. It was the lead item on the entire website, news as well as sport, and also the main story on the front pages of all the following morning's newspapers in our stable: the *Western Mail, South Wales Echo, North Wales Daily Post* and *Swansea Evening Post*. Jon Ford was correct, this was indeed major news. Very quickly the story was everywhere.

Cue complete and utter chaos. No-one had the first clue what 'special leave' actually meant at this stage. Would Giggs be straight back as manager, as he wanted, once these three games were out of the way? Would the police quickly dismiss the case, as the FAW hoped? Would the Crown Prosecution Service charge him and take him to court, as the FAW dreaded?

If the latter, what would that mean for Giggs' Wales future? Questions, questions, questions, with Ford having to somehow find some answers amid so much uncertainty. Under the principle of due process and fair judgment set out in Magna Carta, Giggs was still an innocent man in the eyes of the law, remember. The wheels of the legal machinery in the United Kingdom can often drag, but this one took months and months, indeed years in the end. It just rumbled on and on. All the while the FAW were left in the dark, placed in a truly impossible position. They wanted to back their manager, he was Ford's man, they had a duty of care. There was also the little matter of the Employment Act of 1996 to consider, which states staff members have 'the right not to be unfairly dismissed'.

However, in the modern world of social media frenzy you can just imagine the backlash Wales would have received from critics the moment Giggs came off gardening leave. The FAW deserved every ounce of sympathy. How could they possibly win here? This was lose-lose, whichever way you looked at it.

'As manager of your country you are seen as a pillar of society, so we knew this was going to be incredibly difficult for us,' says Ford. 'On the one hand Ryan was an innocent man, on the other he was potentially facing charges. It was a real conundrum for us and we had to take proper legal advice and involve HR at every stage.

'In time the brave thing to do, in a way, was probably to tell him, "Ryan you can't do this any more, you need to walk away." But what if he replied, "Well I'm not prepared to walk away." So do you dismiss him? And if we did that, the League Managers Association, their union, would understandably fight tooth and nail for their man. We couldn't just get rid of him. Under British law Ryan was innocent until proven guilty.

'It became a bun fight. We had to manage the entire process with various "what if" scenarios hanging over us. It was such a difficult position to be placed in.

'We needed to find a solution, but there was no right answer here. As the months dragged on, still without news of whether Ryan was actually being charged with anything, we had to walk a tightrope. We told Ryan that if the case went to court, then we'd have a real problem. If he was found guilty it would spell the end. If he was found not guilty then what came out in court might make things a little awkward for us anyway. If it didn't resolve itself, maybe in time Ryan would have to walk away himself. We knew that, so did he deep down I suspect. That way we could focus upon the football and Ryan could focus upon clearing his name in court. One way or another, the writing seemed to be on the wall.'

In the end Giggs did indeed walk away, his number two Rob Page eventually moving from stand-in manager for three games to the full-time job. The fact that amid the impasse Page was caretaker boss for almost two years and fully 26 matches demonstrates the intolerable position Ford and the FAW were placed in. That must be some kind of world record for a caretaker gig.

Giggs was subsequently relieved to have his name cleared at a Manchester Crown Court retrial after the Crown Prosecution Service chose to withdraw the charges, but the whole saga took its toll on him… and Ford. The FAW boss felt this personally as he had pushed hard to bring Giggs on board as manager after Chris Coleman, doing so against a backlash from a section of the Welsh fan base who launched a Twitter campaign with an *#anyonebutgiggs* hashtag.

Much of the angst towards Giggs centred around rumbling disquiet that he didn't play in a single Wales friendly match for nine years – an issue which saw me clash with his formidable Manchester United manager Fergie, which I detail elsewhere in the book (chapter 3). Comparisons on commitment to the Welsh cause are often made with Gareth Bale, the other megastar of a generation who followed Giggs into the Wales red No. 11 shirt.

Bale won 111 caps for his country, Giggs the ridiculously low number of just 64 for a player of his stature. You certainly couldn't envisage him brandishing a flag bearing the slogan, 'Wales. Golf. Man Utd. In That Order', the one Bale famously posed with which, of course, had the words 'Real Madrid' written on it.

The situations at the start, however, were chalk and cheese. Some context is required. Bale went on to dazzle for the Spanish giants and become perhaps the best-ever to play for Wales, but when he first burst through he was a left-back in the Championship with little Southampton. He played under George Burley who, with respect, hardly possessed the fear factor or gravitas of Ferguson when it came to dictating whether players would turn up for international duty or not. Even when Bale moved for big money to Tottenham, he was still initially viewed as a defender, and for a while wasn't even being picked by their manager Harry Redknapp.

Giggs, by contrast, emerged as a teenage attacking genius in a period when British football had been through troubled times during the 1970s and 1980s and was desperately searching for a new superstar to light up the game just as the glitz and glamour of the Premier League kicked in. Enter this Manchester United whizz-kid with a mop of curly dark hair who was being dubbed 'the new George Best' and who received more fan mail letters a week than Princess Diana. The young Giggs transcended football, stories were as likely to appear about him on the showbiz and celebrity pages of the newspapers as in the sports section – and Ferguson didn't particularly like the hype.

As Giggs' manager, he threw a protective arm around his protégé. He didn't want him speaking to the press, nor risking injury in what Fergie believed were 'meaningless' Wales friendly internationals where Ryan would be out of his own vice-like control at Old Trafford. The fact that Giggs was estimated to put 10,000 on a Wales gate at the time – yes, he was that popular – mattered not one jot to Ferguson. His attitude was that simply placed unfair pressure upon Giggs' young shoulders.

Don't let Giggs' longevity as a player, loss of his searing pace as he got older, or the subsequent off-the-field issues detract from just how special a left-winger he was – a dazzling talent who would 'nutmeg' defenders, take on two or three at a time and leave them standing as if stuck in quicksand as he went on to score or create goals. Bale proved to be better for Wales, but Giggs was very much the next-best wonder. His record-breaking Manchester United career speaks for itself. The one thing missing on that glittering CV was playing in the finals of a major tournament for Wales. With Ford pushing his cause hard, he determined to make up for that as manager of his country.

I was accused of showing bias, backing Giggs for the Wales job because of my supposed relationship with him and how it would get me stories. The truth is no journalist really gets close to Ryan Giggs. Yes, I know him professionally, was often supportive, always got on well with his Cardiff-based grandparents Dennis and Margaret – although she certainly turned on me once, giving me a piece of her mind and then slamming the phone down after I'd questioned in print his ongoing withdrawals from those Wales matches. Don't upset Mrs Giggs senior was the lesson I learned that day. Trust me, her fire was fiercer than Fergie's! I know, I've been on the wrong end of both. Such was her desire to protect her grandson, to be fair.

The reality in my case though is that I've always worked better with Giggs' two rivals for the Wales job at the time in 2017, fellow Welsh legend Craig Bellamy and Osian Roberts, who was Chris Coleman's number two mastermind during the magical march to the semi-finals of Euro 2016. Indeed, three years earlier, Bellamy had invited yours truly to his luxury house on the outskirts of Cardiff to announce his sudden retirement from football through me. Now remember, Bellers had never been particularly fond of His Majesty's press, so I guess being taken into his inner circle and asked to reveal this major news for him was indeed an honour. 'Make sure it goes on that Sky Sports tickertape mind,' he laughed, after acknowledging that first we would need to break it via the Welsh media. I was absolutely chuffed when Bellamy did subsequently land the Wales manager's job in the summer of 2024, his FAW boss Noel Mooney describing him to me as 'a football genius' who he is adamant 'will one day become manager of one of the biggest clubs in the world'. That is some statement, but let's hope Mooney's bold prediction comes true because it will mean Bellers has excelled with Wales.

I've always found Osian Roberts to be extremely amenable, a brilliant football mind well worth tapping into. Indeed, Osian has been a terrific help with key sections of this book, particularly in charting the inside story of what really happened behind the scenes in the build up to and during the Euro 2016 fairy story. Any one of Bellamy, Roberts or Giggs would do really well as Wales manager, I determined, but I just felt that the winds were with Ryan at that particular time and, perhaps in the eyes of some, that was misconstrued as bias. In many ways my instincts were proven correct. Giggs was doing a superb job... until the off-field controversy blew up in his face. So the cynics who felt Giggs was an accident waiting to happen were right too, I guess.

I spoke to Ryan about this book and there is no doubt that events have left him with a deep sense of unfinished business with Wales. Yet, despite the not guilty outcome, he wasn't even considered when the manager's job came up again a few years later as the FAW chose to give Bellamy the nod. There were a lot of contenders. High-profile, glamour candidates like Thierry Henry. Low-key figures in club jobs at the time such as Luton's Rob Edwards and even Des Buckingham of little

Oxford United, who was so unknown we had to Google his name. In conducting my research for this book I've learned that Eric Ramsay, the former Manchester United number two under Erik ten Hag, was deemed as the next-best alternative if Bellamy said no.

Yet, while each of those names were considered, Giggs wasn't. He has since quietly returned to the dugout as director of football at Salford City, the club he co-owns with fellow members of the famous Manchester United Youth Class of '92, and only time will tell what level of job he is able to attain again. But the big opportunities Ford feels invariably would have cropped up post-Wales clearly didn't materialise given the timeline of events.

Looking at a parallel universe, Jonathan Ford says: 'If it had not happened, I believe Wales would have done a little bit better at the Covid-delayed Euro 2021 finals with Ryan in charge. He'd then have stayed for the World Cup, done well there too. Then it would have been thank you, I'm off, his career going in a very different trajectory with a decent club job either in the Premier League or at the very least the top end of the Championship.'

November 2011 – the harrowing phone call

The same could have been said for Speed, the subject of an even more catastrophic telephone call Ford was to receive nine years previously, this time early on a Sunday morning. Once again, as with Giggs, Wales' future was starting to look golden under their popular young manager. Speed's team were on a roll, four wins out of five, rampaging up the FIFA rankings in record fashion, wonderful days seemed around the corner. They had just battered Norway 4–1, Gareth Bale and Aaron Ramsey were beginning to razzle-dazzle.

Minutes after that Norwegian thrashing a small group of Welsh soccer scribes gathered in a little huddle around Speed in the press room at Cardiff City Stadium when he shocked us by declaring he would never have got into his own team as a player. Naturally I queried what he was saying, given Speed was Wales' record cap holder for an outfield player at the time, a true giant of the midfield. He doubled down. 'I mean it, I wouldn't have been good enough. There is quality in this side, from goalkeeper through to centre-forward, which exceeds any Welsh team I have known. They are classier players than I was. These are the ones who will qualify Wales. That's the aim.'

Buoyant words, but Speed was clearly excited. The exhilarating performance that day was full of panache, perhaps more akin in style at times to Barcelona or Brazil than a traditional British team. Welsh fans were starting to realise what lay ahead was indeed... well appearing to be a very bright shade of red. They were going to enjoy watching it, too. FAW bosses built upon the feel-good factor by taking out giant advertising slogans, on the buses, at Cardiff Central railway station and other prominent destinations, bearing a picture of Speed with the words: 'Your Manager, Your Team.' You couldn't help but get caught up in the buzz.

Just 15 days later came the news so harrowing that, a bit like Princess Diana and John Lennon, many of us remember where we were upon first hearing of Speed's death. In Ford's case it was via a telephone call from Detective Inspector Peter Lawless of Cheshire Constabulary. Ford wasn't given full details at first, but clearly knew something tragic had occurred when he was asked to ring a different number and give a special case reference code to verify himself. Upon being told what had happened in the garage at Speed's Chester home, Ford quickly realised there was a limited time before the weight of the world was about to fall upon Wales. As Speed's employers they needed to own this tragic news, in conjunction with his widow Louise, before the rumour mill went into overdrive.

How on earth, though, do you deal with an unprecedented situation like this? FAW officials had recently attended a UEFA workshop on crisis management and elements of what was learned during that seminar were now put to use as Ford liaised with his colleagues and Louise before the awful announcement was made late morning on the FAW's official website. Within 20 seconds, the website had crashed.

'Getting hold of people early on a Sunday morning was not the easiest of tasks,' says Ford as he reflects upon that terribly sad day. 'Phones were either off, or people were having a lie-in and not answering. Eventually, when I did track them down the reaction was the same as mine had been when Cheshire Constabulary first rang – shock, disbelief, bewilderment and questions of why and how?

'We were working closely with Louise, who still had family members to tell, before we could press the button on the news. I needed to go for a walk to clear my head, but just before leaving the house I went over to the computer and did a Google news search on Gary. Three completely unrelated stories came up, none to do with his death. Within five minutes of my walk police rang again to say we could release the statement. Upon returning I pressed refresh on the laptop and in that short space of time it had gone from three to more than 100,000. By the end of the day it was nearly 20 million.'

All sorts of conjecture and conclusions immediately started about Speed, many of them ridiculous. Such was the state of shock. Why, why, why? This was something no-one could explain and still can't to this day. The reasons for what he did will never be known.

I knew Gary well myself – as an emerging player, respected captain and then manager of Wales. He never once turned down an interview request, was always polite, courteous, friendly and happy to talk Welsh football. That subject was his passion. 'Nice little scoop you've got there,' he'd invariably say after our chats. A few days earlier I tried to ring Speedo to discuss the 2014 World Cup qualifying draw which had just been made. What did he make of the countries Wales would face? Was he happy with the running order of matches? Would his team get to Brazil and finally end a qualifying hoodoo which stretched back to the Wales World Cup Class of 1958? My call went to voicemail, nothing unusual in that. He was always a man in demand, probably speaking to someone else. I'd try again in a few minutes and this time he'd pick up, I deduced. Only he didn't answer again, nor the third time I tried. Gary Speed clearly had far more pressing issues on his mind. After his death I was asked by a top London publishing company to write a book celebrating his life, called *Gary Speed Remembered*. I hesitated at first, but then realised it would be a lovely way for everyone to recall how special he was. It speaks volumes that so many leading figures in the game, his former managers, team-mates, chairmen, colleagues, and indeed the Wales players he managed, were so willing to speak for hours on end about their fond memories.

At the time, however, Welsh football was plunged into crisis. Perhaps get the tissues out here, because it led to the extraordinary scenario whereby Speed's young son Ed left some of the biggest names in the sport with tears in their eyes at a Wales versus Costa Rica memorial match held in Gary's honour three months after the tragedy. Aged just 14 back then, and wearing a red Wales No. 11 shirt with his dad's name on the back, Ed stood in the home dressing room at Cardiff City Stadium, the very same spot Speed senior had occupied 13 weeks earlier for the thrashing of Norway, to address the Welsh team he had left behind.

'We've lost tonight but don't worry about it too much,' Ed began after the 0–1 defeat. 'My dad always said to me what is important is that you always try your best; as long as you do, that's good enough and you all tried your hardest this evening.' He went on to thank them for 'turning up here tonight and playing for my dad', saying they would get to a major tournament as Speed senior predicted, 'because you're good players'.

With that, young Ed walked around the dressing room and

shook everyone by the hand. Those battle-hardened players were welling up at the moving words they had just heard. They were distraught at the loss of their much-loved manager, but couldn't believe this young boy was being so unbelievably strong and speaking so wonderfully well.

The man placed in charge of the team that night was Speed's trusted deputy, Osian Roberts, who says: 'It was an emotional but perfect speech. We had people in that dressing room who had lost dads or brothers themselves and young Ed's words affected them in different ways. One thing everyone agreed upon was how amazing it was for a 14 year old to stand there in front of them, on a night like this, and be so mature with such a brilliant team talk.

'This had been our first time back in camp without Gary and no coaching manual could tell me what to do. It all had to be on the hoof. I knew Gary wouldn't have wanted us to stand still, that game became part of the mission to reach a major finals, but everyone struggled to cope with the loss. We gathered in the team room and showed the players a video we'd put together. "Here's something to remember him by," we told them. They hugged, linked arms, there were quite a few tears. Everyone had to deal with it their own way. We just tried to be as supportive as possible.

'On the night of the game I remember Ashley Williams saying to me at half-time, "Osh, I can't move my legs out there." He was a top Premier League player, a perfect specimen of a sportsman, yet I realised he was physically affected because he was mentally and emotionally drained by what had happened. The last thing I needed to do was talk tactics; I just told the players they should simply give their best in the most difficult of circumstances imaginable.'

A couple of hours earlier, ahead of kick-off, there was another tearjerker up in the stadium's Redrow Suite hospitality lounge, where many of Speed's old team-mates and former managers for club and country had gathered for the night. Among them were Alan Shearer, Ian Rush, Ryan Giggs, Mark Hughes and Howard Wilkinson, who was Leeds United boss when Speed won the league title with the Elland Road giants in 1992. After Louise thanked them all for attending, young Ed, 13-year-old brother Tom by his side, stood up on a table to tell the 400 guests how much he missed his dad, how his mum's soothing words helped, how he and his brother had been set on the right path by their parents.

The master of ceremonies on the microphone in the banqueting room was Roger Gibbins, a former Cardiff City and Tottenham player. 'Remember his dad had died just three months earlier, yet here was Ed being so courageous,' Gibbins told me. 'It was not just what he said, but how he said it, with composure, a bit of humour when appropriate, and supreme confidence. There were 400 of us in the room that night, some real big names among them. Yet Ed stood up in front of everyone, in circumstances you wouldn't wish upon any 14-year-old boy, and had every single one of us in tears. He must have been hurting like mad inside, but spoke in such a wonderful way. When he finished there was rapturous applause which lasted well over a minute.'

More than a decade on, Ford feels the same way about what Speed would have achieved with Wales, and the path opened up for his future managerial career, as he does with Giggs.

'It's always a little romantic talking about Gary's legacy, I suppose, because he was so young people put him on a pedestal,' reflects Ford. 'However, there is no doubt in my mind he would have been a success, qualified us for the World Cup, taken us on. Gary broke down barriers, started to reinvigorate the team. In my mind the wonderful success we were eventually to achieve at Euro 2016 would have happened even sooner had Gary stayed in charge.'

What Speed made clear was that he wanted an end to the boom-or-bust era he himself had experienced as a player with his country – heart-breakingly close qualifying calls for the

1994 World Cup when Wales lost their final group game to Romania, and the 2004 Euros when Russia won a Millennium Stadium play-off, with years of desolation, desperation and a team in the doldrums in between. The extremes had to end. His plan, which unfortunately Speed never got to see through, was for Wales to finally get over the line by reaching a major finals for the first time in six decades, then to do it again and again. Or at the very least, take everything down to the very last game.

For that to happen, which it suddenly started to do with the regularity Speed had foreseen, Wales needed a new talisman to emerge. Ryan Giggs had dominated the headlines as a player for 16 years. Now it was the turn of his brilliant successor in the red No. 11 shirt to burst to the fore, although even Gareth the Great had some major early struggles.

2

Enter Superman Gareth

DECCA Records famously turned down the Beatles. In other news, Gareth Bale was overlooked for the Wales Schools under-16s team – just a year and a bit before making his record-breaking senior debut under John Toshack.

'Which Fool on the Hill' made that decision, I hear you asking?

Like John, Paul, George and Ringo, Bale didn't go on to do too badly for himself after the snub, did he? The 'Long and Winding Road' to fame, fortune and superstardom. His own 'Ticket to Ride'.

But enough of Beatles songs!

Looking back, it does seem preposterous that, despite being picked by Toshack still seven weeks short of his 17th birthday, Bale was earlier snubbed by those Welsh Schools selectors. In their team that year were Chris Gunter and Neil Taylor, who went on to become long-standing colleagues of Bale at senior level, plus Aaron Ramsey, at 14 a year younger than the rest but who was so special I'm told 'he wanted to take the corners and head them in too!'

There were also a host of others chosen ahead of Bale who simply fell by the football wayside. Thankfully, the brush-off didn't last. Bale was too good to keep down. The moment Toshack spotted that enormous potential, making him Wales' youngest player at the age of just 16 years and 315 days in a friendly win over Trinidad & Tobago, it was the start of an incredible journey which saw Bale go on to become, for many, the greatest footballer to pull on the red shirt.

Others contend Bale has eclipsed rugby union icon Gareth Edwards and undefeated world champion boxer Joe Calzaghe as the most outstanding sports star produced by Wales. I make no judgement on that here. I've had numerous dealings with all three down the decades. Great guys, each fully deserve the legendary status afforded to them and, if truth be told, you could make a case for any of them as Wales' finest. To this day Edwards is still revered as the best rugby player in history, an explosive pocket rocket of a scrum-half who dazzled as Barry John's partner during the Welsh team's 1970s sunshine days and starred when the British Lions won in New Zealand for the only time, and then on their 'Invincibles' tour to South Africa. Calzaghe retired with an unblemished record, 46 wins from 46 fights, world champion at super-middleweight, conquering America on the way. Given the brutal nature of boxing, the ultimate Welsh warrior you might deduce.

Let's just say they make for some trio. Where the three superstars totally differ though is that through their formative years, when already totally dominant in their respective sports at age grade level, Edwards and Calzaghe were always destined for greatness. You couldn't imagine those two not making the Welsh Schools rugby and boxing teams by the time they were 15.

Bale, by contrast, had to do it the hard way and at one stage it really looked like he might struggle to even make it as a footballer. That seems a ludicrous thing to write today doesn't it, when you look back so fondly upon a stunning career which saw Bale become Wales' record cap holder and goal-scorer, the world's most expensive player when he joined Real Madrid for £85million, bag five UEFA Champions League medals and three Spanish La Liga titles. In doing so, he scored 106 goals in 258 Madrid appearances, one every two and a half matches for the biggest club in the world, and in his pomp was being ranked next to Lionel Messi, Cristiano Ronalo and Neymar as among the best players on the planet.

Bale had everything – pace, power, poise, panache. Those left-foot thunderbolts flew into the goal, his blinding speed saw him race beyond bewildered defenders as if they were mere shadows, his heading was imperious, his tackling and work-rate for Wales set an example for all the lesser mortals around him. He scored 41 goals in 111 appearances for his country, many of them as captain. No one man makes a team, but it was Bale who dragged Wales from the doldrums into their golden era as they stunned the football world by reaching those Euro semi-finals in France, and then ended 64 years of World Cup hurt by qualifying for Qatar 2022.

It couldn't have happened without him. His place in football folklore is guaranteed. But... let's rewind to Bale's teenage years, 2004 and 2005, and how things nearly turned out so very differently. Back then, troubled by growth spurts which made it difficult for him to run, train or play without pain, and thus lacking in co-ordination and balance, it really did look touch and go for a while. Squeaky-bum time.

Bale himself has conceded: 'At the age of 14 growing pains almost forced me out of the game. I was quite small, then shot up. My back was out of alignment, meaning I couldn't run properly.'

Those early struggles meant that, by the time Bale was 15, a year before being picked by Toshack at senior level, the Welsh selectors didn't feel he was ready to play for their Victory Shield schools side who participated annually in home internationals against England, Scotland, Northern Ireland and the Republic of Ireland. He was too small for the step-up to international football, they deemed. Others were better options.

For the record, the Bale-less Wales XI that lost to a Daniel Sturridge-inspired England in Llanelli that year, having drawn 2–2 with the Republic in Dublin three weeks earlier, read as follows: R Taylor (Chelsea); S Bantock (Brighton), C Gunter

(Cardiff), R Moon (Plymouth), N Taylor (Wrexham); A Ramsey (Cardiff), I Jones (Southampton), C Jones (Swansea), M Noble (MK Dons), C Jones (unattached); M Jones (Cardiff).

No, I don't know who some of those are, either. But 'I was picked for Wales ahead of Gareth Bale' is not a bad little tale for one or two of them to dine out on.

Now, before we hang the Welsh selectors out to dry too much for deeming that Bale wasn't good enough, chirp that ignoring a player of his talent was evidently an act of football lunacy, reckon these guys couldn't organise anything in a brewery, plus the usual clichés, it should be pointed out his club Southampton also possessed the same significant doubts at the time.

Bale, in fact, was one match away from being released by the south coast club. Just 90 minutes of football. Talk about the course of sporting history being altered!

Southampton had handed out six scholarships, one of them going to Bale's room-mate Theo Walcott, who went on to shine for Arsenal and play 47 times for England, but who, with the greatest of respect, didn't come remotely close to matching his close Welsh friend's achievements in the game. A seventh scholarship was potentially available, with a number of individuals, Bale among them, vying for it. However, back then, as with the Wales Schools management, some of Southampton's coaches had genuine concerns about Bale and feared he might not make the grade.

This little-known tale was outlined brilliantly by Malcolm Elias, then Southampton's Academy head of recruitment, himself a fellow Welshman from Swansea and who more recently worked for Fulham in the Premier League. Sadly, Elias passed away shortly before this book was published, but he was among the many who were a great help to me in offering the inside track – in his case revealing what actually happened with Bale. Elias, it should be stressed, always believed in Gareth and proved to be one of his early mentors, urging him to keep up his spirits during those dark days, but he acknowledged it was a tight call.

'We were probably nine hours away from letting Gareth go as a free agent, which looking back seems utterly daft given what he went on to achieve,' reflected Elias. 'It would have meant circulating his name and his parents' information to Cardiff, Swansea, the Bristol clubs and others in the area. Then Gareth would have had to start afresh, go on trial like thousands of others and try to get himself a scholarship for the following season.

'Fortunately it didn't come to that. Thankfully, we got it right in the end, but it does show how sometimes there can be a thin dividing line in sport.

'Upon reflection it seems so strange that Gareth was only the seventh of the scholars we took on from his age group, that so many doubts were there at the time, but his example also offers hope to every budding young footballer out there. Never give up. Gareth Bale is the best evidence of that.'

Cardiff-born Bale, from the same Whitchurch High School in the Welsh capital also attended by two-times Lions rugby captain Sam Warburton and Tour de France winner Geraint Thomas (now there's a decent little sporting hat-trick for you!), had ended up at Southampton after being spotted by one of their scouts as a nine year old. Rod Ruddick, a jovial guy who in years to come would frequently telephone me to proudly talk about Bale's progress, was in charge of Southampton's satellite academy in Bath and on the lookout for young Welsh talent when he attended an August Bank Holiday six-a-side tournament being held in Newport.

From the moment he set eyes upon 'a little lad a few pitches away who just kept running at people', Ruddick was sold on Bale. 'He was playing for a team called Cardiff Civil Service and was head and shoulders above anyone else at the tournament. I'd never come across anyone else like this before,' Ruddick was to reflect. Upon his recommendation, Southampton acted quickly. Thus, weekly from the age of 11, Bale would head by car across the Severn Bridge with his parents Frank and Debbie to the club's Bath training base. Making the regular 270-mile round trip to Southampton was deemed too much for someone so young, but Bale would head down to the south coast intermittently on Sunday mornings for matches. From the age of 14, Bale would then go to Southampton on day release on a Tuesday, sharing a room with Walcott, the two becoming great mates, training on Wednesday and heading back home to Cardiff that evening.

How his home-town club Cardiff City missed him, and the multi-millions he would have netted the Bluebirds in a transfer fee, is a different matter. It's not the first time. Craig Bellamy is another prodigious talent from the Welsh capital who somehow slipped through the Bluebirds' net. Whatever, even though Bale had an obvious skill-set, doubts persisted among Southampton's hierarchy and they were on the brink of releasing him at 15 years of age, worried this shy Welsh youngster needed to beef up physically and come out of his shell more.

Elias, who with Rod Ruddick always fought Bale's corner against the south coast doubters, told me: 'The thing that really stands out, looking back at those days, is Gareth had lots of growth spurts and, as such, missed an awful lot of football between the ages of 13 to 16. Unfortunately it meant the coaches didn't feel they could make a decision on him getting a full-time scholarship. It seems ridiculous now, doesn't it, but there were extenuating circumstances. He was missing matches and there was a feeling from one or two that he might be a little bit soft.

'February was our cut-off date for scholarships and in Gareth's case it went down to the very last possible day. Doubts persisted over him in the eyes of some. There were question marks over his physicality for professional football. Then we had the game that changed everything.'

That career-defining match Elias talked of was an under-18s fixture between Southampton and Norwich. It took place early in 2005 in the tiny village of Colney, three miles west of Norwich, where the Canaries had their training headquarters. Low key though the occasion was, it turned out to be probably as important a 90 minutes as any Bale went on to star in for Real Madrid or Wales when you look back in terms of what was at stake.

'Gareth knew the importance of the match for his own future,' continued Elias. 'It was everything or nothing, really. He was playing left-back – and was absolutely outstanding. We won 5–1 and he ran the show from start to finish, rampaging up and down that flank. I'd always backed Gareth's corner; he was left-sided, could run for fun, looked like he'd be exceptionally quick in time, possessed wonderful skills. My view was that eventually, once over the growth spurts, we would see the real Gareth Bale. Well, everything I knew Gareth had in his locker came together that day at Norwich. I couldn't have been happier.

'That Saturday his parents had driven up from Cardiff to East Anglia for the make-or-break game. Some journey that, as you can imagine. I made a point of going up to them afterwards, smiled and said, "You make sure you have a good trip home." I couldn't out-and-out tell them Gareth had made it, because others were also in contention for the remaining scholarship. We were not announcing it until the Monday and we had to be fair to everyone. But it was a kind of nudge-nudge, wink-wink from me, I suppose.

'I was so pleased for Frank and Debbie. They were the most unassuming, supportive parents I have known. Despite the doubts over Gareth, they were never pushy, none of the "Well, what's happening with him, then" type of attitude. They stood back and waited for our decision, when perhaps one or two others might have thrown toys out of the pram. Amid the uncertainty Frank and Debbie remained calm and I think that attitude helped Gareth. I'm not going to sit here 20 years on and pretend they weren't concerned. They clearly were, but they also trusted us to make the right call. Fortunately we got there in the end, managed to get Gareth over the line. Looking back, it seems crazy that it went to that final day. But it most certainly did.'

Very quickly, confidence boosted, growth pains behind him and belief now starting to soar, Bale became Southampton's next rising star, making his first-team debut aged just 16 years and 275 days when he featured in a Championship clash versus Millwall in April 2006. The following month, still short of his 17th birthday, he became Wales' youngest player in history. A year later he joined Spurs in a £10million transfer, an extraordinary sum of money back then for a left-back from the Championship.

Ten million reasons right there, you might deduce, to fully vindicate Elias' confidence in a young Bale and the decision belatedly reached by Southampton. Yet, despite the bumper fee, Elias explained he felt a need to keep encouraging Bale because game time wasn't coming readily at White Hart Lane.

'At first, it seemed Spurs also had some doubts. If you remember there was even talk of them offloading him in a couple of transfer windows, maybe sending him out on loan. Nottingham Forest were among the clubs mentioned. Fortunately for Gareth he was injured at the time and nothing happened,' said Elias. 'I spoke to him every week, saying "Believe in yourself Gareth, this is another challenge and you'll eventually thrive up there." Then came that night in the autumn of 2010 when he scored a hat-trick versus Inter Milan in the UEFA Champions League. I was watching that game at home on TV, turned to my wife and said, "Gareth Bale doesn't need me any more. He's cracked it." That's part and parcel of the job for me, recognising when someone requires your help and the point when they don't any longer. The world was now his oyster.'

So it proved, but Elias remained adamant that those testing early days at Southampton, the danger of being released, and being snubbed by Welsh Schools gave Bale the mental resolve required to ensure his talent flourished at the top level for club and country. In sport it's not how you deal with the good times, but how you respond to adversity and pressure situations that defines you. Thus, when Real Madrid fans turned on him in the latter years, when Harry Redknapp wasn't picking him for Tottenham amid talk Bale was a Premier League curse for the club because they failed to win any of his first 24 games, when he needed to step-up to score a crucial free-kick or penalty for Wales, Gareth just took it in his stride. Yes, these were all far more high-profile situations, the pressures and scrutiny intense, but perhaps nothing was quite as challenging for Bale as the danger of being discarded at such a tender age and seeing his football dreams go up in smoke.

Elias explained it thus to me.

'Just for a moment, put yourself in Gareth's position back then. He can't train or play because of the pain the growth spurts are causing. He doesn't know when he is going to be fit, he's going to the physio all the time. Then he sees others, his fellow peers, getting scholarships ahead of him, while he's left to wait and wonder. You cannot underestimate the psychological issues that can cause for someone so young.

'Gareth would have gained immense strength from those experiences. Some get scholarships straightaway, the game of football comes easy to them. Others don't – and in Gareth's case he had to wait until the very last day with that game at Norwich. Then he had to travel all the way back to Cardiff, before coming down to Southampton 48 hours later to hear the news one way or the other. Put that jigsaw together and it's one heck of a psychological drama. Gareth isn't one of those who had it easy, he had to learn the hard way, yet strangely enough in the end that benefited him. When he experienced any tough times in his career, he was able to draw upon the resolve of what happened when he was younger.

'Trust me, after coming through that he was mentally hardened for any challenge. So if there is the pressure of a free-kick versus England, or a big Euro 2016 game, or Champions League final, Gareth could cope. Which he always did.'

In light of Elias' comments, perhaps we shouldn't judge too harshly the management who opted not to pick Bale for Wales Schools. One of the men involved in the coaching set-up at the time was Chris Whitley, a retired head teacher who has represented youth football on the FA of Wales ruling council for more than 30 years. He maintains that Bale was always in the age grade system, part of the squad and highly-rated behind the scenes, but back then he was small compared to the other players. That lack of physique, pain from the growth spurts and missing so much football meant a young Bale's confidence was affected.

'There's no embarrassment from us about not picking Gareth. We didn't feel it would have been right to expose him to too much physicality against the other countries at that stage,' insists Whitley. 'If we had put him into that level of football, in our eyes he'd have struggled and regressed. We just didn't want to ruin him.'

The man in charge of that Welsh Schools team was Aberystwyth-born Rob Sherman, who worked as a director of football in a number of countries throughout the world. He, too, defends the decision to ignore Bale, pointing out how Gareth put on close to 20 kilograms, three stone in old parlance, and five inches in the space of a year. Suddenly the smaller, introverted youngster those Welsh Schools selectors were loathe to throw in with the bigger boys became a Welsh footballing version of *Superman*, rippling muscles, standing tall at over six feet, awesome strength and a return of the blinding pace which once made him the second fastest 50-metre runner in Wales, speed which had temporarily disappeared amid the growth issues. In due course, no less a judge than Usain Bolt, eight times an Olympic sprint gold medal winner, dubbed Bale 'the fastest footballer in the world'.

Well, who's going to argue with the quickest man on earth when it comes to his specialist subject?

Sherman reflects: 'Gareth was always with us in the squad. We knew he was a highly intelligent and gifted player, but when you have parts of your body outgrowing other parts, it causes problems. Your co-ordination and balance goes. Back then England and Northern Ireland were picking the biggest, fittest and strongest players; the game had started to head in that physical direction. We didn't want to risk Gareth in that environment. I explained to him that the growth spurts troubling him at the time were quite normal in lots of teenagers and made sure I encouraged him by stressing, "Don't worry, you'll come through this."

'We always knew he would, it's just that at the time he wasn't able to execute things to the level he wanted to and which we knew he was capable of. It may seem daft to people today that Gareth wasn't picked by us, it's easy to say that, but even Southampton were talking about releasing him. When I first heard of that my immediate response was, "You've got to be joking!" I knew he would become far too good a player for them to be letting go. Once Gareth had grown physically, his confidence started to fly, he suddenly stood out among his peers – and never looked back.'

Indeed he didn't. That was in no small part to the belief afforded in Bale by Wales Youth guru Brian Flynn, the 66-times capped diminutive former midfielder who, standing at just 5ft 3in tall, was a giant of the game in his own way. He played for Leeds United and Burnley, before managing Wrexham during their previous golden period of the early 1990s prior to the more recent involvement of Hollywood owners Ryan Reynolds and Rob McElhenney.

'I don't know what a growth spurt is myself,' laughs little

Brian, as he looks back at those early days of Bale's development. 'But what I do know is that putting on five inches in a year is an awful lot at the age of 15. By the time he was 16/17, Gareth had grown to what he is today.'

In his role as Welsh talent spotter from the years 2004 to 2010, placed in charge of the under-17, under-19 and under-21 teams, Flynn's task was to note and nurture the country's finest teenage footballers and then push them forward into Toshack's senior side. 'Flynn's Fledglings', or 'Tosh's Teens', were to become the nucleus of the Euro Class of 2016, the young guns promoted so early they were still in their mid-twenties, but had already turned into seasoned international footballers by the time those European Championships in France came around.

Before any of them became famous, Flynn told me: 'There are three absolute gems to look out for and write about, Paul. Trust me, they are all going right to the very top.' Now, in sports journalism, there's nothing quite like the feelgood factor of seeing highly gifted young players bursting through, thrilling teens and early twenty-somethings the fans can rally behind. Thus, armed with Flynnie's detailed inside knowledge, I excitedly wrote the story about this talented trio with Welsh football's destiny in their hands.

One of the three was Gareth Bale, another was Aaron Ramsey. The third was a guy called Lewin Nyatanga, a defender who actually preceded Bale as Wales' youngest player, who did win 34 caps for his country, but who had a rather less stellar career, shall we say, at Derby County, Barnsley and Northampton Town.

Ah well, two out of three's not bad, is it?

I wrote a subsequent back page banner headline story for the *Western Mail* about top Premier League clubs offering Cardiff City £1 million for a then 15-year-old Ramsey, who was the jewel in the Welsh club's academy. He really was that good, it appeared, brimful of belief in himself and oozing with ability. Now it's fair to say the *Western Mail*, the national title of Wales, has always been viewed as a rugby newspaper. Anything to do with the oval ball sport was historically a massive selling point for the publication. Hence rugby, rugby, rugby dominated – very often on the front page, never mind the back. Imagine the shock and disbelief then among one or two of our rugby writers when I explained we were leading the following day's paper with a story about an unknown teenage footballer.

'Whaaaat,' was the initial response, followed for a few months by sarcastic, but very much tongue-in-cheek 'How's that Alf Ramsey doing, then' remarks. As it happens, the new Ramsey was actually doing rather well, destined for greatness, and in the years to come his match-winning exploits for Arsenal and Wales ensured he would go on to command many more back page banner headlines.

Not as many as Gareth the Great, though. Bale turned out to be the real 24-carat jewel in the crown, having been first spotted by Flynn at a Welsh under-17s training camp held at the BP Llandarcy sport facilities on the outskirts of Swansea. There were 28 players in total. Bale was only 15 at the time, younger than the others, but he stood out like a beacon as Flynn could barely believe what he was setting eyes upon. He recalls that particular training camp as if it were yesterday.

'We split them into three groups, rotated them around over three days,' starts Flynn. 'After the first day one of the coaches said to me, "He's unbelievable, that Bale. I've never seen anyone like him before." I replied, "You won't believe this either, but he's a left-back." Straightaway I could see he was too good to play in defence, he had everything in his locker and needed to be further forward where he could wreak havoc.

'Gareth then came with us to a four-nation under-17s tournament held in Larnaca – ourselves, Spain, Slovakia and our Cyprus hosts. Gareth dazzled, took that tournament by storm. He absolutely ripped Spain apart.

'Now to save on costs, UEFA encouraged teams to stay at the same hotel, and we were in with the Spanish. They had two senior coaches there, the ones who produced Xavi, Andrés Iniesta, Gerard Piqué and others from that golden Spain generation who went on to win the World Cup and Euros. On the last night they called me over, and via a translator asked, "Do we have your permission to inform Real Madrid and Barcelona about this Gareth Bale youngster?" I told them it wasn't my place to give permission, but that I would tell the Southampton manager, George Burley, not to be too surprised to see Real Madrid and Barcelona scouts turn up at their games.

'These two coaches were employed by the Spanish FA, not Real Madrid or Barca. But because of that tournament, and how well Gareth played, by the time he was 16 or 17 Real Madrid would already have known about him. It was only a matter of time before he signed for them, I guess!

'Word spreads fast in football. Sir Alex Ferguson was never off the phone to me. Every time we had a Wales squad get-together he'd ring to ask how Gareth was faring. He was only doing his job, he was very keen to sign Gareth for Manchester United. Everyone started to look at Gareth. I felt he was too important to play left-back, so we were the first to move him forward. I did that in an under-21s friendly against Cyprus in Port Talbot with the instructions, "Don't come back past halfway. Stay up there, we'll get the ball to you and you just do your stuff."

'He was amazing again that day, so much so that after Gareth joined Tottenham I sent a DVD of our game to Joe Jordan, my old Leeds United team-mate, who was Harry Redknapp's coach at Spurs. "This is worth watching," I told Joe. "He's never going to be a left-back. He needs to play centre-forward or left-wing." Joe showed the DVD to Harry, not too long after Gareth was moved to left-wing, and his position was settled then.'

Bale was still only 16 when that under-21s match against Cyprus, Flynn talks of, took place. For avoidance of doubt, that is a big age difference at that level, but his early troubles were well and truly behind him and he was ready to take on the world. Just 11 days later, 27 May 2006, Bale was appearing for Toshack's senior side against Trinidad & Tobago, eclipsing by a year a record once held by Ryan Giggs as Wales' youngest player. Predictably, he made an immediate impression, setting up Rob Earnshaw's late winner in a 2–1 victory.

The Trinidad game was only a friendly. Flynn's under-21s team had a crunch Euro qualifier of their own at the same time, but he felt Bale had already done enough, despite his tender age, to be elevated into the main set-up under Toshack's tutelage. Throughout his outstanding managerial career, mainly on the Continent, Toshack was never averse to giving youth its head. If you're good enough, you're old enough, was his mantra. He certainly wasn't one of those managers, and there are plenty of them out there, who only wanted to rely upon experienced pros.

Indeed, Tosh once told me a brilliant story of how, when boss of Real Madrid for a second spell at the end of the 1990s, he threw in an unknown, untried and untested 18-year-old goalkeeper for UEFA Champions League and Spanish La Liga games. This infuriated Bernabéu board members, who had paid a substantial sum that summer to sign experienced Argentinian World Cup goalkeeper Albano Bizzarri, and felt Toshack needed to pick him instead. Toshack slated Bizzarri in public, saying he was responsible for errors 'that made me weep' and insisted on giving a debut to this teenager from the Real Madrid Academy who had caught his eye. He refused a request from the club's president, Lorenzo Sanz, to change his mind.

'I can't stand board interference and told the Spanish media there was more chance of a pig flying outside the window than me letting the directors pick my team,' Tosh told me. 'Unfortunately, something got horribly lost in translation, maybe that saying isn't as well known in Spain as it is in the UK. The following day one newspaper printed a picture of a pig flying through the air with the president's head superimposed onto it. They thought I had called the president a pig, which, of course, I hadn't.'

The damage was done though. Shortly afterwards Toshack lost his job. The 18 year old then unknown goalkeeper he had picked, by the way, was called Iker Casillas. He went on to play more than 500 times for Real Madrid, made a record 167 appearances for Spain, captained his country to their 2010 World Cup triumph in South Africa and had won three UEFA Champions League medals by the time he was 23. Maybe Toshack was correct in that judgement call after all.

The Casillas 'pig flying' incident happened in the autumn of 1999. So when just seven years later Flynn told Toshack, 'He's only 16, but I think Gareth Bale needs to come with you, rather than my under-21s,' Toshack had no hesitation in throwing him into the cauldron of senior international football. Bale only had 180 minutes of first-team action with Southampton in the Championship behind him, low-key games against Millwall and Leicester, but he was now to become a fully fledged international.

'I picked a whole host of teenagers and, because they were still learning the game at that age, I'd have to stand on the touchline and tell them what to do, where to go,' recounts Toshack. 'Not with Gareth – he had already gone into the right position before I could say anything to him. He just had this sixth football sense which, coupled with his ability, marked him out for greatness. Often what you see on the training ground, or sometimes in their character, can let these young players down and stop them fulfilling their potential. Not with Gareth, he ticked every box.'

In any case, by this stage Brian Flynn had warned Bale. 'I told Gareth that my neck was on the chopping block if it went wrong. Whenever a player moved up a level I told them to make sure they stayed there, that there could be no coming back down. "If I've recommended you, but you're not good enough at the higher level, then I'm not doing my job properly," I explained to them. I was obviously aware of Gareth's earlier struggles. In fact I think Malcolm Elias sat down with Gareth's parents to tell them how hugely important that Norwich v Southampton game was, and how the message to him might be better coming from them, rather than the club. The only thing I can say is that, right from the moment I set eyes on him, I never had the slightest doubt that Gareth would become one of the very best. Once his body formed, the strength, pace and power appeared, suddenly he was explosive.'

From that Wales debut onwards, there was to be no turning back. A superstar was born. Bale joined Spurs for £10million, then Real Madrid for more than eight times that sum, and, for me anyway, he seemed to be man of the match pretty much whenever he played for Wales. OK, admission time here. Being the top guy that he is, Bale agreed to come along and hand out the trophies at a summer Sunday afternoon presentation function being held by my local Cardiff-based club Lisvane Panthers FC, who have always had a large youth set-up. When you have the kind of job I do, with the connections and contacts it opens up, you're often asked if you can try to get celebrities along to certain events.

Well, in for a penny... no harm in asking the main man himself I guess, was there? What better role model for the Panthers' seven to 16 year olds than the superstar who, like them, used to kick a ball about on the same local parks' pitches, in his case for the Cardiff Civil Service team, before going on to fame. Much to my delight, Bale readily agreed to the request to pop along. He turned up and absolutely charmed the youngsters, staying the best part of three hours, to the very end, to hand out countless trophies to all players in the various age grade teams. Everything done with a beaming smile upon his face too, amid incredible patience shown for the non-stop requests for selfies and autographs.

Forget Gareth Bale the footballer, this was Gareth Bale the

human being. That day, he really could not have been more friendly and accommodating. Well, how could I not be nice to him in print after that? It became something of a standing joke in the office when we were preparing the popular Wales player ratings ahead of a game. 'Shall we put Bale down now as your man of the match again, Abbo?' I'd be asked somewhat sarcastically by my colleagues.

Only I didn't need to be biased – more often than not Bale really was Wales' best player, whoever the opposition, wherever the game, whatever the occasion. Even when he wasn't being picked by Spurs in the early days, or Real Madrid at the end, and thus lacking in match sharpness. These ratings are always the biggest talking point among fans – and indeed often among the players themselves. It's always about opinion. You're far more likely to hear, 'How the heck can you give Player X 8 out of 10, he was rubbish,' than 'That's a brilliant set of ratings.'

So I remember with a smile the criticism I took from some Welsh fans in the aftermath of a World Cup qualifier with Moldova, the first game after the stunning Euro 2016 run, which Wales won 4–0 at Cardiff City Stadium. Joe Allen was magnificent that night, but much to the chagrin, and indeed annoyance of some supporters, I gave Bale man of the match in the newspaper – again.

'You got it wrong. Allen should have been star man, not Bale,' I was being told. Now, wee Joe played well. He was always a key part of Wales' success under Chris Coleman. If Allen wasn't of the standard of Bale and Ramsey, his efforts in a red shirt nonetheless should never be downplayed. But that night, however good Allen was against Moldova, I pointed out the following. Wales' first goal, headed home by Sam Vokes, came from a brilliant Bale cross no-one else on the pitch could have produced. The second, scored by Allen from a corner, came after Bale had tried a spectacular shot from distance that was tipped behind by the goalkeeper. No-one else would have attempted such an audacious effort in the first place, I argued. Wales' third was scored by Bale, a sublime finish past the goalkeeper after a solo run took him clear of the Moldovan defence. No-one else could have done that. The fourth came after Bale was fouled in the penalty box. He got up and coolly slotted home the spot-kick himself.

'So Bale was directly, or indirectly, responsible for every one of Wales' four goals. What's not man of the match about that?' I responded to one of my critics.

'Oh, when you put it like that…'

Of course Bale had ordinary games for Wales – yes, he really did – though they are hard to remember now! When that happened I marked him down, well a teeny bit anyway. But it wasn't often. As a rule of thumb I staunchly backed and talked up Bale from the very early days when first alerted to his talent by Flynn, right through to the end when he was receiving severe flak from Real Madrid fans. For Wales he delivered, his 41 goals not so much surpassing but blowing to smithereens the scoring record previously held by fellow legend Ian Rush.

It would be entirely wrong, of course, to say Bale single-handedly ended Wales' qualifying hoodoo, which stretched right back to the John Charles-led Class of 1958 and the World Cup in Sweden. However, it is also entirely fair to say that the jinx would never have been broken were it not for Bale. He was absolutely instrumental in Wales' march through to the semi-finals of that never-to-be-forgotten Euro 2016 tournament in France. A 'once in a 100 years footballer', as Craig Bellamy described him upon becoming Wales manager himself. How Bellers must have pined for a prime Gareth Bale in his own team.

Bale's impact on that golden period simply cannot be overstated enough. Forget the emotion or opinion, just deal in stone cold facts and figures which amply demonstrate why he was more important to Wales than any other player was to any other nation in Europe. Of the 11 goals Wales scored in finally getting over the qualifying line, Bale netted seven himself and created two others. In other words he was responsible for 82 per cent of the team's total goals. Next on the list, but trailing well behind, was Zlatan Ibrahimović, who scored 11 of Sweden's 19 goals as they reached the Euros, but recorded no assists. Ibra's 58 per cent ratio of Swedish goal involvement was highly impressive in its own right, but Bale eclipsed it by miles. Robert Lewandowski was involved in 48 per cent of Poland's goals, Cristiano Ronaldo 45 per cent of Portugal's, Kevin De Bruyne 33 per cent of Belgium's, and England skipper Wayne Rooney 26 per cent of the Three Lions goals. These were Europe's real big hitters, but they tended to be surrounded by better players. Bale didn't exactly have to do it on his own, but if he hadn't dazzled so brightly it's hard to see how Wales could have.

At the Euro finals Bale scored three times as Chris Coleman's side topped a group containing England, Russia and Slovakia and also had two tournament assists to his name, meaning he was involved in 50 per cent of Wales' ten goals en route to the last four. That was a feat bettered only by Cristiano Ronaldo, whose three goals and three assists gave him a 66 per cent ratio for winners, but low scorers Portugal, and Antoine Griezmann, who scored six and set up two of beaten finalists France's goals for a 61 per cent ratio.

Ronaldo, the best player during the finals, and Griezmann were quite rightly recognised in UEFA's official Team of the Tournament, joined by Welsh duo Aaron Ramsey and Joe Allen. France's Dimitri Payet was chosen ahead of Bale. Judge that as you will, but given the uniqueness of Bale's feats in qualifying as well, we can fairly say no footballer had a bigger impact upon Euro 2016 than the Wales talisman.

When it came to the crunch for the World Cup in 2022, it was Bale who rolled back the years with two stunning goals against Austria in the play-off semi-finals, and whose free-kick resulted in a Ukrainian own goal to send Wales through to Qatar. It is a shame that, at 33 years of age, his body having given up on him (echoes of those early days there), we didn't see the best of Bale on the biggest stage of the lot. He did score Wales' only goal of the tournament, a penalty during a 1–1 draw with the USA, but was largely ineffective in subsequent group defeats to Iran and England as Wales bowed out in somewhat lame fashion.

At least Bale had delivered the World Cup dream though, one which eluded genuine world-class talent preceding him, including Ryan Giggs, Ian Rush, Mark Hughes and Neville Southall, and indeed every Welsh player since the 1950s. Was Bale a better footballer than Giggs? That's a really hard one to call. They may have worn the Wales No. 11 shirt for 30 years between them, but they were actually different types of players. Technically, Giggs was flawless, silky, skilful, graceful, quick and with the ability to adapt his game so he could still hit the heights for serial Premier League title winners Manchester United until he was 40. Giggs was unique at the time. Creative players didn't last that long in the game then. Bale was full of power, pace, fearsome shots and athleticism. What the two men had in common was this knack of getting fans, including grown men and women well into their sixties and seventies, off their seats in excitement and expectation whenever the ball landed at their left foot and they started one of those zig-zag runs at bamboozled defenders.

When it comes to what the two greats achieved in the red of Wales, however, Bale clearly stands apart, his stunning goal and goal assist exploits at key moments of key games comfortably over-riding anything even Giggs achieved. And trust me, despite what some fans rewriting history might have you believe, Giggs had plenty of truly fantastic performances in the red of Wales. To eclipse Ryan, you had to be ultra special. Bale was.

Welsh fans adored Bale. He didn't just possess match-winning ability, he also displayed full-on commitment, drive, desire and passion which became infectious among the lesser team-mates around him. If the world's costliest player could race back 40 yards to put in a crunching tackle for the

Wales cause, then they most certainly could do, too. That was another, somewhat unseen, impact he had on the side. He was a brilliant individual, but a great team player at the same time who led from the front in every sense. Everything put together, it afforded Bale a special love affair with the Welsh public to rival that of any other player with any other set of fans of any other team worldwide. Think Liverpool supporters and Steven Gerrard, Real Madrid followers with Cristiano Ronaldo, Barcelona's love-in with Lionel Messi and that is the kind of deep-rooted, unconditional affection handed to Bale among his own people.

During his latter days with Real Madrid, when he wasn't being picked and found himself hounded by the fans and press, Bale would turn up for Wales and still bedazzle. Some of the Spanish media couldn't comprehend how pulling on that Dragons jersey somehow transformed him from bit part, past his best Real Madrid player, into an international version of Popeye who could still power past defenders and strike stunning goals at the highest level of the lot. Good old Welsh laverbread in the diet rather than spinach, perhaps? The answer to the riddle was rather more simple; Bale felt loved whenever he came home. He couldn't wait to get on the plane. It doesn't matter who you are, how much money you have in the bank, what your status is, we are each human beings with emotions and feelings. Being wanted and encouraged brings the best out in all of us. Bale with Wales is ample evidence of that.

His last years at the Bernabéu, by contrast, were riddled with controversy, some of which Bale perhaps fuelled himself by posing for a photograph with that famous – or should it be infamous – flag. You know the one, bearing the slogan: 'Wales. Golf. Madrid. In That Order.' In other words, his priorities were firstly playing for his country, then having 18 holes of the other sport he excels at, followed by his club very much in third place. The argument from the dressing room goes that what Bale did at Cardiff City Stadium that night was spontaneous, just part of the jubilant celebrations after Wales qualified for Euro 2020 by beating Hungary. One of his team-mates spotted the flag in the crowd, went over to get it and the whole squad posed together. Bale isn't actually holding the banner; Welsh striker Kieffer Moore grips it on one side, a member of the backroom staff the other, but he is right there in the middle, grinning away like the proverbial Cheshire cat.

To Bale, and his colleagues, it was just a bit of fun. Given Real Madrid were paying his reputed salary of £350,000 a week after tax, perhaps it's not surprising it wasn't viewed quite the same way in the Spanish capital. Bale was already having a tough time out there, so this simply cranked up the pressure further. While Welsh fans rejoiced, sang songs about the flag and made replicas of their own, Madrid sports newspaper *MARCA* went on the warpath, slamming Bale with a banner headline declaring: 'Disrespectful. Wrong. Ungrateful. In That Order.' Later on, the same paper would go on to label him 'a parasite who sucked the club's Euros without giving anything in return'.

You could argue Bale brought some of this on himself by his own actions, but the *MARCA* assessment does seem overly harsh given he helped Real Madrid secure 15 trophies during his nine years in Spain, including scoring crucial goals to win Champions League finals against city rivals Atlético Madrid and Liverpool. Unequivocal love in Wales, absolute fury among some in Spain. Coincidence or not, after the flag photograph appeared in media outlets, Bale made only six La Liga starts in the remaining six months of that season, was shipped out on loan to Tottenham the following year and then, in his final Spanish campaign, Real Madrid picked him just seven times in 52 matches, when he scored a solitary goal versus Levante. At least he was given ten Wales games that 2021–22 season – bagging a hat-trick in a World Cup qualifier in Belarus, before delivering those three decisive goal moments that drove Wales through the play-offs against Austria and Ukraine. For good measure he also netted in a Nations League clash with the Netherlands. See what I mean about producing your best when you're feeling wanted?

It may have turned terribly sour for Bale by the end, but his 106 goals and 67 assists from 258 Real Madrid matches compares favourably to the 104 goals and 27 assists by Brazilian legend Ronaldo and 49 goals and 63 assists from French maestro Zinedine Zidane when they were playing for the Spanish giants, albeit their spells with the club were shorter.

Yes, he lags way behind Cristiano Ronaldo, an astonishing 450 goals from 438 games over a ten-year period, but the fact is Bale's strikes place him among the top 20 highest scorers Real Madrid have ever had – a stellar cast list of feted Bernabéu luminaries which also includes Alfredo Di Stéfano, Ferenc Puskás, Karim Benzema, Raúl, Emilio Butragueño, Vinicius Junior and Mexican sensation Hugo Sánchez. Fair to say each and every one of those other icons will always have a special place in the hearts and minds of Real Madrid fans. Bale may or may not after the way it ended with 'Wales. Golf. Madrid', but it demonstrates the company he keeps and perhaps why he, too, should be viewed as something of a legend of the world's biggest football club.

There are obviously way too many brilliant Gareth Bale goals to start charting them all here, but four in particular stand out for me, evidence of the special and, at times, unique talent he possessed. If you get a chance, Google them and watch them on YouTube for yourself. You won't be disappointed. In chronological order, the first came in a Cardiff City Stadium World Cup qualifier against Scotland in October 2012. There was context to that game as Chris Coleman had just lost his first four matches in charge. There was plenty of disquiet from the fans about his appointment, no Welsh manager had been defeated in his first five. Who knows what might have happened to under pressure Coleman and how the course of

Euro 2016 history might have altered, had the Scots managed to hold on to, or build upon, the lead given to them that night by James Morrison. Cometh the hour... Bale equalised with an 81st-minute penalty, then scored what was described in the London media as a 'bombshell winner' when he picked up the ball in the centre circle, drove past a hapless Charlie Adam, and from 25 yards out unleashed an unstoppable thunderbolt into the far top corner of Allan McGregor's net. Given how this took the heat off Coleman, I've seen that described as one of the most significant goals in Welsh football history. I'm not so sure about that, but what is beyond dispute is the sheer quality of the strike.

Goal number two, better than the Scotland one in my opinion, came in a 3–1 win over Iceland in March 2014. Same Cardiff City venue, same solo wonder run, but what makes this one extra special is how Bale wards off ungainly, rugby tackle attempts to stop him. He collects the ball well inside his own half, tight by the right-hand touchline, and pushes it a further 15 yards up the pitch to back his searing pace against Iceland centre-back Sölvi Ottesen. To elude the cumbersome effort to stop him, Bale actually runs off the pitch and has to come back on, from out to in, so he can re-gather possession. Not before Ottesen first tries to stop him by almost grabbing his neck, then when Bale shrugs that off by swiping at his legs. Bale is by the advertising hoardings at this stage and could easily have been badly injured clattering into them, but that strength built up after his formative years holds him in good stead. He shrugs off Ottesen, zeroes in on goal, takes no notice of three other Iceland defenders closing in, shifts the ball to the left and hammers home low into the corner of the net. Stunning. For what it's worth, Bale had also set up Wales' first two goals that night for James Collins and Sam Vokes. Man of the match. Again! Surprise, surprise.

Uncannily, just one month later, Bale scored an almost identical goal – this time in the Copa del Rey final as he bagged an 85th-minute wonder winner for Real Madrid versus a Barcelona team containing Lionel Messi, Neymar, Xavi, Inietsa and a host of Spanish World Cup winners. On this occasion Bale is by the left-hand touchline, again receives the ball inside his own half and once more shifts it several yards up the line to back his pace against Marc Bartra. The Barca defender closes the space, shoving Bale off the pitch and forcing him into the manager's technical area. Bale runs straight for 15 yards and then returns to the playing surface, once again out to in, ahead of the 14-times capped Spanish centre-half. He takes the ball forward a few more strides and calmly slots it into the Barcelona net. The Madrid media and TV commentators go wild. Galactico Gareth has well and truly arrived. Given the magnitude of the match, a Cup final versus your most bitter rivals as opposed to a friendly international, this goal will have meant far more to Bale, but to score two comparable solo wonders like that in the space of a few weeks was truly extraordinary.

The fourth Bale goal I pick out is his more publicised overhead dazzler for Real Madrid against Liverpool in the 2018 UEFA Champions League in Kiev, an effort that has been described as the greatest scored in the showpiece European final. No-one anticipates what Bale is about to do as Marcelo's cross comes into the Liverpool box, but he displays acrobatic athleticism to lift two feet off the ground and send the bicycle-kick goal soaring beyond a bewildered Loris Karius. Jude Bellingham earned rave reviews for his last-gasp overhead effort for England against Slovakia at Euro 2024, but his wasn't even in the same ballpark as Bale's – not as high, not as far out, not as spectacular, not as good. Poor Liverpool keeper Karius was so spooked that he fumbled a 30-yard Bale piledriver that also ended up in the back of the net as Jürgen Klopp's men were beaten 3–1.

There were many, many other Bale crackers of course, for Tottenham, Real Madrid and Wales. I haven't even factored in his famous hat-trick at the San Siro for Spurs against Inter Milan which led to 'Taxi for Maicon' calls, the Brazilian right-back great unable to cope with Bale's solo brilliance. But it's those four aforementioned stunners which stand out the most for me, although a couple of free-kick specials at the Euros will last in the memory too.

The end for Bale was somewhat sudden as he announced his retirement from the game early in 2023 and midway through a contract he had signed to play in Major League Soccer (MLS) with Los Angeles FC. The previous summer, a free agent as his lucrative Real Madrid contract had been run down, Bale was pondering his next move ahead of the World Cup in the winter of 2022. He'd done enough at the top level, Bale decreed. This time it boiled down to a straight choice between his home town club Cardiff City or a move to America. Cardiff fans were understandably hugely excited by the speculation. The club's chairman Mehmet Dalman put together what was described as 'an extremely inventive package' to try to entice Bale home, centred around percentages for sales of replica shirts as well as bumper bonuses should the Wales captain have managed to drive the Bluebirds into the Premier League and keep them there.

Bale was happy with Cardiff's terms, the club weren't having to pay an unaffordable monthly wage. After the travails at Real Madrid this looked a win-win situation for player, fans, club and country as Bale wanted to get himself into tip-top shape for the upcoming World Cup. The fact that the Wales medics were based in the same training HQ as Cardiff, and thus could keep close tabs on Bale ahead of Qatar, would be a bonus. However, that option to move to the USA was also always on the table and MLS certainly wouldn't be as demanding on Bale's body as the hurly-burly of week-in, week-out Championship football. In the end, after careful consideration, Bale telephoned Cardiff's chairman Dalman in person to say that he had decided upon California. It is a measure of the man that, after weeks of negotiations, Bale wanted to deliver the bad news himself, rather than let Dalman hear it from his agent.

Dalman reflected upon it by telling me: 'It's a bit embarrassing for me to admit it, but I thought we'd done a deal with Bale. His agents approached me, they explained Gareth would like to come to Cardiff. I said we'd love to have him at Cardiff. We spent three weeks thrashing out a contract that met with their expectations. Obviously, LAFC came in and he chose to go there, different country, different challenge. We respected that decision. He was professional to deal with, his agents were professional in how they dealt with us. We were disappointed, but I wished Gareth the very best.'

Perhaps, upon announcing the LAFC move, it wasn't the wisest move Bale has made to have photographs taken right by Cardiff's training ground on the outskirts of the Welsh capital. That angered quite a few Bluebirds fans at the time, but the annoyance subsided quickly enough and it doesn't dim Bale's idol status in their eyes. Indeed, there is a giant mural of Bale in the Whitchurch area of Cardiff, just a stone's throw from the street where he grew up, to honour what he has done for the area, the city in general and Wales as a whole. Despite the huge wealth available to Bale and the fame that goes with his exploits, his parents Frank and Debbie never moved away from the modest-looking house they own in a busy through road in Whitchurch. They love the location, have made countless friends and memories, and evidently haven't been interested in uprooting to some luxury £1 million gated abode in the leafy suburbs of the city.

Bale has also never forgotten his Cardiff roots and, despite the fame and fortune, remains as humble and down to earth today as he was when coming to do that trophy presentation for Lisvane Panthers FC many years back. Intriguingly, he said upon retiring that giving up the Wales shirt was 'by far the hardest decision of my career. My journey on the international stage is one that has changed not only my life but who I am.'

Right to the very end it was about that love of the red shirt, which is why Welsh fans in turn love Bale so much.

Back to that question at the beginning of the chapter – who is Wales' greatest sports star? Much as I have the utmost admiration for Gareth Edwards and Joe Calzaghe, and the stunning deeds that handed them unparalleled status in rugby and boxing, it's hard not to come down on the side of Bale given the nature of football as the most popular game on the planet. Soccer has something like five billion fans across the world and the name of Gareth Bale is known throughout all continents. He has helped put Wales on the global map in a way that was beyond even Calzaghe or Edwards. Given he has never had any of those salacious front page headlines in the red-top tabloids, you could argue Bale is the ultimate ambassador for Wales.

Mind, he'd better remain friendly with his old Welsh Youth guru Brian Flynn, to whom Bale owes so much. 'I know his secrets. I keep telling them all "I know too many things about you lot, so you'd better stay nice to me!"' laughs Flynnie.

Gareth, you have been told!

3

Getting the Fergie hairdryer treatment

FRIDAY AFTERNOON IN the *Wales on Sunday* office, we were putting the feature pages to bed for that weekend's newspaper ahead of a busy Saturday of live action when the telephone rang on my desk. Yes, we all had landlines as well as mobiles back then – and mine hardly ever stopped!

'Can I please speak with Paul Abba... Abband... Abbandona...'

It was hardly the first time someone has had difficulty pronouncing my rather long Italian surname, although phonetically it's actually not that difficult. Accustomed to it, I tried to put the caller out of his discomfort by saying, 'This is Paul speaking.'

'Oh, hello Paul. It's Alex Ferguson here.'

'Yeah right, who is it really?' I replied, guessing one of my own Sunday League playing colleagues was attempting what he believed to be a funny prank.

'No, it *is* Alex Ferguson,' came the reply. And it was, too.

The legendary Manchester United manager, the most powerful man in British football at the time, was calling to discuss critical articles I had written about Ryan Giggs missing too many Wales games. Fergie's team had just overcome Porto to secure a UEFA Champions League semi-final spot. Job done, now he wanted to focus on putting the record straight about the growing hoo-hah over Giggs not turning up for Wales friendlies. 'Unfair' criticism, he felt, which was 'upsetting' Ryan.

This was the spring of 1997. At that stage, Giggs had missed 21 out of 39 internationals since making his debut as a 17-year-old superstar-to-be against Germany six years earlier. Over the same period, I pointed out in the newspaper, goalkeeping legend Neville Southall had missed just two. Giggs had recently been absent from yet another friendly, a 0–0 draw with the Republic of Ireland, and a phone poll we ran in the paper saw 63 per cent of fans vote that he should be dropped for a looming World Cup qualifier with Belgium. In hindsight that was naive, Wales needed Giggs more than any other player, but it demonstrated the depth of feeling over his continued absences.

Staunchly supportive of his young protégé ahead of that Belgium game, and aware of the backlash in Wales, Ferguson wasn't having any of it. He was about to catch a short flight, he explained, but would telephone again to discuss the matter properly when he landed. OK. I didn't really expect to hear from him again, Sir Alex declining my request for his mobile number so I might ring him instead. 'No, best I call you,' he stated. To be fair, an hour and a bit later he was back on the line again.

If I didn't exactly get the infamous Fergie hairdryer treatment littered with expletives – the phrase coined by Mark Hughes to describe Sir Alex tearing into his players close-up inside the dressing room – he still took me to task over what I had written, the fuss it had caused, reckoned it was a publicity stunt by us. Fergie also made clear his unease over what he felt were 'meaningless' friendly internationals.

While on the phone, the United boss also got a couple of other Wales concerns off his chest. Because of the hullabaloo surrounding a young Giggs, he deliberately kept him away from media interviews, wanting him to focus only on playing football. Thus Ferguson wasn't best pleased that Wales had put Giggs up in front of the press ahead of one World Cup qualifier, pretty much the first time he had spoken to a group of journalists. The London-based hacks who also covered Wales games understandably lapped it up, focusing upon Giggs' role with Manchester United and holding back publication of their articles until club action returned the following weekend.

'And there we were on the morning of a crucial game when stories about Giggs this, Giggs that appeared. Wales knew I didn't want Ryan speaking to the press,' an exasperated Ferguson told me.

Sir Alex was also less than happy, it became clear, at Giggs being sent on as a late substitute for his 1991 Wales debut against world champions Germany when Terry Yorath's Dragons were already being battered by four goals in Nuremberg.

'What good do you think that did the boy?' he said, voice rising. When I bravely, or maybe that should be stupidly, countered, 'He was the best player on the pitch too, mind Alex,' I could sense a bit of steam on the other end of the line. 'That may be so, but it was still wrong,' came the blunt response. Or something on those lines, anyhow.

Here's the rub though. Having got his angst off his chest, Ferguson then turned into 'on the record' mode and started to explain plausibly, professionally, politely and for publication why Giggs was missing so many Wales matches. He was charm personified and, dare I admit it, even persuasive in his arguments. Giggs had hamstring issues, Ferguson stressed, and was susceptible to problems because of the type of flier down the wing he was. He needed to be rested from certain matches, including Manchester United ones, to prevent him from sustaining major damage and wrecking his career. Friendly international results didn't really matter, he argued, emphasising he had told England exactly the same thing, but Giggs would always be made available for World Cup or European Championship competitive fixtures.

Remember, this was the start of United's greatest era when

Ferguson and Giggs went on to each win a record 13 Premier League titles, countless Cups and eventually conquer Europe, the first time for Manchester United since George Best and Bobby Charlton back in 1968. So of Giggs missing the Republic of Ireland match, a 0–0 February bore-draw played in front of a tiny Cardiff Arms Park crowd, Ferguson argued: 'We had crucial Champions League games coming up where we were playing for millions of pounds. Was I supposed to risk Ryan in a friendly international before 4,000 people? I don't think so.'

The attendance was actually recorded at 7,000, but you get the drift.

'This may sound selfish, but put yourself in my position,' continued Fergie. 'If Manchester United lose a game we get slaughtered on the front pages of the newspapers. I get castigated, the players get hammered. We also have the biggest support in the world, people pay a lot of money to watch us play. Those United supporters would expect me to put the club first. I think the public debate that has been created in Wales is terribly unfair. Ryan is very upset about it and you can understand why. But I told Ryan he can look anybody in Wales in the eye. He has done nothing wrong.'

In full flow at this stage, Ferguson went on: 'I've a great admiration for the Welsh people. I'm a Celt myself and have the same viewpoint, parochialism, patriotism. I respect all of that and will do what I can to help Welsh football. There is nobody who wants Ryan to do well for Wales more than me.'

When I pointed out some fans had demanded their ticket money back because of Giggs withdrawing yet again, Ferguson countered: 'Is it fair that Ryan is the biggest seller for Welsh football? Because, if so, it puts a terrible responsibility upon Ryan and myself. I'd have to let him play every time, but what would the Welsh public think about paying their money and then seeing him come off injured after ten minutes? It's not just Wales. He's missed a lot of games for Manchester United, too. I have the list right here in front of me.'

Clearly Ferguson had forearmed himself with the relevant statistics before telephoning me to make his case. One of those fixtures Giggs had just missed was the Champions League quarter-final in Porto. Ferguson was clearly concerned about those Giggs hamstrings. Yet, ironically, after forcibly and indeed impressively arguing his corner, Ferguson then stated Giggs would travel down to Cardiff for the game against Belgium the following weekend, even though not 100 per cent.

'After the fuss that's been kicked up down there I have no option but to let Ryan go with Wales this time,' he explained. 'They have seven days to get him fit.'

England were also playing and Ferguson withdrew David Beckham and Gary Neville from Three Lions duty, but Giggs was made available for Wales. Which, of course, prompted my editor to publish a banner headline in the newspaper declaring, 'Victory! We took on Fergie over Giggs for Wales – and won', as we reported what he said about the whole saga. Looking back, I'm not sure it was quite as simple as that. Fergie was his own man, he didn't tend to bend to newspapers. However, it was certainly fascinating to hear the Man Utd chief, for the first time in public, put forward his own viewpoint about Giggs not playing for Wales and attempt to take the heat out of the situation amid evident supporter discontent. Suddenly you could begin to understand the Old Trafford reasoning, even if you didn't agree with it.

Actually, this was the second time I had 'clashed', if that is the correct word, with Fergie over a young Giggs. The previous occasion was during a packed Wembley press conference after Manchester United had lost a League Cup final to Aston Villa in the spring of 1994. Giggs, just 20, had been substituted midway through the second half by Lee Sharpe. Given he was all the rage back then, and keen for a Welsh angle on the final for my newspaper, when the opportunity arose I piped up with a question of my own. 'Alex, can I ask why you took Ryan Giggs off so early?'

Ferguson just looked at me and replied bluntly, 'Did you not see the game?'

Another journalist from one of the London tabloids jumped in to support me, asking if Wembley occasions overawed Giggs a little at that embryonic stage of his career? A theory which Ferguson dismissed, of course. The questioning on other Manchester United matters continued for a further ten minutes or more, at which point Ferguson got up from the top table to leave – but upon doing so he fixed his eyes upon yours truly again. Now in this room there must have been close to 100 football journos, plus all the bright lights from TV and press cameras creating a glare. I was seated right in the middle of the throng, but Ferguson picked me out to make a point of saying: 'That was off the record about Ryan, by the way.' Wag of the finger. Then he was away.

Of course, with so many writers present nothing could be off-limits at such a public gathering, but it was Ferguson's way of looking after Giggs again. He didn't want banner headlines along the lines of why everyone should have seen Ryan was playing poorly so he had to be substituted. Nip it in the bud. Which Sir Alex expertly did. As per usual, I guess.

It is fair to say that from the moment he made that 1991 debut in Germany as Wales' youngest player, until he hung up his international boots in 2007, Giggs tended to dominate the football agenda. Initially that centred around whether he would or wouldn't turn up for certain matches, an issue that started under Terry Yorath, the first Wales manager I had dealings with. For context, perhaps it is important to stress that Wales then was a galaxy away from the set-up players are accustomed to these days. The FAW wasn't exactly awash with money. There wasn't the army of staff, medics, physios, sports scientists and dieticians more recent regimes have been able to call upon. Ferguson, accustomed to the best at Manchester United, knew this, of course. So did Giggs.

The rules were somewhat different, too. Players didn't travel down to be assessed by the Welsh medics and then return to their club if deemed not fit. They just didn't come. Wales had to ensure that if they were picking Giggs, including earlier on at age grade level, Manchester United knew exactly what was happening. Thus the task of informing Ferguson fell to the FAW's commercial chief, Malcolm Stammers.

He takes up the story. 'I'd go into the office between 7am to 7.15, knowing Ferguson was always at the training ground early. Terry Yorath gave me his direct number and I'd ring. "Good morning Mr Ferguson, it's the Welsh FA here. Just to let you know that Ryan has been selected for Wales' next game and the paperwork will be sent up shortly." The response tended to be on the lines of "I will decide whether he's selected or not." And that's how it went. Ferguson's priority was clearly Manchester United, which was fair enough, but we had to make sure that the phone call was made and they couldn't say they had not been properly informed.'

Stammers continues: 'Should Ryan have been tougher with Ferguson? Let's put it this way – he had to manage not only himself but also his club manager, who as we know could be rather persuasive! Ferguson didn't want burnout for Ryan by the age of 26. Fergie and Ryan will point to the fact that he played until he was 40 as evidence they did the correct thing back in those early days. It's fair to say Terry used to find it very frustrating, but he had been a club manager himself and kind of understood Fergie's stance.'

Obviously a hefty number of Dragons fans didn't agree. Even close to 30 years on, when Giggs was named as Wales manager, his absence from friendly matches for fully nine years – that's a pretty chunky time, for avoidance of doubt – was used as a stick with which to beat him. Proves he's not committed to Wales, so the claims went.

Yet, rewind three decades and the Welsh scene was very, very different. Crowds at international games were small; there wasn't the massive post-Euro 2016 interest or publicity of the modern era. Finances were a day-to-day struggle and the national team at a low ebb. The top Welsh clubs, Cardiff City, Swansea City, Wrexham and Newport County were bobbing up and down between the bottom divisions. Malcolm Stammers even talks of how the players had only two sets of training gear – meaning much-loved kit-man Ron Stipfall would take one lot home with him to wash so at least the Welsh stars would have clean shirts, shorts and socks the following day. We're not talking that long ago in the grand scheme of things, but it was a zillion miles from how Wales players are treated today. The team didn't even have a regular home, flitting between Cardiff's Ninian Park, Wrexham's Racecourse Ground and Swansea's Vetch Field for matches.

It was against this difficult backdrop, and after years of near misses in the 1980s under the management of Mike England, that Yorath set about trying to revive the fortunes of Welsh football. He succeeded to a large degree – albeit it ended in rather ignominious fashion, which we'll come on to.

FA of Wales bosses felt Yorath had the characteristics required to become a top manager of his country. TY, as we called him, was a natural leader of men. He'd skippered Wales in 42 of the 59 caps won playing in red as a midfield dynamo – ferocious in the tackle, accomplished on the ball, hard as nails, not the type to take a backward step. Yorath commanded respect, having made more than 140 appearances during the Leeds United heyday of the 1960s and '70s, winning the League and appearing in major European and domestic finals. He may have played second fiddle to Billy Bremner and Johnny Giles, but he wouldn't have lasted so many years under Don Revie if he couldn't play. He went on to star for Tottenham too, acting as midfield minder to the more stellar talents of Glenn Hoddle, Ossie Ardiles and Ricky Villa.

TY was a quiet, reserved individual, very down to earth and never particularly fussed on the trappings that went with the game, but his Welshness burned as deep as that of anybody.

He epitomised the spirit of Wales, *hwyl*, passion, the bearing of the Welsh crest. So once Yorath started to make a managerial mark, winning promotion with Swansea in his second season, it was somewhat inevitable the FAW would come calling. At first Yorath did the job part-time, while also managing at club level, but he was dealt the rawest of raw hands. For Italia '90 World Cup qualifying, Yorath's men were pitched in with the star-studded Netherlands, who had just won the 1988 European Championships with Ruud Gullit, Marco van Basten and Ronald Koeman among those dazzling for the men in orange, and the equally brilliant West Germany, who boasted the likes of Jürgen Klinsmann, Lothar Matthäus and Thomas Hässler.

The reigning Euro champs and the German powerhouses who went on to win that World Cup. Wales had no chance, albeit they only lost 1–0 to a late Gullit goal in Amsterdam and 2–1 at home to the Dutch. The games against the Germans were even closer, 0–0 in Cardiff and a 2–1 loss away, but those two fixtures each had a significant impact on the way forward.

It was that last qualifier in Cologne, in November 1989, that made people sit up, take notice, and start to realise there was a shape, organisation and threat to this Welsh side under Yorath. Perhaps the team could actually go places. Wales had the audacity to take the lead through Malcolm Allen, giving the Germans an enormous fright before Rudi Völler and Thomas Hässler goals saw them squeak home to secure second spot in the table and a passage to Italia '90 as one of the best runners-up.

The same Germans, of course, would lift the trophy just seven months later, famously disposing of Bobby Robson's England in the semi-finals, Gazza's tears and all that. Yorath's Wales had twice pushed them to the brink; Germany were that close to not even qualifying. In defeat then, there was hope for the future as Yorath looked ahead to the 1992 European Championships in Sweden and the 1994 World Cup in the USA. Wales suddenly had a new weapon as well for those games,

Cardiff Arms Park, the iconic home of Welsh rugby, situated on the banks of the River Taff right in the middle of the city.

The FAW had experimented with taking that aforementioned 0–0 home qualifier with West Germany to the 60,000-capacity rugby ground, rather than the traditional, but much smaller, club venues they had used for decades. The players loved the change. Instead of running out in front of crowds as low as 3,000, suddenly they were being roared on by 30,000-plus passionate supporters. It made a significant difference in every way. There were some complaints about a five-figure sum being lost to the oval ball game for hire of the ground from the Welsh Rugby Union, but the FAW hierarchy knew they were able to make substantially more than that from gate receipts and other revenue. So plans were put in place to try to make Cardiff Arms Park their permanent home. The seeds were sown, believe it or not, at the England versus India cricket Test match at Lord's in July 1990, the game where Graham Gooch hit his legendary first innings score of 333.

The FAW's boss Alun Evans and their commercial chief Malcolm Stammers were invited to a hospitality box by a London-based company who displayed advertising hoardings at big sports events. They had got wind that Glanmor Griffiths, the WRU's chairman, was also attending. So Big Al, as Evans was known to us in Welsh football, and Stammers craftily set about finding out which Cardiff to Paddington train Glanmor would be travelling on. They booked tickets for the same service, sat at a table with Glanmor and spent much of the two-hour journey discussing terms and conditions about how to make Cardiff Arms Park their official new home, conversations which spilled over into the cricket. Glanmor, like Big Al, was something of a far thinker in his own field. The FAW duo sensed he already had a vision in his head about a new state-of-the-art bigger ground for the Wales rugby team. In due course, the world-class Millennium Stadium was built, at a cost of £121million compared to the £798million for Wembley, bringing FA Cup finals, world heavyweight title fights and concerts by pop's biggest megastars to the Welsh capital. Glanmor knew there was more likelihood of getting grant monies from the relevant authorities if the new ground was multi-purpose, rather than just for rugby, so having Wales football on board at the old Arms Park, and subsequently at the Millennium Stadium, suited him as much as it did the FAW.

It was a big decision to move away from the more traditional football venues, but Ninian Park, The Racecourse and The Vetch, while iconic in their own right, no longer had facilities or a capacity fitting for top international football. It would be another two decades before Cardiff City Stadium was built. As well as greater ticket revenue, the FAW knew Cardiff Arms Park, with a larger crowd, meant bigger opportunities for corporate hospitality and advertising. Commercially it made sense, the players were happy, there was a decent playing surface – unlike when Wales were to move to the Millennium Stadium itself – more fans would attend matches. It was win-win all round. Wales were nomadic no more. Cardiff Arms Park was their new home. Could they now turn it into a fortress?

It was just Yorath's bad luck again then that Wales should be drawn with those dreaded Germans once more in qualifying for Euro '92. A German side who were not only now world champions, but also boosted by the best from East Germany after the fall of the Berlin Wall. To compound matters, a gifted Belgium team marshalled by their world-class playmaker Enzo Scifo, the Kevin De Bruyne of his day, were also in the group – and only one country would qualify for the finals in Sweden.

Wales started with an Arms Park roar, Ian Rush, Mark Hughes and Dean Saunders an unstoppable goal force as they blew aside the Belgians 3–1 in October 1990. Yorath had fearsome strike power at his disposal, so potent that Hughes, that warrior and world-class front man for Manchester United, Barcelona and Bayern Munich, was forced to drop into midfield to ensure Rush and Saunders could be accommodated further forward. Of the three, Sparky was the one with the more rounded game suited to facing and making the play with ball at feet, the other two using their blinding speed to spin and race into space beyond defenders. 'I started my career as a midfielder and it's no problem whatsoever,' Sparky told me at the time as he happily addressed his shock change of position. He would play anywhere for his country. Ego, and any notion of demanding to be picked where he really wanted, went out of the window for the wider cause.

You sensed Yorath's men were just starting to get on a roll. They beat Luxembourg away 0–1, Rush again scoring, and headed to Brussels top of the table and brimming with confidence for the return fixture with the Belgians towards the end of March 1991. But, as this book so amply demonstrates throughout, Welsh football simply isn't Welsh football without a bombshell – or six. This time it was yours truly who was somewhat innocently caught up in the controversy that rocked Yorath and the team ahead of that crunch game.

Yorath was combining his full-time club job at Swansea with his part-time role as Wales boss. It seemed fine to begin with that 1990–91 season. Yorath won nine and drew three of the 14 Swans matches played between November and January, but things took a distinct turn for the worse as the team then embarked upon a run of 11 defeats on the trot and by March were in real danger of relegation into Division Four, now known as League Two. Swansea's then-chairman was Doug Sharpe, a successful local businessman who loved the club, and one way or another he wasn't going to let them fall through the relegation trapdoor. It was against this backdrop that I was conducting an interview with Sharpe on the club's dip in fortunes when he dropped his grenade ahead of the upcoming Wales match.

'Terry can't do the two jobs, it's too much for him,' Sharpe said. Gulp. Was he genuinely suggesting Yorath could no longer continue as Wales manager, and needed to resign that part-time role if he were to remain in charge of Swansea? Or vice-versa, of course.

Yes, he most definitely was saying that, Sharpe made it clear. The Swansea chairman felt too much of Yorath's time was being spent planning for Wales and it was to the detriment of his club. Sharpe was a backer of the international team, it must be pointed out, with close links to the FAW hierarchy. His priority, however, was to Swansea City, and losses to Crewe, Tranmere, Southend, Torquay, Bury, Mansfield and Exeter, among others, convinced him they weren't getting the best from Yorath.

'So you mean this, do you? Can I run the story in the *Wales on Sunday* this weekend?' I asked.

'Yes, he can't do the two jobs properly,' Sharpe reiterated again.

I did wonder what Yorath's reaction would be to such banner headlines, particularly ahead of such an important Euro qualifier, but Sharpe maintained he had already told his manager the same thing anyway. 'Terry knows what I think,' Sharpe continued. Thus, that weekend, in massive typeface, the words 'You can't do two jobs' landed with the Sunday morning cornflakes on the front page of the newspaper, accompanied by a picture of Yorath, and Sharpe's explanation. Cue pandemonium. Within days Yorath parted company with the Swans, albeit things got rather messy amid claims from Sharpe that he had asked his manager to resign, while Yorath insisted he had been sacked. Lawyers were consulted, confusion reigned. And amid this chaos, Yorath's Wales players were due to gather within the next 48 hours to begin preparations for Belgium. Hardly ideal.

Bearing in mind I was something of a rookie sports reporter at the time, this proved to be a massive learning curve for me – one of two very big lessons I took from Yorath's time in charge and which I have leaned on ever since during my writing career. I always got on well with TY, found him excellent company, enlightening and easy to deal with, but word reached me he was unhappy with my story. Given our close relationship, I realised I had made the fatal journalistic error of not telling him what was going into print. Bad decision, Paul. I'm not for one second suggesting that Sharpe hadn't actually previously informed Yorath of his views and got me to do his 'dirty' work for him, but let's just say once the story was in the public domain the writing was clearly on the wall. Yorath's Swansea career was over in a flash. TY knew how things worked. He wasn't going to shoot the messenger, but it was important we spoke to clear the air. Having done that, and accepted I should have had the decency to contact him before going into print, we were able to put it to bed and our football writer–manager relationship continued as normal. Yorath wasn't the sort to bear resentment. 'Nothing wrong with the article, Paul. You should have let me know, though,' TY explained. He was right.

From that day on I've always tried to make a point of ensuring those I get on famously with – managers, players, coaches, top officials, directors, referees, whoever – know about anything majorly contentious that is going in the paper about them. They may not like the story, but at least forewarned is forearmed and all that. Frank Burrows, for the record, was named Swansea's new manager shortly after. So Sharpe, as any good chairman should, evidently had his ducks in a row and the relegation fears just about eased.

The second major journalistic lesson I learned with Yorath came when his contract as Wales manager wasn't renewed amid huge controversy at Christmas time 1993. I was one of two journalists to bat TY's corner, spelling out in print how outrageous and unfair we felt the decision to be and that, instead of losing his job, he should in fact be handed a new, improved deal to take Wales forward. The pro-Yorath press campaign, if that is the correct phrase, was to absolutely no avail. Several years on, TY had been long forgotten about – yet the same FAW council members who got rid of him, many in their sixties, seventies and even eighties, were still holding down their own seats of power.

Memo to oneself and perhaps to any budding young sports reporter out there: when a decision is taken to dispense with a manager's services there is no point harping on about it, whatever your personal misgivings, however popular he might be with the fans. The hierarchy make their call and they aren't going to change their mind. I quickly learned these are the people with the real power. So, as time went on, and countless managers I liked and got on well with unfortunately lost their jobs, I knew I needed to quickly focus upon the next man in line and start building a new working relationship. Malky Mackay, a big favourite with Cardiff City supporters but ruthlessly sacked by Bluebirds owner Vincent Tan, was just one example of this. I was close to Malky for a while. There was massive, and understandable, disquiet about his departure among the fans who admired him for taking Cardiff into the Premier League, but Tan held the real clout and wasn't budging on his judgement call. Again, like Yorath, Malky was soon forgotten about while Tan was still in situ more than a decade on, hiring and firing plenty of other managers. Even Brian Clough, back in the 1970s, couldn't win a power struggle with Derby County chairman Sam Longson despite an uprising from the club's fans, so what chance did Yorath have, or Malky for that matter?

Anyway, before all that was to happen, and just six days on from his ugly Vetch Field departure, Yorath put the Swansea controversy behind him to mastermind a splendid Wales 1–1 draw in Belgium. Even better, on 5 June 1991, his side beat the world champion Germans on an epic Cardiff Arms Park night, 34,000 fans roaring louder than for many a year as Ian Rush grabbed a never-to-be-forgotten second-half winner. Not many teams overcame Germany in those days. This truly was a win for the ages, one of those special 'I was there' sporting moments. Rush was unstoppable. What a striker, what a goalgetter. Three weeks on the FAW rewarded Yorath by giving him a full-time contract – on a grand salary of around £40,000. Well, I did say finances were tight. They were improving, but not overly significantly at that stage. As time went on those salaries were thought to increase to around £60,000 for Bobby Gould, £130,000 for Mark Hughes, £250,000 for John Toshack and Chris Coleman, and double that for Ryan Giggs. Not exactly the £20million per year Manchester City were said to be paying Pep Guardiola, or Gareth Southgate's £5million-plus England package. Money was never going to be the driver for anybody taking the Wales job – it was more about love of the country, or someone looking to make a mark in their first management job, a rung on the career ladder.

Shortly after defeating the Germans, Yorath's men had another major scalp to their name when a Dean Saunders goal saw them beat Brazil 1–0 in an Arms Park friendly. So, in the space of three months, Wales had wins over the reigning world champions and also the side who went on to lift the next World Cup in 1994. Compared to what had gone before, and alarmingly what was to come after, these were truly heady days. Throw in an early friendly victory out in Brescia, and Yorath could put victories against Italy, Brazil and Germany on his CV.

Sadly, the Euro '92 campaign fell off the rails the following month when Wales were thumped 4–1 in Germany, the hosts going on to top the group by a single point, and leaving the Dragons with one of those agonising near misses. However, that game in Nuremberg is perhaps best remembered for another reason – the debut of a fresh-faced, hugely exciting new Welsh sensation, the like of which we'd not seen before. Unfortunately even Ryan Giggs, when he was actually playing, couldn't prevent one of those truly surreal Wales rise-and-fall moments.

4

Wales' *Sliding Doors* moment

FULLY FIVE YEARS before Gwyneth Paltrow was to star in the Hollywood blockbuster *Sliding Doors*, the Wales football team beat her to the punch. In an alternative reality Terry Yorath's side would have changed the course of sporting history by reaching the 1994 World Cup in the USA and helping football eclipse rugby two decades before the Euro 2016 aces did actually achieve that feat.

Gareth Bale, Aaron Ramsey and their mates were mere toddlers at the time of Wales' extraordinary 1990s high to low extremes. At least by the time they appeared for their country they were to be grateful for some sound decision-making by the FA of Wales powerbrokers. Previously, instead of the riches of the World Cup and everything that would have brought to a success starved football nation, catastrophe was to follow.

For several years. Utter doom, gloom, despondency and downright embarrassment.

You wouldn't have thought one solitary result could make such a chasm of difference. But it did. Paltrow's rom-com script, of course, centres around two very different storylines for her character Helen, depending on whether she catches a train or not. In Wales' case the good, or the very bad, outcome hinged on a win-or-bust qualifier against Romania in the late autumn of 1993 and the messy manner in which the FAW dealt with the fallout.

Oh, what might have been.

Perhaps Yorath should have got Wales over the line, so he needs to take a portion of the blame for what happened next, but let's just say some of the eyebrow-raising calls made afterwards didn't exactly help matters.

Looking back, Yorath possessed a truly magical blend of stars. Ian Rush, Mark Hughes and Dean Saunders made up a formidable, goal-laden forward unit, arguably as good as any on the planet. Neville Southall was the world's best goalkeeper. Kevin Ratcliffe, while no longer in his pomp, could bank upon vast know-how and big game experience from captaining Everton to two League titles and various major Cup triumphs. Back-up players like David Phillips, Mark Bowen and Barry Horne may not have been of that quality, but they were nonetheless among a clutch of trusted Premier League regulars Yorath could turn to.

Suddenly, this highly impressive group of battle-hardened warriors was bolstered even further by the emergence of two hugely gifted young guns who supplied flair, flamboyance, fresh-faced exuberance and extra goal power. Gary Speed was already a League title winner with Leeds United. Ryan Giggs, soon to become one many times over with Manchester United, had the football world at his feet.

What a lineup it made for, in my opinion edging it man for man over the Wales side who rampaged to the Euro semi-finals under Chris Coleman. If only for a midfield maestro like Aaron Ramsey to knit everything together too, but that would be getting really greedy.

Just like Coleman's aces, I've not the slightest doubt Yorath's Class of the 1990s would have rampaged on the biggest stage had they reached the World Cup. It is hard to say how far they might have progressed out in the States, but that kind of theatre appeared ready-made for many of these exceptional talents. Getting to a major finals was the perennial problem. There were no play-offs or backdoor routes via the Nations League in those days.

At least this time, after horrendously tough draws previously under Yorath, there were no super-powers standing in the way. Wales' group promised to be a keenly contested showdown for two qualifying spots between Yorath's Dragons, Romania, Belgium and a combined Czechoslovakia and Slovakia (RCS) team, with Cyprus and the Faroe Isles making up the numbers, albeit those two still had to be beaten.

The breakthrough of a teenage Giggs, in particular, suddenly gave Wales fans everywhere extra hope. He had made his debut at the tail end of the previous European Championship campaign, sent on as substitute six minutes from time in that 4–1 Nuremberg thrashing by Germany. In doing so, Giggs became Wales' youngest footballer at the age of 17 years and 321 days, eclipsing a record previously held by fellow great John Charles from the 1950s. It was a feat Giggs was proud of and which he retained until Bobby Gould awarded a cap to a little-known defender called Ryan Green, then on Wolves' books, who was picked against Malta at the age of 17 years and 225 days. An evidently unhappy Giggs described that as a 'typical Gould gimmick'. Green only had one further cap. I often see and speak to the 'other' Ryan, now in his mid-forties, at my local gym in Cardiff. He played afterwards for Hereford, Bristol Rovers, Port Talbot and Merthyr Town, so it's a great quiz question to throw at our fellow gym-goers – 'What has that guy got in common with Ryan Giggs and Gareth Bale?' No-one gets the answer, until I tell them he sandwiched the two megastars as Wales' youngest footballer. It's some achievement, to be fair, and one which Green remains humble about.

Giggs' club manager Sir Alex Ferguson didn't describe his protégé's international debut as a gimmick, but he wasn't exactly dancing jigs around the streets of Manchester about it, either. Fergie felt there were much better games for Wales to give Giggs his bow than when you're being bashed by the German mean machine, but these had to be Yorath's calls.

At first it was slowly, slowly for Wales and Giggs. Their

World Cup campaign would be bookended with fixtures against Romania, and no-one foresaw the disastrous start as Yorath's defence leaked like a sieve to let in five goals within the first 35 minutes on a sweltering Bucharest afternoon. Ian Rush's second-half consolation goal and another Giggs appearance off the bench mattered little as the Dragons crashed 5–1, the imperious Romanian playmaker Gheorghe Hagi scoring twice for the hosts. Ferguson would hardly have been enamoured with that one, either. Giggs' first Wales game was as a substitute in a side already four down to the Germans, now his third appearance, in the 57th minute for Mark Pembridge, came with Wales even worse off in Romania. At least there were 27 minutes in a 1–0 win over Luxembourg in between!

Yorath got World Cup matters back on track with a 6–0 Arms Park thumping of the Faroe Isles, Rush netting a hat-trick, while a Hughes goal accounted for Cyprus 0–1 in Limassol, before a 2–0 defeat in Belgium put them on the backfoot again. It was a mixed start at best, those results coming in 1992, which meant Wales couldn't afford to slip up in the six remaining qualifiers during 1993. Almost every game was make or break.

Cometh the hour, cometh the young man. After five substitute showings, Giggs could be held back no more. March 31st, 1993, at Cardiff Arms Park, was a red-letter day for Welsh sport as Giggs made his full debut in a cracking 2–0 win over the Belgians, predictably marking the occasion with a wonder free-kick goal and man-of-the-match performance.

There had been so much hype about this now 18-year-old sensation bursting through at Manchester United, but suddenly Wales fans could see what the fuss was about for themselves. They positively drooled about what they were viewing close up. The boy wonder dazzled throughout, his dynamic, positive and pacy running bewildering the Belgium defenders as he cut inside and outside of them, tormenting, teasing, thrilling. He richly deserved the standing ovation given by 27,002 fans when substituted for Mark Bowen in the 89th minute.

Earlier, a roar of 'Ryan Giggs, Ryan Giggs, Ryan Giggs' started behind the goal and quickly spread right around the ground. This was a new football phenomenon we were witnessing and invariably the following morning's front and back pages were about this then new darling of Wales, many, many years before more unsavoury headlines, shall we call them, were to emerge.

Among the admirers present inside the ground that night was the legendary Wales and Lions rugby scrum-half Gareth Edwards, widely recognised back then as the greatest sportsman Wales had produced and who himself had graced the famous Cardiff Arms Park turf with his own brilliance on countless occasions. I interviewed Edwards about what we had just seen. He reckoned that any unofficial mantle he may have held of Wales' finest was about to be obliterated. The ballyhoo surrounding Giggs appeared to be fully justified. Here was a magician turning out in the red of Wales. Crikey, to think we could look forward to another 15 years of this brilliance, many of us thought at the time.

Extraordinary, isn't it, that somebody even better then came along in the Wales No. 11 jersey. Talk about Welsh fans being privileged.

Little story here. My first sighting of Giggs came when he was a 16 year old, playing for a Wales Youth team managed by Brian Flynn versus England Youth in Yeovil. Word had reached us on the grapevine about this sensational Welsh wizard coming through at Manchester United, amid comparisons to the great George Best, so time to pop down to Somerset to see for myself. Giggs wore the red No. 10 shirt that night – and tore the cream of England apart. Without wishing to sound disrespectful to his Welsh team-mates, it was as close to one person against 11 that I have seen on a football pitch. England won the game, but the question on the lips of their players afterwards was, 'Who the heck was that Welsh No. 10?'

Ryan Wilson, as he was on the team-sheet, wasn't particularly well known at the time. That night he regularly dribbled past three or four flatfooted England defenders in one go, ball seemingly super-glued to his mesmeric left foot, trying to score. It was like watching a young Welsh version of the great Diego Maradona. It didn't take a journalistic genius to work out this guy was going right to the very top. As a bonus I spoke to Giggs afterwards and got the phone number journalists up and down the UK were to covet, albeit he changed it pretty soon! Ha, bet Giggsy has done that a few times.

After the wondershow versus Belgium, the genie was out of the bottle and everybody knew who Ryan Giggs, née Wilson, was. The golden future of Welsh football for the next decade or more had seemingly arrived. Teenager or not, opponents would double up, often treble up on Giggs, but that would create extra space for the superb Welsh strikers around him as Wales drew 1–1 away to the RCS and won in the Faroes 0–3 to set up a thrilling trio of Cardiff Arms Park autumn games that would determine their World Cup fate. At times, Yorath used to bemoan the fixture scheduling. Back then FIFA or UEFA didn't get involved, the countries had to sort out the sequence of matches among themselves. Wales, lacking clout, rarely got what they asked for. Indeed, Yorath explained it to me along the lines of: 'Everyone meets up in a room. We each put forward suggestions, try to compromise, but Eastern Europeans, wearing these black leather coats, just say no, no, no until they get their own way. It's not particularly pleasant.' Suddenly, though, with three back-to-back home matches to conclude the group, that scheduling had worked out very much in Wales' favour. Could they make the Arms Park factor count?

Giggs and Rush scored during a rip-roaring 2–2 draw with the RCS, a thrilling 90-minute affair which ebbed and flowed and was a credit to the two sides, before Saunders and Rush goals accounted for Cyprus 2–0. Thus everything hinged on the

17 November 1993 showdown with Romania, among the most significant fixtures in Welsh football for decades, before and since. Win, and Wales were at the World Cup for the first time since John Charles and his 1958 team. Lose and… well, let's not go there just yet.

It was a scenario which ushered in unprecedented interest. Tickets were the hottest property in town, sold out in a few days. Football shirts began to outstrip rugby jerseys for the first time. Everybody, it seemed, wanted a piece of Giggs and Wales. The Andy Williams hit 'Can't Take My Eyes Off You', synonymous with the Welsh team, boomed from our TV screens as the BBC got us in the mood with their brilliant trailers for the match.

Welsh rugby was in a right old mess, 15 defeats in their last 20 Five Nations games. They had even embarrassingly lost at home the week before to Canada and previously, ironically, against Romania, meaning oval-ball regulars were turning to Yorath's burgeoning side as something better to cheer for national pride. Football fervour began to sweep a nation as men, women and youngsters from Cardifff to Caernarfon, Newport to Newtown, Bangor to Barry, Llandudno to Llanelli began to eye the big prize.

The feel-good factor was extraordinary. Yorath urged his team to embrace the sense of occasion and for the fans to drive Wales over the line. How did those players get away from the hype and relax amid the mounting pressures? During the Yorath years they would travel together from their hotel base on the outskirts of Newport to a little backstreet pub called The Exchange in the Llandaff North area of Cardiff, a local hostelry so hidden away you wouldn't know it was there unless you resided nearby. This was hardly Stringfellows or a glamorous nightclub, of course, but Yorath knew of the pub because it was a stone's throw away from where he had been brought up in the Welsh capital. At first, locals were stunned to see Giggs, Rush and others ensconced in the corner, winding down with a quiet drink, but they appreciated the privacy the players wanted, didn't make a song and dance about superstars being in their presence, and The Exchange continued to be Wales' big secret.

Given the hope and massive build-up for Romania, the letdown was all the harder to take as Wales lost 1–2 in the most agonising fashion with that infamous Paul Bodin moment. Gheorghe Hagi had put the visitors ahead, a rare Neville Southall error as the ball squirmed under his body, but Dean Saunders equalised and within two minutes Gary Speed was bundled over by Dan Petrescu. Penalty. The crowd went wild, the Romanians looked as if they were about to wilt, Wales' players appeared to grow ten feet tall in stature. This dream was on – only for Bodin to strike the crossbar. The joy turned to deflation, Florin Răducioiu grabbed a winner near the end and Romania, not Wales, were going to the USA along with group runners-up Belgium. The top two finished on 15 points, with Wales back on 12. Not even Giggs could turn this one around.

If possible, it hurt those of us who knew Bodin even more because a nicer guy you could not wish to meet. He was an easy target, for obvious reasons, but that night, and in the aftermath, I could only feel sympathy for the likeable left-back. Why was he taking the penalty in the first place, you might wonder, when Giggs, Rush and Saunders were in the team (Hughes, unfortunately, was suspended)? The answer to that is Bodin had become something of a spot-kick expert for Wales, had scored from his previous attempts and was confident he would this time too.

'I just hit it as hard as I could. That was how I took penalties, by drilling them rather than placing them,' says Bodin. 'The crossbars at the Arms Park were oval, not round. It hit it on the apex, so it came right back out. If it had been half an inch lower it might have hit underneath the bar, and bounced down and in. All of the boys told me it wasn't my fault, but for me it was like the world had come to an end, and I did not get any sleep that night, or the night afterwards.'

What compounded Wales' woe was the news which emerged four days later when Bodin was playing for his club side Swindon against Ipswich. The Robins were awarded a penalty – and guess what? You've got it, Bodin scored. As he normally did.

Bodin never played for Wales again and reflects upon the events of that night by saying: 'It still sits there in my head and is obviously still talked about. The most disappointing thing for me is that, unlike some players who miss a vital penalty, I never got the opportunity to put things right.'

It proved little consolation to Wales and their demoralised fans that Romania went on to wow in the USA the following summer. They topped their group, knocked out Argentina 3–2 in a last-16 classic, and only went out on penalties to Sweden in the quarter-finals. Many pundits, this author included, felt Wales would have performed just as well in America had that penalty-kick gone in.

Instead, the loss triggered a sequence of events that saw Yorath controversially lose his job and Wales utterly collapse, entering the international wilderness for the best part of a decade. Even Gwyneth Paltrow, aka her *Sliding Doors* character Helen, would have struggled to match quite the differing fortunes Wales now managed.

A £1million sponsorship deal, unprecedented sums back then, had been agreed with Ford Motor Company if Wales qualified, which Yorath had helped to broker. That was lost to the Welsh game. So too the buzz, excitement and interest Rushie and the team would have received as the UK's only representatives at USA '94. England, for a change, had already failed to qualify, losing out the previous month to Norway and the Netherlands. Scotland had been ousted by Italy and Switzerland. Wales were the big British hope, and with Giggs, Hughes and Rush in the side – top stars at Manchester United and Liverpool – they were perhaps the glamour team, too. BBC and ITV cameras were preparing to follow them everywhere, beaming everything the players did into front rooms nationwide and providing a profile never seen before. Just imagine how many new followers Wales would suddenly have received. Shades of Euro 2016, only on an even grander scale as this was the World Cup. The stakes were incredibly high.

Goodbye to that, then. Travesty enough. Just as bad was the saga that developed over Yorath, whose contract was running out. He wanted a pay increase, the majority of Wales fans appeared to back him to carry on as manager for the next European Championships when Wales would get it right, but FAW boss Alun Evans and his ruling council evidently disagreed. It led to a 'Will He, Won't He' tedium over a new deal which dragged on until Christmas. At which point Yorath was told his contract wasn't being renewed.

Merry Xmas Terry, enjoy the festive cheer!

An inevitable outcry erupted among the Welsh public and in certain sections of the media. Yorath had taken Wales up to 27th in the FIFA rankings, unchartered territory as their highest position at that point. He had restored respect, galvanised the people, had a decent enough win ratio. But, as mentioned in the previous chapter, it was to prove irrelevant that a couple of us in the Welsh press came out strongly on his side. The FAW's president Tommy Forse responded to the criticism coming their way by urging me rather forcibly to back down, stating dogmatically: 'Terry has failed. He only had to win two of three home games, couldn't even manage that – and we struggled to win the one that we did, too.'

That was me told, then! Although only Welsh football could be conducive to the kind of perverse twist we were to witness next. Alun Evans, to be fair to him, pulled off a masterstroke by persuading John Toshack to succeed Yorath. Bobby Robson, who had led England to the World Cup semi-finals three years earlier, was also spoken to as the FAW showed real ambition in a bid to ward off the backlash against them. Tosh was at the peak of his powers at the time, having recently led Real Madrid to the Spanish League title, and he agreed to do the Wales job part-time while carrying on in his full-time position as manager of Real Sociedad. On the one hand, going part-time again could be perceived as a backward step. On the other, if there was a way to silence the critics, yours truly among them, this was it. Even those of us supporting Yorath knew full well Toshack was clearly another couple of levels above him as a manager. How could his appointment not be anything other than a brilliant coup?

In the big man breezed for Wales' next game, a March 1994 friendly against Norway at Cardiff's Ninian Park, with his revolutionary 'Systemar Toshack' tactics – otherwise known as the Christmas Tree – and so-called because there were five at the back, Gary Speed and Barry Horne in midfield, a slightly deeper Ian Rush and Nathan Blake just ahead of them, and Mark Hughes on his own as the focal tip up top. Tosh, as always, was ahead of his time. Many other managers would quickly follow this blueprint that Toshack had utilised so successfully in winning La Liga with Real Madrid. Terry Venables copied it for England at Euro '96 and was feted as a genius. Toshack's problem was that after jetting in from northern Spain on the Monday night, Real Sociedad's weekend La Liga clash with Racing Santander dealt with, he only had a single training session on the Tuesday to prepare the team for Wednesday night's game. His message, and wishes, clearly didn't come across strongly enough in that short space of time as Wales' players ran around looking like strangers and were 0–3 down within 51 minutes. A Chris Coleman consolation goal at the end didn't really matter.

Still, there had to be hope with Toshack in charge once those players became accustomed with his methods, surely? A manager of his stature was exactly what was needed to end Wales' qualifying jinx. Then, on the Saturday morning, three days after the Norway defeat, came the telephone call at home that made me realise things were a lot more complicated behind the scenes than anyone realised. Toshack, now back in Spain and preparing Real Sociedad for their next game with Tenerife, was ringing to ask for my guidance on the Yorath situation. What exactly had happened with his former Wales team-mate from the 1970s? Why wasn't Terry's contract renewed? What did the Welsh fans think about it all? What was this 'political' situation he now realised he'd stumbled into?

I started off by saying it wasn't my place to be answering these questions. He should direct them to his FAW employers. But Tosh pressed. 'I'm asking as a friend,' he said. So relenting, I responded as honestly as I could, but made it clear that, despite the controversy, he was now the manager of Wales, not Yorath, and we all needed to look forward, not back. However, when Toshack then said, 'I don't have to put up with this rubbish you know,' my antenna was raised. 'I could hear people singing "Toshack, Toshack, Go Back to Spain". I'm not stupid, I can see things aren't quite what I thought they were,' he continued.

Clearly Toshack had been stung by unexpected criticism from his own Welsh people, and at the Ninian Park ground where he first made his name as a teenage Cardiff City star, but I felt we ended our conversation on a positive enough note, agreeing things could only get better – and would with him in charge. Nonetheless, I put the phone down in a little bit of a daze. Later that day in the office I confided in work colleagues. 'Don't laugh, but I get the feeling Toshack may walk away – already.' I didn't feel comfortable enough with the information at that stage to run the story on the back page of the following morning's *Wales on Sunday* but, sure enough, within 48 hours news began to leak out from Spain that Toshack was indeed quitting – after just one match and 47 days in charge.

This was real egg on face time for the FAW, already facing fierce flak after ditching Yorath, and their response was to close ranks and turn to Toshack's assistant, Mike Smith, as a steady pair of hands. Smith was one of football's good guys, rarely had a bad word to say about anyone, nor anyone about him either. Whether he was the right man to guide Wales through this crisis was another matter entirely. Smith had been manager of the Wales Class of 1976, who Toshack played for, and took them to a European Championship quarter-final against Yugoslavia. They had topped their qualifying group, the only Welsh side in history to do so, and something beyond even the more recent Gareth Bale-inspired team. Unfortunately, back then, only four countries contested the Euro finals – UEFA expanded the tournament from 1980 onwards – and Smith's Wales lost out to the Yugoslavs. Smith clearly had decent history, but it was somewhat wishful thinking to expect him to turn back the clock and repeat those feats two decades on.

Regrettably, as many feared, results were woeful. Wales lost six of the ten games Smith took charge of between 1994 and 1995, but worryingly they included two of the worst defeats in history – a 5–0 European Championship thrashing at the hands of Georgia and an equally embarrassing 3–2 setback in Moldova. Former Soviet bloc countries can be tough nuts to crack in the modern era, but in those days they were expected to be cannon fodder. At the very least, a Wales team containing Rush, Hughes, Southall, Speed and Saunders were expected to win. Giggs was missing from the two games.

Wales returned from the horror trip to Georgia to a banner headline in the *South Wales Echo* declaring 'Sack the Lot' – which was a criticism directed not at the manager or his players, but the FAW's 28-man ruling council who had got rid of Yorath 11 months earlier, overseen the Toshack one-game fiasco, and then plumped for a sadly out-of-his-depth Smith. The Blazer Brigade, as they were known.

'Once again Wales is a laughing stock. Once again it is the FAW rulers who stand convicted in the dock – guilty of murdering a dream,' read the stinging back page comment piece, which also demanded: 'The pens of FAW chief executive Alun Evans and the others who appointed Smith should be drained of the ink, emptied by letters of resignation.'

Strong words. Now I wasn't particularly slow in coming forward to criticise the FAW, but this particular bold piece wasn't written by me, but by the *Echo*'s then chief soccer writer Rob Phillips, who went on to become a commentator for BBC Wales. His stinging assessment probably echoed what a lot of fans were thinking, exasperated by what had happened post-Yorath. Needless to say, the resignation letters were not forthcoming. The *Echo* is a Cardiff evening newspaper and with only so many of the FAW's 28 council members residing in and around the Welsh capital, and no newspaper websites at the time to broaden the readership, sadly most of them probably didn't even see the article. Even if they had, they'd have brushed it off.

Smith could not hide quite so easily. While acknowledging he was 'shell-shocked and ashamed' at the abysmal back-to-back results, he stated he wasn't resigning and wished to see the job through. I had sympathy for Smith. He loved being Wales manager, his principles were the right ones, but he should never have been placed in this pressurised position in the first place. In private conversations, and I had many with him, what came across loud and clear was the deep hurt Smith felt from the flak coming his way. Sadly, and perhaps predictably, results didn't get better, and more and more you sensed Smith was just a stop-gap until the next proper appointment. A commendable 1–1 draw in Germany was offset by three-goal losses to Bulgaria home and away. A change of manager was clearly required and the FAW duly stepped in to relieve Smith of his duties following a 0–1 defeat in the Cardiff return game with Georgia in the summer of 1995.

Yet another embarrassing loss. Just 19 months after Wales had been on the World Cup brink, ready to completely alter how Welsh sport was perceived, they were now deep, deep,

deep in the doldrums. Staring into the abyss. Gwyneth Paltrow couldn't possibly have dreamt up such starkly contrasting storylines.

At least, as pop star Yazz would sing, the only way is up. Unfortunately, things were actually about to get a whole lot worse.

5

Conflict, chaos, controversy and captain Vinnie – the bizarre Bobby Gould era

THE BOBBY GOULD Wales years were so surreal at times, crazy you might even say, that it is hard to know where to start. Just when everyone needed a bit of stability and normality, chaos, confusion, conflict and controversy defined the era to such an extent that the Wales football team often dominated the front pages of the newspapers as well as the back – and not for the right reasons.

So much happened that stretched credulity during that spell between 1995 to 1999, including an uncouth training ground fight before a crunch World Cup match after Gould called out his own star centre-forward, much to the bewilderment of other players. Somehow you couldn't envisage that happening with Gareth Southgate and Harry Kane.

There was a racism row, the team were ordered to use a prison as their new training base, Robbie Savage was contentiously thrown out of the squad on the morning of a huge Euro game, and humiliating setbacks led to a furious Gary Speed ripping into his manager in a dressing room dressing-down to beat any other – with a little bit more on top, too.

Vinnie Jones, an out-and-out Watford geezer, member of Wimbledon's infamous Crazy Gang, and soon to become

Hollywood superstar, was named captain for one game after a dressing room vote was held. Let's just say the move raised an eyebrow or three.

There was also the rather strange day when Wales' preparations for a big clash with powerhouse Germany involved a Cardiff Arms Park practice game against the finest from the Welsh press, an XI yours truly was honoured to captain. It was only a bit of fun, a real privilege for us scribes and wannabe footballers, it helped build a bond between team and media. What was a little more bizarre was the twist it threw up as Gould was said to have axed one of the players due to face the Germans on the back of what he witnessed during that kick-about.

'You'd be amazed how much I learned from my players in a little game like that,' pointed out the manager. At least Wales beat us. Rather humiliatingly, they lost another warm-up game to Leyton Orient!

Fair to say this was an incident-laden period which certainly didn't leave us journalists with a shortage of headline-making material to write about. Bobby Gould was good copy, as we say in the newspaper trade, meaning there was always a story. You took it in your stride at the time, just part of the job. Looking back, it is flabbergasting to think some of these things actually happened with an international football team, particularly one containing big name stars like Ryan Giggs, Mark Hughes and Gary Speed.

Despite that, those who knew Gould couldn't help but warm to the man. He was liked by most, easy to talk to, never afraid to answer your questions no matter how contentious they may be, a real gentleman. He was just, he might accept, a little out of his depth in the prestigious job he had been given. As things began to go so badly wrong, you had to feel a little bit sorry for him, albeit he brought some of the criticism upon himself.

Perhaps it's best to rewind to the very beginning with how Gould was surprisingly appointed in the first place. Welsh football was in a mess, the FAW needing to find a suitable person to take the team forward following the departures in quickfire succession of Terry Yorath, John Toshack and Mike Smith.

Gould was never meant to be in the frame. The job was lined up for Brian Flynn, then working wonders as manager of lower division Wrexham, albeit not amid the Hollywood glare we've been accustomed to more recently up at The Racecourse. Flynnie's biggest rival was Ron Atkinson, who had managed Manchester United for five years, led Aston Villa to a Wembley League Cup triumph, and who was then in charge of Coventry City. Some FAW bigwigs believed Atkinson possessed the flamboyance and managerial gravitas required to get Wales back on track, even though finances dictated it would have to be on a part-time basis. Another ambitious candidate was Howard Kendall, mastermind of two Everton League title triumphs during their mid-1980s trophy-winning era, but who had since dropped down to become manager of Notts County. Flynn, Atkinson or Kendall. After the recent troubles it seemed Wales couldn't really go too far wrong with any one of those three. The speculation intensified about which one it actually would be, with Flynn always viewed as the number one choice.

The first inkling that other eleventh-hour candidates were also in the frame came when I received a telephone call after a meeting of the six-man FAW sub-committee tasked with going through the applications and whittling them down to a shortlist. 'Can you give Jimmy Shoulder's name a push?' I was asked. Shoulder was the largely unknown Wales Youth development guru and manager of the under-21 side, and there was a view from some committee members that a low-key appointment from within might actually prove the best way forward. Thus, in early August 1995, the banner headline in the *Wales on Sunday* read 'Shoulder Charge', as we revealed Jimmy was indeed one of seven men the FAW planned to interview. Also on that shortlist, we pointed out, were Flynn, Atkinson, Kendall, Welsh legend Neville Southall, plus another Welshman, Mike Walker from Colwyn Bay, who had made a mark as manager of Norwich City. Tucked away right at the bottom of the list was the left-field choice. Bobby Gould. The interviews were to take place that coming week and I remarked in the office that Gould, full of bubbly enthusiasm and certainly capable of talking a good game, was exactly the kind of personality who would charm the men in suits, potentially coming from nowhere to land the job.

Flynn remained the front-runner, but his work at Wrexham was not yet completed and complications with a compensation package to the Robins, on top of the salary the FAW would have to pay, ruled him out. A shame. At the peak of his managerial powers at the time, it would have been fascinating to see how Flynn and Wales got on together. By the time he did land the role, on a two-match part-time basis in 2010, it proved a little too late for Brian.

I'm not sure Atkinson was even interviewed in the end. The attraction for him would have been the chance to manage an international team; the downside was the £60,000 salary on offer, absolute chickenfeed for a man who had bossed Manchester United, Aston Villa and Spanish giants Atlético Madrid. Shoulder, Kendall and the others were then to fall by the wayside as my hunch about Gould bewitching his FAW interviewers proved to be true. To be fair, Gould had decent pedigree, winning the FA Cup with Wimbledon, one of the biggest shocks in the grand old competition's history as his Crazy Gang overcame Kenny Dalglish's title-winning Liverpool team, while he also took little Coventry City to the top of the Premier League for a spell.

Gould had been without a club, enjoying a sunshine break in the West Indies, when his mobile telephone rang. It was his best friend on the line, a guy called Bill Smith, who said, 'I've got a job for you mate. Wales want a manager.'

Gould smiles: 'There I was sunbathing on a beach in Grenada, piña colada in my hand, chance to relax. "Yeah, I really want a job at the moment, Smithy!" I told him, followed by, "Anyway, why would a bloke who's 50 per cent English and 50 per cent Scottish expect to get the Wales job?" However, upon my return, unbeknown to Smithy, I put in an application and was invited to an interview with FAW council members at a hotel in Wrexham. I knew I'd got the right venue when I saw the zimmer frames outside!'

The night before, Gould had visited Wrexham's Racecourse Ground to watch Flynn's team in European Cup Winners' Cup action against Romanians Petrolul Ploieşti. Little did Flynn know the Wales job he coveted so much was instead about to go to the man looking down from the stands. The following day, at the interview, Gould says the FAW committee formed a U-shape around him in the room as he sat down, and his first words were, 'There was a black gentleman in the USA who once said "I have a dream". Well gentlemen, I too have a dream – to become your international manager.'

A good communicator, brimful with ideas and a deep thinker on the game, Gould then outlined his vision – which in effect meant shaking up the Welsh structure from the bottom upwards. You can't keep just relying upon volunteers and amateurs to run Welsh intermediate and youth sides, Gould argued. He felt things were a little archaic and outlined the semblance of a set-up which would lead to better coaching and see younger players move seamlessly through age grade teams into the senior side. Living in Portishead, just the other side of the Severn Bridge near Bristol, Gould was prepared to commute most days to the FAW's offices, then in Westgate Street right in the centre of Cardiff, to push through his ideas with staff.

He believed part of his mantra was to talk up the much-criticised League of Wales, then in its infancy, and to promote the Welsh domestic game. Indeed, once in situ Gould came up with the brazen idea to try to get Princess Diana to present the trophy at a Welsh Cup final. The wonderful old competition, dating right back to 1877, had completely lost its way after Cardiff City, Wrexham, Swansea City and Newport County were kicked out because they didn't play in the League of Wales. Those teams not only boasted fabulous Welsh Cup and European pedigree, they also had by far the biggest support bases. As soon as they were barred, the competition nosedived, losing sponsorship, publicity and interest. Against that backdrop, and with tiny mid Wales village side Llansantffraid meeting Barry Town at Cardiff Arms Park in the first final of the new era, Gould tried to whip up support with the biggest marketing coup of the lot by approaching the Princess of Wales. He knew her attendance would generate enormous publicity and a decent-sized crowd. Unfortunately, the bold plan didn't come to fruition, just 2,666 fans turned up in a 53,000-capacity stadium, but at least Gould had a go.

It was this kind of energy, passion and vision that saw the FAW plump for Gould ahead of the more obvious names. Support from the men in suits was fine, having imaginative ideas was great, but first and foremost Gould was there to win international football matches, and his bigger issue was to earn the respect of the players and Welsh public. Deep down he knew he was on the back foot from the start, having never played the game at international level.

The first sign of perhaps a teeny bit of paranoia came just a couple of days into the job. Having been alerted to the fact Gould wished to broaden his options by eyeing Anglos who might have Welsh ancestry, a laudable thing to do in order to bolster the squad, I wrote a story saying he had drawn up a list of targets. Those players, we stated, included Southampton goal ace Matt Le Tissier, Nottingham Forest wide-man Steve Stone, and Everton midfielder Vinny Samways. Gould was on the phone straightaway, concerned the Welsh public might perceive this as an English manager seeking to bring in English players to the Wales national side. In any case, Gould pointed out, Samways wasn't particularly his kind of player.

Fair enough on Samways, but Gould shouldn't have been the slightest bit perturbed about looking to improve the team. Did his concerns express a little early insecurity? Put it this way, he had to very quickly learn on the job. As it happens, and for differing reasons, none of the aforementioned stars went on to play in the red shirt, but not without a fight from yours truly, and the brilliant readers of the *Wales on Sunday*, to try to persuade Le Tissier to throw in his lot with Wales.

From Guernsey, the mesmeric Southampton front man could have played for any one of England, Wales, Scotland or Northern Ireland as the Channel Islands did not have a team. Perhaps predictably he was picked by the Three Lions, appearing in a Dublin friendly against the Republic of Ireland in February 1995, a game infamously abandoned after rioting fans caused trouble. As that was a non-competitive fixture, Gould knew Le Tissier was still available to Wales, FIFA confirming he could indeed switch allegiance. England had a plethora of quality forward options: Alan Shearer, Teddy Sheringham, Les Ferdinand, Robbie Fowler, Andy Cole, Steve McManaman and Darren Anderton among them, with a teenage Michael Owen on the horizon. Wales weren't exactly short in that department, with Ryan Giggs, Dean Saunders, Mark Hughes and a young John Hartson available, but Le Tissier was a goal machine and we figured Gould needed his skills far more than England boss Terry Venables did. He would make way more international appearances playing for Wales and would be feted by the Welsh people.

So, over a number of weeks, we ran a 'Please Play for Wales, Matt' coupon in the *Wales on Sunday*, a hugely popular and well-read sports section back then, asking readers to sign with their name and address and send back in if they wanted Le Tissier. The response was overwhelming, those coupons absolutely flooded into our offices from Welsh fans everywhere.

As such, armed with a massive box of these damn things, I was dispatched down to Southampton to present them to Le Tissier to try to turn his head.

As I arrived at the training ground he came across to meet me with a genial smile. This was real people power, could he be persuaded? Sadly, the answer was no. Le Tissier was polite, clearly touched by the will of the Welsh public, and made clear he was hugely respectful of and grateful for their wishes. However, he calmly explained he had already appeared for England, albeit for only 26 minutes in that abandoned match. 'I'm really humbled by this, please thank everyone in Wales via your newspaper. But it just wouldn't feel right to me after already appearing for England,' he explained.

Thus the door was closed. We gave it everything, it just wasn't to be. A pity. Le Tissier would have been a sensation for Wales, earning legendary status. His skill-set was made for international football. Who knows how many caps he might have won in red? Certainly a darned sight more than the eight he attained for England, a criminally low number for a mercurial footballer of his quality who scored sublime goals on a regular basis. He was contentiously overlooked by Terry Venables for England's Euro '96 squad, then by Glenn Hoddle for the 1998 World Cup. What a waste, although doubtless England fans would argue eight caps for the Three Lions are worth 50-plus for Wales.

Le Tissier or no Le Tissier, Wales started encouragingly enough under Gould as the new manager picked up the final throes of the Euro '96 qualifying campaign left behind by Mike Smith, beating Moldova in his first game and then pushing Germany to the brink before falling 1–2 to a late Jürgen Klinsmann goal. Ryan Giggs was magnificent that night, running non-stop at the German defenders who couldn't work out how to cope with this dazzler down the left flank. Germany, under Berti Vogts, contained an amazing team and would go on to win those Euros at Wembley ten months down the line but, as often seemed to be the case, they were given a real fright by Wales. Early promise then for the Gould era – only for it to become undermined by a whole host of controversies which, put together with poor results, turned the dressing room against him.

Maybe the first indication for Wales' players that things were going to be rather different under this manager came 48 hours ahead of that fine showing against the Euro champs-to-be... when their preparation routine involved that 20-minute warm-up versus the Welsh press! Gould came up with the idea, asking yours truly to cobble together a media XI and we'd play against Giggs and Co. at the end of their Monday morning training session. Now I was a regular Sunday League player, naively liked to think of myself as a mix of a skilful 10, centre-forward and winger, but prime goalhanger was probably the most apt description! Unfortunately, I'd injured my calf and could barely run. No way on earth was I missing out on this opportunity, though. Off I popped to my GP, baffled expression on his face as I explained the situation, and left the surgery armed with a prescription to reduce the inflammation so I could at least play in goal.

At the allotted time, just as Wales' training was winding up, Her Majesty's Fourth Estate trooped down towards the Arms Park pitch in the black and white kit provided for us. I presume the players had been told we were the opposition that day, although there seemed to be something of a startled look upon their faces as we began to line up in our positions opposite them. We were hardly Jürgen Klinsmann, Thomas Hässler and Andreas Möller, the men they were about to face, were we? Gould though would have seen this as an opportunity to bring his players and the Welsh media closer together, which he believed was important for a host of reasons.

Big Neville Southall, love him, spotted me looking terribly lost in my yellow goalkeeper's shirt and kindly jogged over to give me a pair of his gloves. Talk about hands like shovels, those mitts almost came up to my forearm! Anyway, we may be hard-bitten sports hacks but we're also fans at heart. Thus, this was living the dream, an unprecedented opportunity to play on the same pitch with the idols of a nation. I bet the England press have never had the chance to line up against Harry Kane, Jude Bellingham, Wayne Rooney, Steven Gerrard and the rest. Most grateful for the opportunity, we were grabbing it.

We kicked off, and that little roll of the ball forward a couple of yards was pretty much the only time we managed to get inside Wales' half! Let's just say my goal was under siege, as you'd expect in a game between amateur Sunday League footballers, at best, and the finely tuned professionals who represented the cream Wales had to offer. One or two players, glint in their eyes, saw it as an opportunity for revenge for some of the less flattering headlines written about them down the years, or lowly player ratings given. Right from that kick-off, Dean Saunders went over the top on the man from *The Sun*, John Richardson, causing a gash to his shin. Saunders just smiled – he and Rico, as we called John, were pally enough. This was just Deano being Deano.

I'm not sure Gould, as referee, even gave us a free-kick for that. He, too, probably saw the funny side. Anyway, Giggs scored past me with Wales' very first attack, Saunders quickly grabbed a second and the third came from an own goal via a corner. For what it's worth we lost 3–0, but it was an admirable effort given the circumstances – even if I do say so myself!

Three other things stood out. At one point I had the ball at my feet when I suddenly heard a kind of 'woosh' through the air. Giggs, then 22 and possessing lightning speed, had closed me down from nowhere with his attempt at a flying sliding tackle. I have never known anybody move so fast. This was real up-close-and-personal stuff. More by luck than judgement, I managed to drag the ball back with the sole of my foot and clear in a panic. Giggs got up off the floor and just gave me a huge grin. He'd have been proud of that piece of skill himself!

I'm not sure Sir Alex Ferguson would have been smiling, mind, if he'd known his most valuable Manchester United asset, subject of a massive AC Milan bid at the time, was playing in a game like this.

Then Gary Speed tried a shot from 30 yards out which was hit with such venom that I wondered whether I should even get in the way of that one. To this day I'm convinced Speedo, who I got on well with, whacked that thunderbolt straight towards me deliberately as a bit of mischief in his own eyes. Have some of that, Abbo! Luckily for me, the ball hit the BBC's Phil McNulty's flesh on the back of his thigh. It was a while before poor Philip could walk after that.

The third most significant thing that stood out was a suggestion Gould actually changed his team for the Germany game on the back of what he just witnessed. Out, it was mooted, went midfielder Geraint Williams; in came Nathan Blake in a more forward role. Whether true or not, Wales went on to play pretty well against the Germans, only that Klinsmann goal near the end condemning them to an unlucky defeat. Williams did get into the action, as a substitute for Blake with eight minutes to go – and Big Nev let me keep his gloves! I can also tell you from my bird's-eye view down on the pitch next to them that those Welsh players were good. Very, very good.

It was a unique experience for them, and us, but ultimately a bit of amusement. No harm done. Unfortunately the players were soon to come across a number of moments which had much greater significance and caused many embarrassing headlines the team could have done without. The first of those was in May 1996 as Gould prepared his side for the start of the upcoming 1998 World Cup qualifying campaign with a friendly game away to Leyton Orient at Brisbane Road. It was a gentle warm-up ahead of meeting San Marino in the opening qualifier a week on. Fair to say the 90 minutes didn't exactly go to plan. A fully-loaded Wales, including Giggs, Hughes, Saunders and Robbie Savage, lost 2–1 – to a team who had finished 89th out of 92 in the Football League, failing to win any of their last ten matches and who were dumped out in the first round of three Cup competitions that season.

Non-cap international or not, given the nature of the opposition it had to rank as one of Wales' worst results in history. The two unknowns who scored Orient's goals were defender Lee Shearer, who hadn't played a competitive game for the O's and dropped into non-League football with Dover, Margate and Faversham Town, and a trialist by the name of Peter Garland. He didn't score another Orient goal and ended up playing for sides right down the English pyramid like Whyteleafe, Dulwich Hamlet and Greenwich Borough. Angry words were exchanged by the Welsh players at the end. They were humiliated, questioned why the game was played, and not best pleased to have been put in that situation in the first place. What mattered most though was avoiding injury and, club season having finished, getting any rustiness out of the system ahead of the banana skin of a game in San Marino. Wales duly headed out to Serravalle to get their World Cup campaign off to a flier with a thumping 5–0 win on a dangerous-looking, rutted pitch which, coupled with one or two cumbersome challenges, certainly tested those graceful runs down the wing by Giggs.

He scored one, Hughes bagged a double, while Andrew Melville and Mark Pembridge grabbed a goal apiece. When, at the beginning of the following season, Wales followed that up with a 6–0 Cardiff hammering of the same opposition, it prompted an introduction to my match report which I was never allowed to forget by some. 'Two wins, six points, 11 goals scored, none conceded... bring on the Dutch...' I brashly wrote, with group favourites Netherlands next up in back-to-back games. Within three months, after 1–3 and 7–1 hidings, friends would look at me and chirp, 'What was that about bring on the Dutch, then?' Ha. Lesson learned. Guess you don't make idle boasts when you're about to face a team containing world-class talent like Dennis Bergkamp, Clarence Seedorf and Jaap Stam.

Unfortunately for Gould it was no laughing matter as the two games each had consequences by throwing up a couple of the kind of incidents which were to dog his reign. The first Netherlands clash was in October 1996 at the Arms Park. When Dean Saunders gave Wales the lead, which they kept hold of until the closing quarter, my early optimism appeared to be reasonably well founded. Then wham, bam, slam, two Pierre van Hooijdonk goals and one by Ronald de Boer in the space of seven minutes saw the Dutch emerge victorious. Gould was concerned at the way Celtic centre-forward van Hooijdonk had got away from the Welsh defence for one of the goals and he is said to have made those views known in his dressing room debrief. However, one of his own players, Nathan Blake, said he was upset by Gould's alleged description of van Hooijdonk.

'I could not believe what I heard,' said Blake, who stated he was also perturbed by a training ground incident revolving around the different colours of bibs. It resulted in Blake vowing never to play under Gould again, saying at the time: 'Racism is a thing of the past. We're in international football. I'm an established striker and I should not have to listen to it from my own people, especially a manager I play for.' Amid banner headlines claiming 'Gould's job jeopardised by race row', the manager tried to clear the air by apologising and said: 'Perhaps Nathan has finer feelings than other people. In future I will take that on board. I told the players that if there were cryptic comments, nothing was meant. There is a thin line and there is no way I have been involved with anything regarding this before in my career.'

He hadn't been, either. Gould was staunchly supported by his FAW bosses, with the chairman of their powerful international committee, Ken Tucker, saying: 'I know Bobby very well and would not have thought there was any question of racism in his behaviour. He is just not that type of man and I am very surprised at this allegation.' The FAW's president Brian Fear called it 'a storm in a tea-cup' and made clear: 'His job is not in danger for his remarks.'

There were further contentious headlines to come from the return game in Eindhoven a month down the line, although at least this was just for football reasons. Netherlands 7 Wales 1. One of the darkest days in the country's football history. Only Neville Southall kept the score below 20. I kid you not. I was there. I saw first hand what Big Nev has himself described as his best performance. He certainly could not be blamed for any of the seven which flew past him, including a Dennis Bergkamp hat-trick.

The result was bad enough, but what also ensured that game continues to be talked about in Welsh football circles is the fact that Gould named Vinnie Jones as captain, ahead of more established figures such as Southall, Dean Saunders or Gary Speed. Vinnie, with his strong Home Counties accent, had discovered some Welsh ancestry via a maternal grandfather from Ruthin, a north Wales market town 18 miles west of Wrexham. He wanted to become an international footballer and threw in his lot with Wales after an attempt to play for the Republic of Ireland had failed and with England not wanting him.

It led to ridicule from some quarters, but Vinnie's commitment to the cause could not be questioned. Upon first being selected, he travelled by train from London to Cardiff one afternoon to meet me for an interview, keen to spell out his pride in his new-found role, to emphasise what playing for Wales would mean to him and why he was so determined to make a success of it. He'd taken the time and trouble to make that journey straight after training with Wimbledon, wishing to state his case in person, before heading back to Paddington. His eagerness to pull on the red shirt was palpable.

Almost 30 years on, our paths crossed again, this time outside Watford's Vicarage Road ground ahead of a Wednesday night Championship fixture with Cardiff City. By then, of course, Vinnie had quit football to become a Hollywood global star. He was thoroughly pleasant again as we spoke before kick-off, but truth be told I don't think he remembered me. Well, when you've worked with Brad Pitt, Nicolas Cage and Angelina Jolie, who the heck is Paul Abbandonato of the Welsh press?! Nonetheless, we had a decent chat about the good (or should that be bad) old days, reminiscing, recounting some of those Wales matches, before I shouted after him as we parted company: 'Remember now, support the Welsh team tonight.' Vinnie turned around, broke into a massive smile, hesitated for a moment, then pointed across the way and responded, 'I can't mate, I was born just over there.' Fair enough, I guess.

I digress there. During the brief period he was with Wales, Vinnie certainly threw himself into the cause and made a point of learning the national anthem, this at a time when not every player used to sing it before games. His great mate John Hartson taught him the words. Unsuspecting Wales players would be walking around the team hotel when, suddenly, Vinnie appeared from behind a pillar, plant pot, or door, to bark *Gwlad, Gwlad*' and other lines in their faces. Decent enough actor though he may have become, and the film blockbusters he starred in speak for themselves, it's fair to say Vinnie had certain limitations as a top-level footballer. Thus it came as a surprise when Gould named him as captain that night in Eindhoven against the Dutch. The manager held a secret ballot among the players – and Vinnie was pronounced the winner. According to some there was scepticism afterwards about how many had actually voted for Vinnie; Dean Saunders, as one of the more senior players, was claimed to have been the popular choice.

However, two decades after the Gould era had long since ended, I travelled to his beautiful home just outside Bristol to reflect upon those Welsh management years and get his insight into what really happened for an article for *Wales Online*. The true story behind some of the shocking headlines, if you like. Among them, Captain Vinnie.

'The truth is he won it hands down,' Gould told me. 'I was accused of not counting correctly, but no-one else came close. He was chosen by the dressing room. In hindsight what I should have done was make my own decision, not put it to the players.' Before I could even ask, Gould fixed me with a gaze to assert: 'I'd have gone for Vincent too, by the way. We had a rapport after he'd played under me at Wimbledon.'

The following year, Gould was to call time on Vinnie's brief Wales career. He played for his adopted country nine times over three years, was sent off during a 0–1 home loss to Georgia, was never to feature on the winning side, but did have a couple of commendable draws to his name away to Germany and at home to Turkey. Just three matches after making him captain, Gould totally dispensed with Vinnie following a 1–2 World Cup defeat to Belgium. 'That was another situation with him that I handled wrongly,' he conceded. 'When I ended his Wales career I told Vincent by phone, not in person. It was a coward's act – and one thing I've never been is a coward. I should have gone to see him. I regretted that.'

Back to Eindhoven. In my hotel room, shortly before heading off to the Philips Stadium to cover the game that night, I was watching a pre-recorded news clip on Dutch TV of Vinnie looking ahead to the 90 minutes. Wales were big underdogs, but in true Crazy Gang spirit he boomed: 'Well, we've gotta give it some to them… we gotta give it some.' The Wimbledon team Vinnie played in was as hard as nails, got stuck into superior opponents by whatever means possible, could intimidate teams and win matches with such an approach. They 'gave it some'. Unfortunately, 7–1 later, it's fair to say the Dutch didn't appear to get the message from Vinnie and Wales. You'd like to think his Hollywood scriptwriters would have come up with a better ending for someone as charismatic, but this was the reality of international football.

While Vinnie and the rest of the shell-shocked squad returned to Cardiff, Gould flew on to Istanbul to take a look at Wales' next opponents, Turkey, who were in action against San Marino the following evening.

He took up the tale. 'I'm on my own out there, really down after being thrashed 7–1, struggling to accept it. My hotel room was on the tenth floor. I stood out on the balcony, looking at the Bosphorus, and thought "Do I jump?" Sounds overdramatic, but I felt awful.

'Now as manager of Coventry, we were top of the Premier League, six wins in our first eight games. After one match in London we stopped off for a McDonald's. I had a quarter-pounder, strawberry milkshake and apple turnover. Footballers can be superstitious, that meal became the norm. So a few years on, I'm standing there on my tenth-floor balcony in Istanbul, feeling really down, when I suddenly think, "There must be a McDonald's here somewhere. I will have that – then think about jumping afterwards."

'I went out onto the street and asked a little Turkish fellow where the nearest McDonald's was. He was as poor as could be, asked if he could clean my shoes for some money. I felt so sorry for him, let him do it, gave him money and as a treat took him to McDonald's. We each had a quarter-pounder, strawberry milkshake and apple turnover. As we talked, I realised there were plenty of people worse off than me in the world.'

Gould didn't jump, of course, nor did he have long to drown his sorrows because Wales were back in action within five weeks, a home clash with Turkey just before Christmas which had become must-win to get their World Cup campaign back on track after that double-Dutch mauling. Wales drew the game 0–0, a rather nondescript encounter which once again became more famous for what happened off the pitch. Cue more unwanted front page headlines.

By that point, Gould had called an end to Ian Rush's international career; farewell to a true Welsh legend. Rushie, pre-Gareth Bale, was his country's record scorer, a highly impressive 28 goals from 73 matches. Quicksilver pace, lethal shot, sublime finishing, in his heyday he was the greatest striker in the world. For Liverpool and Wales he was also, perhaps, the first exponent of the press-from-the-front tactics, decades before Pep Guardiola used it with Manchester City and Barcelona. Rush wasn't just a great goal-scorer, his work ethic was second to none.

Time stands still for no-one in football however, and as Rush was being pensioned off, John Hartson, then just 21, was the new Welsh centre-forward on the block, playing for Arsenal and itching to become the starting No. 9 for his country. Gould evidently saw things differently, believing Mark Hughes and Dean Saunders were better striking options. He had picked Hartson for the 7–1 demolition in Eindhoven; he was dropping him for the Turkish clash. It led to perhaps the most unseemly incident of the lot as the two men became embroiled in what Gould calls 'rough and tumble' – aka a training ground fight, called by the manager and much to the astonishment of the rest of the squad who had been asked to gather in a circle to witness the ding-dong. Secretly, it seems, they actually enjoyed it.

Gould explained he first got the idea when boss of Wimbledon. If any members of the Crazy Gang had a problem with one another – and there were some pretty forceful characters in that team – previous manager Dave Bassett would instruct everyone to form a circle. 'He let the two in dispute have a wrestle, grapple, whatever you want to call it. No punching, no pinching, it wasn't a fight, just a way of letting off steam. After a while Dave would say "That's enough, shake hands, friends again." And everyone was better for it,' recounted Gould.

And so to the Welsh team's training base on the outskirts of Newport that winter, just ahead of the Turkey game Hartson had been axed for.

'As I walked out on to the pitch, the only thing I could hear was Hartson this, Hartson that. Chirping away. He didn't like the fact I'd picked him for one game, left him out of another,' started Gould. 'I'd had enough. The press and TV cameras were present, so I made sure we walked right to the far end. I explained to the players what they did at Wimbledon, gave Neville Southall my watch, turned to John and said, "Do you want a rough and tumble? Because the only thing I can hear is your voice."

'He's giving me a right old hiding. I'm down on the floor, John's on top venting anger and frustration. We're having a good old rough and tumble. Then I look up and notice Mark Hughes screaming his head off. I've never seen him so animated. "Come on, John," he was shouting, really getting into it. Next thing I look up to the other side and see Ryan Giggs jumping up and down. I thought to myself, "I bet Fergie wouldn't be doing this." At that point I told John enough was enough, he'd got it out of his system. He's a strong old so-and-so and when I got back to my hotel room and took off my top I noticed big red scratch marks down my back. My wife Marge went mad, "You've been with another woman," she screamed. I tried to explain the truth. She took some persuading, but eventually saw the funny side.'

Now I've personally known Hartson since he broke through at Arsenal and have always got on famously with him. We've shared countless chats down the decades, on and off the record, shooting the breeze about all things Wales. Yet I'm not sure this particular incident has ever cropped up in our conversations, although Hartson has talked elsewhere about it. It appears he simply didn't know what to say, or where to look, when called out by his manager, other than to try to point out what was good for the Crazy Gang was definitely pretty stupid for Wales. 'Bob, what's going on here? These are international footballers, they're superstars,' was Hartson's take. 'But the players had already gathered in a circle, there was no way out.

I just grabbed hold of him for two minutes, no punching or kicking.'

It was rather undignified – and to make matters worse neither did poor Hartson get much of a look-in against Turkey, sent on as a substitute for Saunders just nine minutes from time and unable to do anything about the scoreless stalemate. Indeed, Wales didn't win another game of that World Cup campaign, losing a barmy return clash in Turkey 6–4 and finishing above only San Marino.

Despite the poor results and growing controversy, the FAW stood firmly by their manager and backed him to qualify for the European Championships in 2000. Things became rather low key for a few months, with friendlies against Brazil (0–3), Jamaica (0–0), Malta (won 3–0) and Tunisia (0–4) providing the preparation for those Euros. By this stage Gould had unearthed and given a senior debut to a teenage gem of a player called Craig Bellamy, described by him as a huge talent for the future, but a real firebrand.

'I first saw him with the under-18s at Bisham Abbey, ahead of them flying to a game in Scandinavia,' recalled Gould. 'A bundle of football energy, darting here, there and everywhere. I asked our Youth coach, "Who's that?" The reply came, "Gouldy, you don't want to know, he knows everything!" Craig was certainly a straight-talker, even at that young age. OK, he rubs some people up the wrong way, but I saw him in a different light. I have rarely come across someone with so much passion to learn about the game. In Craig's early days as a teenager with Norwich he'd fly to Europe to watch matches just to broaden his football knowledge. I spotted his talent right away and could see it just needed to be managed.'

Over the next 16 years, Bellamy went on to become a Welsh legend as a player. As such, he became a popular choice for manager in 2024. Gould also handed a senior debut to a second youngster he'd noticed in the age grade teams, another character who wasn't exactly shy and retiring and who, too, would go on to make a significant name for himself – on and off the pitch. Welcome Robbie Savage. Who'd have envisaged, while making his Wales debut playing for little Crewe Alexandra, this effervescent individual would go on to star in *Strictly Come Dancing* and host BBC Five Live's flagship football radio phone-in show, *606*?

As indicated, Bellamy and Savage have never been slow in voicing their opinions on all things football – and indeed beyond – but as young players they probably sat open-mouthed in disbelief inside the dressing room as Wales' final preparation match ahead of Euro qualifying, a June 1998 friendly away to Tunisia, culminated in Gary Speed losing it and absolutely tearing into his under-fire manager. By that point Speed had been made Wales captain, Gould having abandoned other experiments, including Ryan Giggs and the contentious Vinnie Jones appointment. 'When I told Gary the good news his first reaction was, "You took your time asking didn't you?" He was a natural leader, knew the job should have been his,' reflected Gould. 'Everybody loves playing for Wales, but perhaps he loved it more than anybody else.'

It was this desire for Wales to do better which led to Speed's no-holds-barred outburst that afternoon in Tunis following another woeful showing as they were thrashed 4–0. It meant that Gould had now won just two matches out of the last 12, and those were meaningless friendly victories over Malta and Scotland. The run of poor results, allied to the various storms, had taken its toll on Wales' exasperated captain. He didn't want to let it go on like this, thus vented his feelings in no uncertain terms.

The Tunisians were meeting England at the World Cup in France 13 days down the line, and wanted to test themselves in a send-off against British opposition. There were 80,000 people watching that afternoon in the sweltering African heat. Given the circumstances, the carnival-like atmosphere, scorching weather and a partisan home crowd, perhaps Wales were on something of a hiding to nothing, but no-one foresaw such a humiliating slaughter in the sun.

Speed's mood hadn't been great when Wales landed in Tunis. Several players had already pulled out of the end-of-season friendly, numbers were so shy Neville Southall even had to wear an outfield player's shirt as one of the substitutes on the bench; now Wales were at a hotel base which Speed felt was not befitting of an international team. He wouldn't accept second best. At his behest, Wales were forced to up sticks and find better accommodation. The Tunisians put the kick-off time back, then forward again, while Wales say they weren't even given footballs to train with. The chaotic preparation hardly helped, and after the team were battered 4–0, according to Bellamy, the manager's take was that, 'Tunisia aren't a bad team so there's nothing to be ashamed of.'

Well, that was the final straw for Speed, simmering like a volcano over everything that had gone wrong from start to finish on that trip. Now he just erupted, ripping into Gould's team selection, tactics, training methods, man-management and just about everything else. Wales had no organisation, played 'like a pub side', they were way too easy to beat, he decreed. And, by the way, Tunisia weren't a good team as Gould claimed and would be on the first flight home from the World Cup – which they were, one point out of a possible nine from a group containing England, Romania and Colombia. There was absolutely nothing left out by Speed. It wasn't intended to be a character assassination, but he felt Gould's approach had set Wales back. Things needed to be said, lessons learned, if the country was to move forward again. As dressing room blasts go, this became something of the stuff of legends within close-knit Welsh football circles.

I had to meet up with Gould immediately after the game as I'd been asked by the *Sunday Mirror* to ghost-write a column for him for the following day's paper. They weren't interested in Wales, but they were keen to learn Gould's views on how

England versus Tunisia in Marseille would play out. Basically that meant interviewing Gould in a sectioned-off media area and then ghost-writing the column for him under his own words. I had absolutely no idea at the time that literally just five minutes earlier Gould had felt the full blast of Speed's wrath. In hindsight, that afternoon Gould did appear to be a little sheepish when we spoke, certainly not his usual ebullient self. I put that down to the shock of a four-goal hiding, but time proved there was clearly more to it than that.

Many years on, upon asking Gould about what Speed said that day in Tunisia, he still preferred to keep it inside the dressing room. Gould described it as: 'Gary was always challenging you, and as a manager I loved that. It was because he cared so much. He had an opinion which, at times, he wanted to put forward for the betterment of the team. If you have an opinion, voice it in the right areas and people will accept it.'

I'm not sure if Gould's FAW bosses were made aware of the manager-captain bust-up, nor if they knew much about the Manic Street Preachers, the sport-loving band from the Gwent Valleys who changed the lyrics of their song 'Everything Must Go' to 'Bobby Gould Must Go' at one of their gigs. Whatever, the Blazer Brigade remained adamant Gould was the right man to take them into eight back-to-back Euro 2000 qualifiers against Italy, Denmark, Switzerland and Belarus in the race to reach the tournament being jointly hosted by Belgium and the Netherlands.

In a bid to raise much-needed revenue, a legacy of the dramatic fall post-Terry Yorath, the FAW controversially opted to take the two biggest games, versus the Italians and Danes, to Liverpool's Anfield ground as the capacity of Cardiff City's Ninian Park was barely able to touch 15,000 at the time. Anfield, The swaying Kop, is a wonderful venue with a rich history, we all know that, but it's not Wales, is it? Before a ball had even been kicked Gould's men needlessly had been placed on the back foot – and it quickly got worse with another of those extraordinary incidents only Welsh football seems capable of throwing up.

On the morning of the opener with Italy, Gould jettisoned Robbie Savage from the squad for what he saw as an unmannerly act towards 126-times capped Italian legend Paolo Maldini. Interviewed by Sky Sports, Savage was handed Maldini's blue No. 3 shirt and upon being asked how Wales would cope with the great man he tossed it away.

'He put it in a bin,' reflected Gould many years on. 'I was absolutely disgusted. It was horribly disrespectful to Maldini.'

To Sav it was a bit of a laugh. His team-mates knew that, it was the kind of character he was. They'd have giggled along with him. Gould saw it differently. He immediately summoned Savage at the team's Carden Park Hotel base, around 40 minutes from Anfield, told him to pack his bags and go home. After the other players intervened, protesting to the manager, Gould relented, telephoned Savage again and said he could come back – but he was being dropped from the starting XI and would have to make do with a place on the bench. As it happens, Savage came on for the final nine minutes, a substitute for Mark Hughes, as Wales went down 0–2 despite a gallant display. Wales played well in this Saturday night fixture, could easily have taken a highly creditable point against a side who would go on to reach the final of the Euros, but the result and performance became incidental with the Savage row dominating the headlines. That continued on the Sunday morning when the midfielder sat next to his manager during a hastily arranged press conference designed to clear the air, but which Gould's critics claimed was cringeworthy.

Savage, arms folded and looking distinctly uncomfortable, was asked to explain the sequence of events, and started, 'I won't say what took place in the room.'

'Why not, why not?' interjected Gould loudly. 'Tell them the truth. You've got nothing to hide, I've got nothing to hide.'

Savage remained sheepish, a little embarrassed and shook

his head. Gould looked at him and urged, 'That's what we're here for. We're not here to be brow-beaten by them. Don't hide a thing because if you do you'll regret it.'

After a couple of sips of water, and ignoring another 'tell them what happened in the room' demand, Savage quietly explained what he did was meant in a light-hearted fashion and apologised for any offence caused.

Reflecting upon the whole incident two decades on, Gould remained unrepentant. 'I'd been out for an early-morning run, was told about the Sky interview, went to my room, waited for the next bulletin and couldn't believe what I was seeing. I wasn't happy with the interviewer either, putting Robbie in that position,' he told me.

'I raced to Savage's room, pretty much kicked the door in, got him out of bed and told him, "Get your bags packed and drive home." I was furious and he knew it. So did his roommate who had a look of shock on his face. Remember, I'd always had a special rapport with Sav, moved him from under-18s into the senior team for his debut. I kind of took Sav under my wing, but I told him he could not behave like this.

'Shortly afterwards I head down for breakfast. The news had got out and a deputation, Mark Hughes, Dean Saunders, Neville Southall, approached me. "We want him back," they demanded. "Well you can't have him back," I responded. They told me the players had gathered in a meeting room and would like to talk to me about it. So in I went. "We want him back," they repeated. I relented a little. "He can come back, but I will put him on the bench and that's as far as I will go," I told them. I phoned Sav, he returned like a shot – but only as a substitute. I had to stand up and say, "Rob, this is the moment where you get into a position where we need to respect football." If he's got to learn the hard way, so be it. There was an ironic twist to this story too. Italy's captain Fabio Cannavaro was magnificent that night. I went into the Italian dressing room to congratulate him and he handed me his shirt. That one is definitely not going in the bin, I thought!'

Some Welsh fans had chanted 'We want Bobby out' near the end of the Italy defeat, pressure was clearly growing, but suddenly, and somewhat unexpectedly, Gould managed to turn everything on its head with dramatic wins versus Denmark and Belarus in one of the new double-header international dates FIFA had just introduced. A teenage Bellamy grabbed a welcome winner versus the Danes in Copenhagen, the best victory of Gould's reign, and four days later defender Kit Symons scored five minutes from time to seal a 3–2 triumph in a gripping clash with Belarus. For a while, as Wales trailed 1–2 and were being outplayed, it looked like being another of those awful nights, but in front of 11,000 fans who created a rip-roaring, passionate atmosphere inside Ninian Park, the players displayed energy, spirit and tenacity to pull through.

Upon seeing Dean Saunders shortly after the final whistle, I joked, 'Well you've wrecked it for yourselves now mate, haven't you?'

'What do you mean?' he responded, a quizzical look upon his face.

'You've just kept Gouldy in a job?'

Deano didn't know what to say at first, before smiling, 'Well, we can only do our best for Wales Paul, can't we?'

There was palpable relief from the manager though – and the FAW suits who so loyally remained behind him as the flak flew thick and fast. Gouldy erupted with joy when the final whistle blew. Facing the heat, with the fallout from the Speed and Savage bust-ups continuing, he had silenced his many critics – for another eight months, anyway. Emboldened, Gould even seemed to take a little delight in moving the team to train at a prison a few miles up the road from Wales' hotel base, supposedly to make it hard for the press just as 'they were making it hard for me'. It was certainly a totally different experience having to go through the security gates of HMP

Prescoed, near the Monmouthshire town of Usk, and then walk into the prison canteen, with inmates around you eating their lunch, waiting to interview Gould and his players. The manager knew it also ensured that journalists and TV cameras couldn't get in to see what was happening behind the scenes at private training sessions.

'I was taking a battering from the Welsh media. I'm going to have them, I thought, they won't get out of this place! It was my way of having a little laugh, making it clear they don't control everything with the Wales team,' reckoned Gould.

The fact that HMP Prescoed also housed what Gould says was a better pitch than anywhere else in the area was perhaps more significant. 'We were like nomads, having to go wherever was available for training and the players deserved much better,' he recalled. 'Someone told me Usk prison had a lovely pitch which was hardly used. So I approached the governor, drove up to take a look for myself, saw it was a beautiful grass surface, and so that's where we went.'

The playing facilities were indeed first class, the players didn't moan, perhaps more was made of it by us in the media than the reality of the situation warranted. 'Wales Superstars Head Behind Bars' made for a good headline, but this was an open prison, hardly the searchlights, barbed wire and armed guards of Alcatraz or Colditz. That said, there was to be one moment Gould certainly didn't anticipate. The prison guards would wait for the players to get into their kit, then, to be on the secure side, lock the changing room while they trained for two hours. One morning the team were waiting out on the pitch for their manager... and waiting. And waiting. Where was Gouldy? You've got it. Turns out he was accidentally locked in the changing room. Fair to say a few were in fits of laughter when they realised what had happened!

Even though the team seemed happy enough with their new base, training in a prison added to the Gould 'crime sheet', no pun intended, as far as the manager's foes were concerned, and everything was to come crashing down on a balmy June Saturday night in Bologna in 1999 when Wales were smashed 4–0 by Italy. Instead of flying out two days before the game, as was customary, Gould took the team down to the Adriatic coast near Rimini for the best part of a week to prepare. It was a beautiful part of the world, but a long 1998–99 club season had just concluded and it is suggested some players felt they might have been better served training back home.

When the game commenced, while it would be wrong to say the players threw in the towel, that was the night Gould accepted he couldn't get the best out of them any more. The moment to go had arrived. First he ripped into front pair Ryan Giggs and Dean Saunders at half-time, saying they weren't doing anywhere near enough for the team. Indeed, Deano was substituted straightaway, replaced by John Hartson. By the time the fourth Italian goal had gone in, Gould was up from the dugout and pretty much off down the tunnel, with a request of 'Get me the president' to the FAW's media chief Ceri Stennett.

And so, with 11pm approaching, Stennett and FAW bigwigs Des Shanklin (president) and David Collins (secretary-general) stood outside the dressing room while Gould spoke to his players for one final time. The door opened and Gould emerged to say, 'We need to talk.' They went into the nearby doping room and spoke for 20 minutes as the manager quickly negotiated his pay-off.

Last deadlines had pretty much gone for the Sunday papers back home and the journalists who had flown out to cover the game, match reports long since filed, were impatiently waiting for Gould to attend his customary post-match press conference, ready to grill him on the heavy defeat and see if there was anything worth trying to squeeze into their titles. We were unaware of the behind-the-scenes drama taking place a few yards away inside that doping room. When Gould belatedly arrived he announced straightaway that he was standing down as manager. He'd tried his best, but this had been the final straw.

This was major news. In a panic I rang the sports desk back home in Cardiff to see if anyone was still around and we could hold back our editions to get this breaking story in. Thankfully, my sports editor hadn't yet left and I reeled a 400-word piece off the top of my head so we could get it on the front and back pages of the *Wales on Sunday*. The internet was in its infancy, *Wales Online* did not even exist, this was the only way to get the news out there. All my early training as a general news reporter, making daily police, fire and ambulance calls to check what had happened overnight and get it straight into the evening paper, came to good use at that moment to enable me to deal with this dramatic development. We couldn't possibly let the newspaper come out without covering Gould's resignation. After all, this was what many Wales fans, our readership, had been waiting for.

Because I was so busy sorting that out, I happened to be the last journalist back on the media bus which was parked outside the main VIP entrance of a now deserted stadium, ready to take us back to our hotel. It was gone midnight. At least the driver and my reporter colleagues had patiently waited for me. Poor Gould wasn't so fortunate. The team coach had already departed without him. Thus he jumped on our bus instead, sat quietly at the front, and politely bid us all goodnight as he was dropped off at the team hotel, before we were taken on to our own a couple of miles away.

For Gould it was a sad ending to a day which had started in unpleasant fashion when he fell victim to a thief on the morning of the match. 'We went on a usual staff walk to relax, settle nerves,' he explained. 'When I got back to the hotel I realised my wallet was missing. A pickpocket had been at work. So a few hours on there I am, deep into the Bologna night, we've lost 4–0, I've resigned – and I've got no wallet or money! It hadn't been a great start to the day for me and it wasn't a great ending, either. You'd think it couldn't get much worse than that.'

However, eyes lighting up, he emphasised: 'Let me tell you. Nothing, and I do mean nothing, will dampen my enthusiasm for my time in charge of Wales. It was an absolute privilege and I loved it, whether good or bad moments. Remember too, I wasn't sacked. I chose to resign. I just thought I'd taken the team as far as we could possibly go.'

Perhaps Gould had a sixth sense of what was in store because, the previous evening, at Wales' under-21s game in Italy, he had confided in a senior FAW official, 'I just wish I could have another couple of years in this job.' He was somewhat melancholy, almost semi-resigned to his fate and what might happen against a very decent Italian outfit in 24 hours' time. Yet even then Gould went out on his own terms. That night in Bologna he told Ryan Giggs, synonymous with the No. 11 shirt of course, that he was wearing No. 9 instead. He was the manager, he would determine who played – and who wore what jersey. Gary Speed, for the record, donned 11 against the Italians instead of Giggsy.

So, how do we assess the controversy-laden Gould era? Intriguingly, his lowly 29 per cent win ratio from 24 matches is exactly the same as the figure achieved by his successor Mark Hughes from 41 games, yet the two regimes are regarded as chalk and cheese by players and many fans alike. Gould is certainly an affable individual. He tried hard to win over the people, even taking the full Welsh team to play in charity matches against local sides. He had a vision for the game at all levels which, in his eyes, replicated what we were eventually to see come to fruition under different management structures and with greater backing from the FAW almost 20 years on.

'When I saw Wales doing so well at Euro 2016 – a group who had come through the age grade system together – I remember thinking that's exactly what I wanted to implement. Gareth Bale would have been about eight at the time,' reflects Gould.

To be fair, Gould threw himself into the job, pushing for better kit, training facilities and top hotels for away matches, if not always getting his way. He even made a point of standing up to Sir Alex Ferguson, going to visit the legendary Manchester United manager to try to ensure Giggs was available on a more regular basis. 'I was apprehensive because he's such a formidable figure,' explained Gould. 'But I had to put down some ground rules. Giggsy would put 10,000 on the gate. I did a newspaper article saying I was not prepared to con the Welsh public by telling them Ryan was going to play and then have him pull out. I was driving across the Severn Bridge one day when my mobile rang. It was Fergie in meltdown; the hairdryer at maximum setting. He didn't like how his stance had been portrayed. Our rapport was affected, although I know Sir Alex would have taken the identical position as me if he had been an international manager.'

Enthusiastic as he was to push football at every level in Wales and put in place a better youth and coaching set-up, ultimately Gould was going to be judged by top-level results, and his record of just seven wins from 24 matches was never going to be deemed anywhere near good enough. In Gould's last 11 competitive fixtures, Wales only managed two victories. Much as he attempted to get his methods through to the players, it became apparent too many senior pros just weren't being sold on them.

Not that they had much time to reflect because, four days on from Bologna, there was another important game, this time at home to Denmark. I use the term 'home' somewhat loosely because, as with the opening game of the group versus the Italians, the fixture was to take place at Anfield. I felt this was entirely wrong and after Wales' victory over Belarus in front of a febrile Ninian Park crowd of 11,000, who made so much noise it sounded more like 100,000, we had campaigned very strongly in the newspaper to get the FAW to bring the Danish match back onto 'proper' home soil. A play-off spot was at stake. Wales had a better chance of taking three points from their closest rivals for second place in the group by staging the game at Ninian Park, we believed.

Thus, over a number of weeks. we wrote a series of articles, forcibly outlining why the eleventh-hour change needed to be made. We were constructive about it; yes, we understood the commercial reasons for choosing Anfield, bigger crowd, greater corporate opportunities, closer to north Wales. However, imagine the vast riches that would come from actually qualifying, we pointed out, inviting fans to have their say, too. They responded in their droves. As such, two-page spreads of letters from the Welsh public helped crank up the pressure. The players also got on board, adding their weight to the clamour for Ninian Park.

Belatedly, amid an Everest-load of press, people and player power, the cash-hit FAW relented by telling UEFA they were changing venues, even though that meant compensating Liverpool FC for loss of revenue as contracts had been exchanged. Exasperatingly, the Danes then complained, insisting they wanted the same playing conditions as Italy when they met Wales in that first group clash. They also told UEFA they would have 4,000 supporters at the game, and Ninian Park could not accommodate such numbers. Perversely UEFA backed the Danes, rather than the home team. As if things weren't hard enough already, Wales had lost home advantage again.

There is a feeling in journalism that there is no point in leading a newspaper campaign, firmly sticking to your guns time and again, unless you finish on the winning side. However, right to the very end we remained dogmatic in our Ninian Park, not Anfield, stance because Wales playing their home games in Wales just felt like the right call. We kind of got our way, with the FAW grudgingly doing a U-turn, only for UEFA to wreck the day. The game would indeed go to Liverpool as originally planned, but those backing the call for Cardiff were the moral victors in my eyes.

Just 10,956 fans, and nothing like the number of Danes suggested, were inside Anfield as the team, jointly managed by caretaker bosses Neville Southall and Mark Hughes, lost 0–2. That was qualifying over yet again, then. Wales continued to be at a low ebb. The issue that now mattered was who would lead the team into their two remaining matches in the group, Belarus and Switzerland, and, more importantly, the next couple of campaigns that were to follow.

On the flight home from Bologna, Southall and Hughes had been seated at the front of the plane next to FAW officials. As the two most senior players, Gould recommended they be put in charge, against Denmark at least. Neither man was the sort to say no to their country. Southall's record of being Wales' record cap holder over many years spoke volumes for his commitment to the cause. Indeed, Ian Rush contacted yours truly to pay tribute to Big Nev when his team-mate surpassed the previous-best tally held by 1980s midfield warrior Peter Nicholas. It was a friendly away to Estonia in Tallinn and Rushie pointed out, 'The fact that Nev is breaking the record out there says everything about him.'

Hughes burned Welsh passion, just like Southall, and would never take a backward step for his country. He was once left out of Gould's squad for a friendly international away to Switzerland, at the business end of the season when his club Chelsea were chasing the FA Cup. Given Sparky's advancing years, Gould probably thought he was doing him a favour, enabling him to rest. Hughes saw things differently and demanded a meeting to find out what was going on.

'We landed back at Heathrow after losing to the Swiss and, given Chelsea's training ground was nearby, I went straight there,' says Gould. 'When we met, if Sparky wasn't exactly pinning me to the wall, let's just say he had a forceful manner. "Don't you dare leave me out of any Wales squad again," he said. I never did. Well, would you have taken on Sparky? Talk about caring so deeply for your country. I loved him, great player, so studious, so passionate.'

Hughes played the full 90 minutes of that clash with the Danes and thus left Southall very much as the front man on the management side, while also offering his own input over selection and coaching. That was the night Big Nev looked rather dapper in the manager's technical area, resplendent in black suit, black shirt and black and white checked tie. Having finished as a top-end player by that stage, Southall was looking for his next challenge and becoming boss of Wales was high on his list of ambitions. The team played well in defeat – who knows, with proper home support at Ninian Park they may have won – and Big Nev reckoned he hadn't so much thrown his hat into the ring, more 'chucked a stetson in there'.

While no-one saw him as manager material at that point, Hughes also put his name forward for the job. The FAW, knowing they simply had to get this appointment right after so many failures, were setting their sights in a more ambitious direction.

The man they wanted was Terry Venables. Cue more drama.

6

Sparky – hit or myth?

TERRY VENABLES, LIKE the great Brian Clough, is the manager Wales never had.

An audacious bid to land Ol' Big Head himself, Nottingham Forest League title and double European Cup winner, was launched towards the end of the 1970s and again in 1988. England may not have wanted the best manager in the country, wary of Clough's brash, outspoken manner, but Wales twice made a formal part-time offer to him. On each occasion the Forest board blocked the move at the eleventh hour. Who knows what might have been achieved with Cloughie, so brilliantly portrayed by Michael Sheen in *The Damned United*, barking orders from the Welsh dugout instead of Mike England or Terry Yorath?

Perhaps the same question can apply to Venables, mastermind of England's march to the semi-finals of Euro '96 just three years before Wales opened positive talks with him as we headed towards the turn of the millennium. As with Clough, it was a hugely ambitious move by the FAW, another attempt to bring a genuine world-class manager on board. Unlike Clough, Venables didn't have a club job, so he was available. Cockney wide boy exterior or not, he was also proud of his Welsh roots from the Rhondda Valley and the move clearly appealed. The evidence tells us nothing comes easy with Welsh football though, and unfortunately this proved to be another of those *Sliding Doors* moments as what Venables dubbed 'complications' meant the talks collapsed.

Venables was described by many players, Alan Shearer among them, as 'the best manager I've worked under'. Landing him would have been a real coup. Would his tactical genius, famed man-management skills, know-how, experience and charisma have given a new Welsh generation of talent at the start of this century the extra dimension required to qualify for the World Cup or Euros?

We will never know, of course. What history does tell us is that the FAW appointed Mark Hughes instead. An inspired decision in its own right given Sparky had no managerial background at all and helped to make the Dragons a competitive force again, but if anything sums up the boom-or-bust nature of Wales over three decades it is demonstrated in a microcosm of Sparky's five years in charge.

This was as rollercoaster as you can get. Hughes started with a horror run of 12 games without a win, equalling the worst sequence of results in Wales' history which had been set way back in the 1800s.

That was immediately followed by the greatest period I had covering Welsh football pre-Euro 2016, a truly wonderful 18-month spell which saw Wales beat giants Germany and Italy, play in front of unprecedented crowd numbers, and go ten matches unbeaten. That was another record, but clearly a much more welcome one. Heady days, those were.

From high to low again. Almost disbelievingly, straight after came another unwanted landmark – a record ten competitive matches and almost two years without a victory.

Sparky's spell as manager was a small moment in the grand scheme of things, but so amply defined the bigger picture over a longer period of time. Boom and bust. At one end of the spectrum, a mere 5,064 fans attended a 0–2 Euro defeat to Switzerland in Wrexham. It didn't quite eclipse the record low crowd figure of 4,839 who watched a 4–2 World Cup qualifying win over Turkey in 1965, again at The Racecourse, but it underlined how bad things had become.

Astonishingly, within a matter of months, Wales went from among the worst supported countries in Europe to the very best as they pulled in 70,000-plus sell-out crowds at the newly built Millennium Stadium. No other nation was attracting such high gates on a regular basis. A mix of everyone wishing to see this new jewel in a Welsh nation's crown right in the heart of Cardiff city centre, cheap ticket prices, and then a winning Wales on top made for a potent triple-pronged cocktail. It led to the scenario whereby nearly 74,000 turned up for a game against those enormous crowd-pullers Azerbaijan. It was a beautiful, sunny spring Saturday afternoon; there was a celebratory carnival feel to the occasion, happy faces all around as Wales won 4–0. Welsh football was fast becoming the hottest ticket in town. I drank the moment in. It couldn't get much better than this.

Sadly it didn't. Suddenly, we had one of those most extraordinary of implosions which was to see Wales enter the wilderness years again – and I've still received no rational explanation about why it all fell off a cliff so dramatically, other than maybe Hughes reached a certain level and couldn't go any further.

As such, even today, more than two decades on, I struggle to judge the Hughes era definitively. Two days after Sparky's departure I penned an article in the *Western Mail* highlighting the various pros and cons of his reign, headlined 'Hughes: Hit or Myth?' There was a lot of understandable love from many in the Welsh public, and certainly his players, for what he achieved. Equally there was angst from others who believed a more canny manager would have got more out of this group of gifted players.

Terry Venables, perhaps? If only.

I'm not sure I came to a proper conclusion on Sparky at the time. Even with the benefit of lots of hindsight and plenty of water passing under various Welsh bridges, I probably still view it the same way. The jury remains out a little for me. While I loved reporting on the enormous highs, I'm also of the opinion Hughes left behind the worst-case scenario in sport – an old team that was also a losing team. It meant his successor had a difficult task picking up the pieces, just as he had to, albeit in a different way, upon inheriting the mess left behind by Bobby Gould.

Indeed, after the disquiet of the Gould and Mike Smith years, the FAW daren't put a foot wrong with their next choice of manager. In time-honoured fashion they discussed the job with a trio of Welsh legends, Hughes, Neville Southall and Kevin Ratcliffe, but very much top of their wishlist was Venables, the man with the most gravitas. This was the glamour appointment to captivate a nation, they felt.

It became a drawn-out process and, aware the FAW were keen on El Tel – the tag given to Venables after he led Barcelona to the Spanish La Liga title – I struck up something of a rapport with him to gauge his interest in the role. Venables spoke fondly of his early upbringing after the war in the Rhondda Valley village of Clydach, of how he regarded himself as half Welsh and of his enthusiasm for the job. That was it then, it seemed, Venables was the Chosen One. He was keen. The Welsh people were hugely excited by the prospect of him coming on board. Finally, after years in the doldrums post-Terry Yorath, a self-implosion, Wales could take several gigantic steps forward again.

As the weeks went by, frustratingly with no announcement, I telephoned El Tel again. This time he was more circumspect. 'There are complications,' he told me, without wishing to elaborate upon what those issues were. 'The job is very tempting and everyone knows about my connections with Wales, but there are still things I need to think about. I honestly don't know which way to turn at the moment – I'm torn.'

Alarm bells now rang in my head. We ran the story

highlighting how the dream move could be off, suspecting it was down to finance. Shortly afterwards those fears were confirmed when one of my colleagues conducted a separate interview with Venables. 'There are lots of managers who will do the Wales job for the money on offer, but I'm not one of them,' he was quoted as saying.

This was a real body blow. Things appeared to have been going so well. My FAW contacts told me they were prepared to give Venables a three-year deal worth around £130,000 per annum, double the money Gould was on but hardly the kind of salary El Tel had been accustomed to in charge of England, Barcelona and Tottenham. The bigger issue, it was explained to me, was that Venables wanted a get-out clause inserted in the contract, which meant he could walk away after 12 months if the role wasn't working, or another big offer came in. That was the deal-breaker as far as the FAW were concerned, with secretary-general David Collins explaining: 'Unfortunately his terms were not acceptable. The package would have been too expensive.'

Undaunted, one bright Welsh entrepreneur contacted me to say he was ready to put up some of the extra salary out of his own pocket and crowdfund for the rest, via publicity in our newspapers, to make up the difference. This was an indication of how much Venables appealed to many fans. Again we ran the story, it gained traction, lots wanted to support the Venables for Wales cause, but it didn't feel right. It was the FAW who needed to finance any deal for El Tel, not the fans.

Former FAW president Phil Pritchard, a key figure in the decision-making process, reflects: 'Yes, we interviewed Terry. He was excellent too. We felt we had an obligation to speak to others as well, which we did. We quickly came to the conclusion some would be good at one thing, others had strengths in other areas. Terry had real pedigree, but the finances made it difficult. Impossible really. Remember, the FAW struggled to make ends meet at the time, we were never awash with money.

Because of that, we never actually formally offered the job to Terry, although we wanted him.'

They did to Hughes though, Pritchard explaining: 'Sparky was the apple of everybody's eye and that tipped the scales. No-one, outside of a small group of us on the FAW, saw him as manager material at the time, but we felt he had good organisational ability, a great demeanour, got on well with the players, would be their confidante as well as their boss, and that he was the one to bring everyone back together again. He also had his backroom team mapped out in his head. A clear vision for how he saw Welsh football's future.

'Just as with Venables, Sparky was used to much bigger salaries. We told his agent Dennis Roach that we weren't like the bigger countries, didn't have money to spend, we hadn't qualified for anything at that stage. His attitude was "I know what Mark Hughes' value is. Mark knows what his value is, but we accept you can't afford that so we'd be interested in listening to whatever you're able to offer."'

In the end the FAW presented Hughes with a similar package to the one they had tried to tempt Venables with. It was small fry for a man of his stature, who had played for Manchester United and Barcelona, but there was the carrot of a bumper £1million bonus if he qualified for a major finals. 'It would be self-funding as we would get five times that figure back from FIFA or UEFA anyway,' explains Pritchard.

And so Hughes, just 35, still playing for Southampton and a complete managerial rookie, was the new man in charge. We didn't know what to expect or how this would play out. What he wasn't, of course, was Terry Venables, the cheeky-chappie who would enchant the people with his witty one-liners.

Sparky is a different type of character, almost a complete contradiction of a man in some respects. On the field of play he was as tough a striker as you can imagine, mixing it with the best, never taking a backward step, winning 72 caps over a 15-year period, always playing with full-on commitment.

When I once questioned Sir Alex Ferguson about his absence from a couple of Welsh squads, wondering if the Manchester United manager might be behind it, he snapped at me: 'Do you really think I'm able to tell Mark Hughes that he cannot play for Wales?' An absolute Welsh warrior, then.

Off the pitch Sparky is softly spoken, almost even a shy individual who rarely loses his temper and keeps himself to himself. Whereas the more gregarious Venables was always charm personified, loved telling stories to the media, Hughes had been brought up in a more circumspect world at Old Trafford. Certainly, in the early days I always felt he was less comfortable holding court at press conferences than more outgoing figures like John Toshack, Chris Coleman or Bobby Gould, who had football anecdotes coming out of their ears and were happy to share them. Hughes preferred to keep things in-house. Not that he ever ducked his media duties; Sparky knew as manager of Wales he needed to speak to the nation and was contractually obliged to do so. I suspected he wasn't exactly drowning his sorrows, mind, whenever those press briefings were wrapped up.

Hughes was certainly a man accustomed to style. Someone who visited his house in the stockbroker belt of Cheshire once explained to me how beautiful it is – big gated property, password to get in, hand-woven carpet which follows the contour of the house, fantastic interior design, and even one room with a full-sized snooker table, plus display cabinets all around containing various trophies he'd won, including player of the year, as well as framed shirts. The trappings of fame and fortune from someone who always played with a steely-eyed determination to be on the winning team.

Fair to say Hughes put that latter trait to good use in his first role as a manager, immediately stamping his own mark on Wales by modernising the format and bringing what he believed were new Manchester United-like levels of professionalism to the set-up. On the basis you never wield more clout than on day one, he certainly went into battle for the team at FAW meetings, staunchly fighting his corner to get the purse strings released so his players could have the best of everything.

He assembled a bumper backroom staff around him, including two former Wales team-mates in Mark Bowen, quiet but studious, and Eddie Niedzwiecki, louder and more outgoing, who were each viewed as coaching innovators ahead of their time. They were aided by the more worldly-wide Eric Harrison, the famed Manchester United Youth guru who brought through the Class of '92 which included David Beckham, Ryan Giggs, Gary Neville and Paul Scholes. Sparky was always the front man, the mouthpiece through whom everything had to go, but he realised the value of tactical and coaching input by the trusted staff around him while he finished up his own playing days.

Hughes insisted upon a state-of-the-art training base, Wales heading to the new Vale Resort on the outskirts of Cardiff, which was already home to the nation's rugby team and where the football men now took over the entire ground floor of the luxurious complex. The two teams would often share facilities. Followers of the oval-ball side would tell me how even the biggest, hardest rugby aces would almost stand in awe when they spotted a global megastar like Ryan Giggs walking towards them in the lobby area.

Hughes also demanded top-notch hotels when Wales played matches in other countries, as well as special charter flights from Cardiff to cut down on the travelling time. He didn't want his players heading 136 miles up the M4 to London before boarding a flight. 'Footballers will always look for excuses, reasons to moan about one or two things, particularly when results are going wrong. Take away those excuses and it leaves them nowhere to go,' Hughes explained the major changes to me at the time.

It was sound reasoning and part of that, Sparky reckoned, was making Wales look more like a proper international team off the field too. Nothing annoyed him more than the Ragbag Rovers image Wales used to have – a tag he himself gave the side – as proverbially speaking they would beg, borrow or steal training gear from here, there and everywhere. Because kit used to be in such short supply, some players would even travel in their club tracksuits. A world away from more recent times.

Instead, Hughes insisted upon his players wearing bespoke FAW outfits before and after matches. Very dapper they looked too in a grey suit with embroidered FAW badge upon it, blue shirt and red tie. Hughes even demanded shirts with cufflink holes. Now, that's not exactly the kind of item players tend to pack when getting their gear ready to go away on international duty. Many was the time FAW employees Mark Evans and Ceri Stennett, who looked after the team, had to dash into Cardiff city centre to buy sets of cufflinks, and indeed black shoes that players could also forget. This new image was important for Sparky. He wanted to prove to the public that under him Wales meant business. It was his way of saying his players deserved respect for who they were and what they were representing. If he could fight their corner to get the very best for them off the field, then he would expect the same in return when they crossed the white line.

His captain Gary Speed was certainly impressed. 'They should give Sparky a ten-year contract,' was the message he wanted to send out via the Welsh media. With an influential figure like Speed fully on board, Hughes very quickly won over the dressing room. The players loved him and his methods, yet that wasn't remotely translated in terms of early results. Hughes started with a 1–2 victory in Belarus, when Ryan Giggs scored a late winner, but what followed was that dismal 0–2 European Championship home defeat to Switzerland in front of barely 5,000 fans.

Clearly, the Welsh public would need a lot of convincing that Hughes was the manager to revive the nation's fortunes.

Yet suddenly, something quite remarkable started to happen. Wales embarked upon the joint worst run in the country's then entire 125-year history, a woeful 12 matches without a win, but at the same time they began to draw bumper attendances which made them the envy of the rest of Europe.

The FAW didn't know what to expect from their move to the brand-new Millennium Stadium, the sporting citadel which was owned by the WRU, so they pitched ticket prices at just £3 and £5 for the opening game versus Finland, then £5 and £10 thereafter. No more than a single banknote was the FAW's marketing strategy. Well, something radical probably needed to be done because a repeat of the lowly gate at the previous game in Wrexham would have been embarrassing inside such a huge venue.

Wales' first match at their official new home was a friendly international towards the end of March 2000. The Finns were hardly a glamour draw like England, Brazil or Germany. This was uncharted territory, the FAW were wary, just hoping their cheap tickets policy would lead to a little upturn in the gate at least. No need to worry. Every single ticket, all 66,000 of them, were snapped up within 48 hours. Sold out signs. It would have been more were the capacity not slightly reduced for security reasons as the authorities bedded in the venue. This demand for tickets was so startlingly unexpected I found myself fielding calls from senior FAW figures based in mid and north Wales asking me if what we were reporting from Cardiff was really true? Well, to be fair, it did defy belief. Something special, indeed extraordinary, was occurring here.

The bumper crowd figure wasn't the only eyebrow-raising moment. So, too, was the news that Ryan Giggs was playing his first friendly game for Wales. Yipee, hang out the bunting, shout it from the rooftops. But, fully nine years after making his debut, and after 16 successive friendly internationals missed, Giggs finally lined up in one. Less than five weeks earlier he had been absent from number 16, a mid-February 0–1 win in

Qatar, which saw a fresh fuss kicked up in the Welsh media and in turn a robust response from Manchester United boss Sir Alex Ferguson.

'Which bright spark at the Welsh FA thought it was a good idea to arrange a friendly game in Qatar with an eight-hour flight at this stage of the season?' he questioned.

Fergie had a point, to be fair, but cry wolf and all that. This was hardly the first time Giggs had been deemed 'injured' when a Wales friendly came around. Nonetheless, the barren run was to be broken and Giggs came out fighting. We conducted a big interview with him ahead of the Finnish clash where he insisted he was fully committed to the Welsh cause and even revealed he had the Three Feathers, famous emblem of the Wales rugby team, embedded on the bottom of the swimming pool at his plush Manchester home.

'The criticism hurts, and particularly the people I'm close to, because they are Welsh, reside in Cardiff and have to read this sort of thing about me,' stated Giggs. 'I have won a lot with Manchester United, but I've always said there's no better achievement than playing for your country. The proudest moment of my career was when I first captained Wales. Sir Alex has also rested me for Man Utd games, he didn't want me burned out at 26.'

For the record Giggs went on to play in nine out of Wales' next 24 friendlies, including against Liechtenstein, New Zealand and Canada, before hanging up his international boots. In total he missed 30 out of a possible 40. He certainly gave an excited Welsh public a glimpse of what they were missing that night versus Finland because Giggs was absolutely magnificent, tearing into discombobulated defenders, running past them non-stop and causing carnage. Wales lost 1–2, through a Nathan Blake own goal, but Giggs was comfortably man of the match and marked the occasion by scoring Wales' first goal at the new ground.

Another huge attendance, more than 72,000 this time as

the Millennium Stadium capacity was increased, turned up a couple of months later as Wales lost a glamour game against Brazil. Indeed, such was the lure of the ground at the time, the fans just kept on coming during the 2002 World Cup qualifying campaign despite the alarming and record-equalling 12-match winless streak. In all, the barren run saw Wales lose friendlies to Finland, Brazil and Portugal, World Cup clashes against Belarus, Poland and Norway, and draw other qualifiers with Armenia (twice), Ukraine (twice) and the reverse fixtures with the Norwegians and Poles. Not since the end of the 1800s had any Wales team experienced such misfortune.

Now, on the one hand Hughes needed to rebuild dressing room morale which had hit the floor under Gould. He explained it was a slow process, but in time the defeats would become draws and the draws would turn into wins. Fair enough, we could buy into that. On the other hand this wasn't a good set of results, however you dressed it up. By this stage Hughes had been in charge for more than two years, ample time in my opinion to put his own stamp upon the side. As such, I argued in print that given the World Cup draw had been kind to Wales for a change, with no superpower in the group, it represented a massive opportunity missed. Far from being in the top two, dreaming of a trip to South Korea and Japan, Wales were battling it out with Armenia for the ignominy of finishing rock-bottom. Everything came to a head with the last game at home to Belarus on a Saturday afternoon in early October 2001.

Six days before the match, we ran a banner headline in the *Wales on Sunday* which read 'Wales' Worst – Or Are They?', outlining how Sparky's Wales had already equalled the unwanted record. Failure to beat Belarus, we pointed out, would make it unlucky 13 and put them into the history books on their own. The question element to the headline was quite deliberate as, while stating the stark facts, I also queried how on earth a team containing talents such as Ryan Giggs, Craig Bellamy, John Hartson, Simon Davies and Gary Speed could earn such an unwanted tag. Why were they not winning football matches?

I think Sparky and his players were caught off-guard a little by the article, perhaps unaware of the label they were about to be saddled with. Being dubbed 'Wales' Worst' jolted a few, not least the manager who, as kick-off drew nearer and an agenda having been set, was forced to contend with the damning statistics thrust in front of him. 'Trust me, I have played in far, far worse Wales teams than this one,' Sparky defiantly declared. 'Such a label is unkind and unhelpful.' He went on to admit: 'My pride has been hurt. There were a lot of things said that hurt.'

It was time to lance the boil. Fired-up Wales produced their best performance yet under Hughes, winning 1–0 through a Hartson goal, but playing with such a swagger it could easily have been four or five. It was only Belarus, that must be emphasised, but the winless hoodoo was over and there was always a feeling within the dressing room that one spark would lead to lift-off.

Suddenly it just clicked. And how. Sparky's men became an unstoppable force. From worst to best, this time they went ten straight matches without defeat, eclipsing previous record runs achieved by the Wales Class of 1958, who saw an eight-game unbeaten streak ended by Pelé and Brazil in the World Cup, and then the team under Mike England at the start of the 1980s.

There were a couple of huge scalps in there too, home victories over Italy and Germany, plus an unprecedented run of four wins out of four in the opening Euro 2004 qualifiers which had everyone dreaming about a place among the elite in Portugal. The fans turned up in their droves to marvel at this new-found Wales. No other team in Europe, possibly even the world, was attracting such sizeable numbers to games. Not England, with Wembley being rebuilt and thus capacity at other venues reduced, not Germany, not Spain, not Italy.

Interest levels were unprecedented. Even rugby, historically the dominant sport in Wales in terms of wall-to-wall media coverage, was knocked off the back pages, and indeed front pages, of the newspapers, as well as prime time TV news shows.

In a bid to keep the feel-good factor going, and encourage even more fans to witness first-hand what was happening here, I wrote an article arguing the chance to watch Ryan Giggs and Craig Bellamy strut their stuff on the international stage in a winning Wales team for only a fiver or tenner had to represent the greatest value for money bargain anywhere in world sport. Sparky's Wales were on the rampage, everything came together, they were riding the crest of a wave. Bellamy scored in an impressive 1–1 draw with Argentina at the start of 2002, Rob Earnshaw bagged the winner in a 1–0 triumph over Germany; there were creditable draws with a crack Czech Republic team and away in Croatia.

Wales were taking on some of the very best to prepare for the real business of Euro 2004 qualifying, which started in stunning fashion. First up, in September 2002, were Finland at their Olympic Stadium in Helsinki. A difficult opener, but John Hartson and Simon Davies were on target in a thoroughly professional performance as Wales won 0–2. That set the ball rolling. The following month saw what at the time had to rank as Wales' greatest ever result, that never-to-be-forgotten 2–1 Millennium Stadium win over Italy. Think back, what a night that was. The Manic Street Preachers and Bryn Terfel sang on the pitch beforehand, the great John Charles, revered in the two countries after shining for Juventus and Wales, was introduced to a rapturous ovation in front of a sell-out crowd – and goals from Simon Davies and Craig Bellamy tore apart an Italian defence containing Fabio Cannavaro, Alessandro Nesta and Gianluigi Buffon, men who would win the World Cup less than four years later. It was an evening of raw passion, Welsh *hwyl*. Sparky's side, feeding off the energy from the fans, were so superior it could easily have been an Italian thumping like no other.

That win for the ages was followed up with a third autumn triumph, another dominant showing as Sparky's sizzlers beat Azerbaijan 0–2 in Baku. Into 2003 and Wales made it nine games unbeaten with a 2–2 friendly draw with Bosnia, then a record ten with a 4–0 thrashing of the Azeri in the return Euro clash in Cardiff. Playing at home against a team like Azerbaijan in the past might have drawn a 10,000 attendance at most. That Saturday afternoon, in the Cardiff sunshine, I recall looking around at a sell-out Millennium Stadium crowd enjoying themselves amid a party-like atmosphere and just thinking 'Wow'. Heady times indeed, made all the more magical because of the dark days we had experienced previously. Goals from Craig Bellamy, after just 60 seconds, Gary Speed, John Hartson and Ryan Giggs ensured the party continued well into the night.

The 4–0 thumping meant Wales were soaring away at the top of their Euro group at the halfway point. Only France, Zinedine Zidane, Thierry Henry and their other greats, could match the four wins out of four perfect record. Well, we couldn't resist it, could we? A head-to-head comparison between the two sides simply had to be made. Some composite XI it was, too. Of course the French had the greater numbers, much as we tried to cram in as many Welshmen as possible, but this Sparky team was beautifully balanced in its own right. Paul Jones, Mark Delaney, Andrew Melville, Danny Gabbidon and Gary Speed made for a perfect blend of young and old, pace or know-how, at the back. Robbie Savage and Mark Pembridge were nuisances in midfield, perfectly suited to the up-and-at-'em approach Hughes demanded, with Simon Davies providing the silky skills further forward. Big John Hartson, among Europe's form centre-forwards at the time, combined up top with Giggs and Bellamy who flew down the wings at breakneck speed. Like Terry Yorath's great team of the 1990s, that 2003 line-up, with talents including Jason Koumas and new goal machine Rob Earnshaw waiting in the wings, was again every bit as good in my eyes as the Euro Class of 2016.

I was convinced Sparky's side would continue their surge and roar at the Euro finals in Portugal the following summer, a tournament which was won by huge underdogs Greece remember. That kind of stage was perfect for Wales' counter-attacking style and quick, highly skilful players like Giggs and Bellamy in full flow. Getting there still remained the age-old issue. In those days only the top team went through automatically, there wasn't the luxury of finishing second and still qualifying, as happened with Chris Coleman's Euro 2016 group runners-up behind Belgium.

Still, while you never count your chickens in football, the feeling was it seemed much harder for Wales to blow it from here than to finish first. What followed was an inexplicable meltdown that saw Hughes' team fail to win any of their remaining four matches to fall behind Italy, lose a two-legged play-off with Russia, and then continue the barren run in the opening four games at the beginning of the next World Cup qualifying campaign. A new record low of ten competitive games and 19 months without a win. To go from such extremes in quick-fire fashion like that – Wales' joint worst, Wales' brilliant best, Wales' worst again – was plain barmy. It made no sense whatsoever.

The first sign that things were to go wrong came with something totally out of Hughes' control. Four days after battering Azerbaijan, Wales were due to go to Belgrade to take on Serbia. Full of confidence, with everyone fit and a real buzz in the camp, everyone strongly fancied their prospects of making it five wins out of five. Then they really would have had a giant foot inside those Euros. Instead, it proved to be yet another of those moments that only seems to affect Welsh football. The game was called off at the eleventh hour after the assassination of Serbian Prime Minister Zoran Đinđić, which led to a state of emergency being declared. Wales couldn't travel in those circumstances and were told they needed to play instead in the searing 30 degrees Balkan heat during August, the closest designated international friendly date. By the time they reached Belgrade all the splendidly built-up momentum had been lost.

It began with an utterly pointless end-of-season friendly in the United States, an 11,000 mile, 28-hour round trip to California which did more harm than good. Wales lost 2–0, the end of the unbeaten run, but that wasn't the chief worry. More concerning was the fact that 18 of Hughes' original party pulled out of the game, almost an entire squad, leaving the manager scratching his head. We ran the obvious newspaper headline, 'Do You Know the Way to San Jose', based, of course, upon the Dionne Warwick international best-selling hit, reporting at the time how Hughes spent much of the build-up locked in telephone conversations with players and clubs trying to stress the importance of the fixture as the only warm-up for Serbia. There were always going to be withdrawals, it was the scale of them which shocked everyone involved. To compound matters, the match was played on an American Football pitch which curved downwards towards the touchline. There was a three-foot space, then a brick wall. No-one was particularly keen on doing a sliding tackle.

Looking back, I can't help thinking it was that San Jose moment which kick-started the sudden downward spiral. When Wales finally did land in Belgrade three months later, the missing players back on board, they walked into a very hot, oppressive and hostile situation. The RAF had previously bombed Belgrade during the Balkans War, a point the team were reminded of upon arrival when the Serbian liaison officer explained they would need to take a longer route to the hotel as one of the main bridges in the city still hadn't been repaired. At the stadium there certainly wasn't a warm Welsh welcome.

The Serbian fans were loud, while the bottom five rows of the stands were filled with armed soldiers dressed in menacing all-black T-shirt, trousers and berets. The FAW's media chief Ceri Stennett was wearing the correct 'all areas' pass around his neck, but found his path blocked as he attempted to walk towards the press section. When he protested, a rifle was pointed.

The ring-rusty players, in tip-top March condition immediately after blitzing Azerbaijan 4–0, now had just one Premier League game behind them. Against that backdrop, and in such sweltering heat, they produced a tame display and lost 1–0. Had the Serbia fixture taken place as originally planned five months previously, the mindset and outcome might have been entirely different. Instead, it proved to be a defeat from which Wales never recovered. Another chastening night followed 17 days later when Wales were thrashed 4–0 by Italy in Milan, a particularly disappointing experience for the 8,000 travelling Welsh fans, an incredible number, who made the trip to the San Siro in such hope. A 1–1 home draw with Finland, followed by a 2–3 loss to Serbia, each played again to sell-out Millennium Stadium crowds, meant that after initially roaring away with the group Wales took just one point out of a possible 12 in their final four fixtures and now finished behind Italy. They had done football's equivalent of Devon Loch, the horse which inexplicably fell 40 yards from the winning post when five lengths clear in the 1956 Grand National, and it was to get worse.

A two-legged play-off with Russia beckoned. Cue more drama and controversy. The hard part of the equation was done on a bitterly cold November Saturday afternoon in Moscow when Wales produced a performance to be proud of, backs-to-the-wall, trading a few blows of their own, but emerging happy with a 0–0 draw. I travelled with the team, sitting at the back of the plane, players up front, and recall the horrendously long time it took to get through Moscow airport upon arrival and then back out again afterwards. A cynic might claim the Russian authorities wanted to make things as uncomfortable as possible for Hughes' men. I couldn't possibly comment. Nonetheless, the feeling was Wales were now heading back to the Millennium Stadium to finish off the job in front of their own passionate fans. Instead of being an 'I was there' moment as part of yet another capacity crowd, it was one of those desperately disappointing nights, exactly a decade on from the 1993 World Cup setback against Romania, and every bit as demoralising.

The players were pensive on the bus heading into Cardiff; even the normally ebullient Robbie Savage, whose antics and wisecracks were brilliant for team morale, was quiet. And anyone who has been in Sav's company will tell you that's not normal! Hughes was negative with his selection and it is well documented that Vadim Yevseev scored what turned out to be the only goal of the game midway through the first-half. Wales were out, 0–1 on aggregate, and like Romania this was going to take some recovering from.

When I criticised Hughes' tactics, arguing he should have utilised the huge goal threat of Rob Earnshaw at the expense of a fourth midfielder in Andy Johnson, he dismissed my reasoning by retorting: 'We finished with four centre-forwards on the pitch, Paul – how many do you want?' That alluded to the fact that by the end John Hartson and Ryan Giggs had been joined by second-half substitutes Earnshaw and Nathan Blake. I couldn't accept Sparky's argument and it made me wonder if he had taken the team, this gifted group of players, as far as he could. Wales were chasing the game by then. I felt they would have been far better served with a more adventurous approach from the start, making the most of raucous home support, going for the jugular and putting Russia under the pump. The visitors might well have crumbled in that scenario. Instead, the strangely passive nature of the Welsh performance handed the initiative to the Russians.

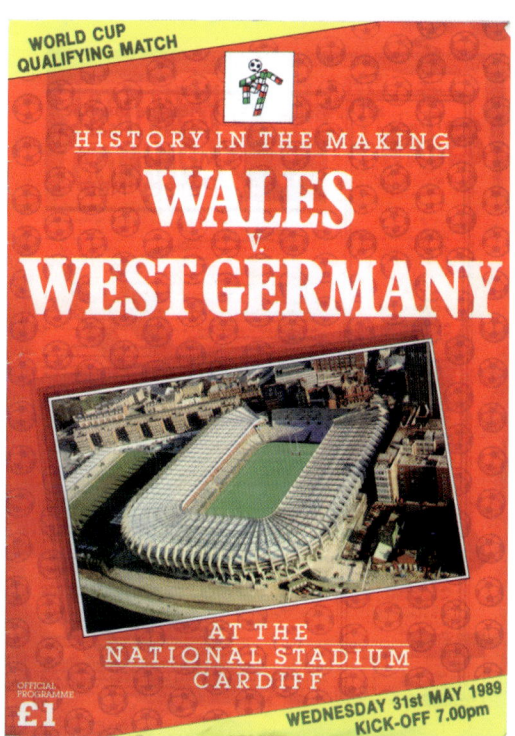

The historic match-day programme (a bargain at just £1) for Wales versus West Germany in May 1989. This was the first football game to be staged at Cardiff Arms Park, home of Welsh rugby. It finished 0–0.

More Arms Park history-making versus the Germans, the big Euro night when Ian Rush downed the then world champions with a never-to-be-forgotten winning goal in 1991.

Wales' *Sliding Doors* moment in November 1993 – Terry Yorath and his team take pride of place on the front cover of the programme for the gut-wrenching World Cup loss to Romania, one of Welsh football's darkest nights.

Welsh-language channel S4C get us in the mood for the big game – Ian Rush, Ryan Giggs and Dean Saunders certainly made for a goal-laden trio up front.

The agonising moment as Paul Bodin's penalty strikes a Romanian crossbar.

Getty Images

Wales versus Wales! Ryan Giggs (standing next to me, in yellow) and Dean Saunders pose with a Welsh Press XI after we played against them at Cardiff Arms Park ahead of them meeting Germany. We lost 0–3. Not a bad effort, considering!

A night to forget – Netherlands 7–1 Wales in Eindhoven 1996. The Dutch programme had a special feature inside entitled 'Ryan Giggs is Magic', but the young wing ace didn't play.

Bobby Gould shows me the stunning view from his home across the Bristol Channel towards Wales, meaning he will never forget his controversial four-year spell in charge.

Mark Hughes hated the Ragbag Rovers image hard-up Wales used to have. Here he is looking resplendent in the bespoke suit, shirt and tie outfit he insisted his Wales team wore.

PA Images/Alamy

Paul Jones, John Hartson, Gary Speed and Andrew Melville are helpless as Vadim Evseev gives Russia a 1–0 Euro 2004 play-off win at the Millennium Stadium – another of those Wales *Sliding Doors* moments as they entered the doldrums.

Independent/Alamy

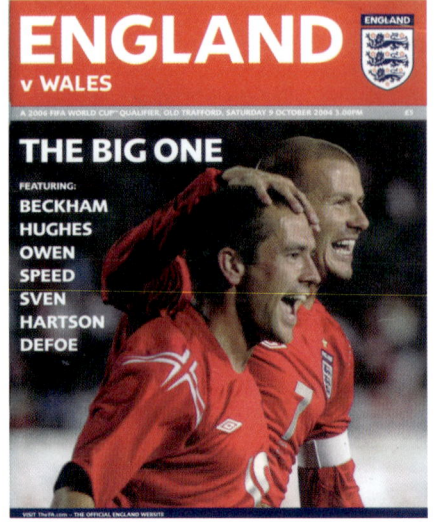

Even England were labelling an October 2004 World Cup qualifier against Mark Hughes' Wales as 'The Big One'. Unfortunately, David Beckham and Michael Owen featured on the front of the FA's programme, had the last laugh with a 2–0 win in the first game between the countries for 20 years.

John Toshack looks studious as he plans and implements Wales' much-needed youth revolution during the Noughties.

Phil Stead

A young Gareth Bale, handed his debut at just 16 by Tosh, displays the skills which lit up the Wales No.11 shirt for many years.

Phil Stead

Bright new dawn – a teenage Aaron Ramsey takes pride of place on the programme cover for Wales' first match at their new Cardiff City Stadium home, versus Scotland, in November 2009. Toshack's team won 3–0 – and Ramsey was Man of the Match.

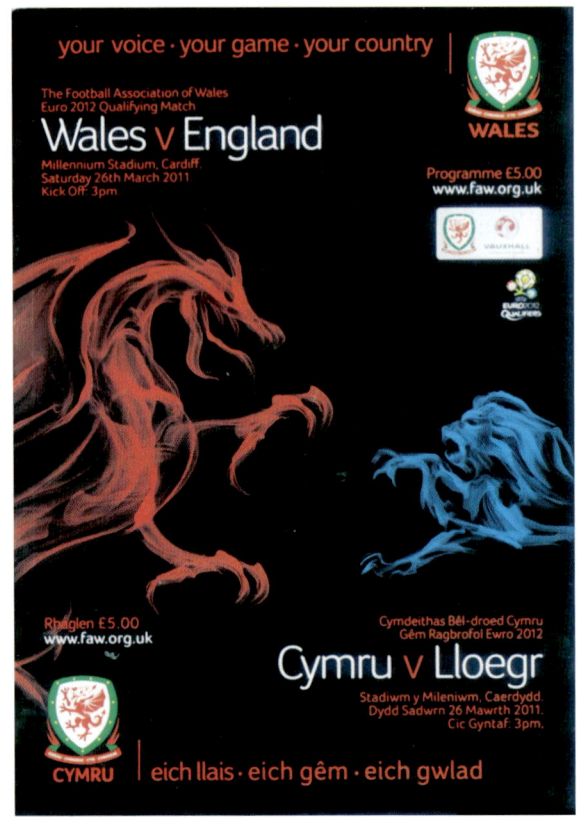

your voice · your game · your country
WALES
The Football Association of Wales
Euro 2012 Qualifying Match
Wales v England
Millennium Stadium, Cardiff.
Saturday 26th March 2011
Kick Off: 3pm
Programme £5.00
www.faw.org.uk
Rhaglen £5.00
www.faw.org.uk
Cymdeithas Bêl-droed Cymru
Gêm Ragbrofol Ewro 2012
Cymru v Lloegr
Stadiwm y Mileniwm, Caerdydd.
Dydd Sadwrn 26 Mawrth 2011.
Cic Gyntaf: 3pm.
CYMRU
eich llais · eich gêm · eich gwlad

The last competitive match to be played at the Millennium Stadium, versus old enemy England in the spring of 2011. Amid disquiet, Wales quit the venue halfway through their tenancy agreement with the Welsh Rugby Union.

Happier days as Gary Speed is unveiled as Wales manager in 2010 by FAW President Phil Pritchard (left) and Jonathan Ford (right). The two officials had to sit side by side a year later to announce the sad news.

PA Images/Alamy

BRAINS BEER
faw.org.uk
faw.org.uk

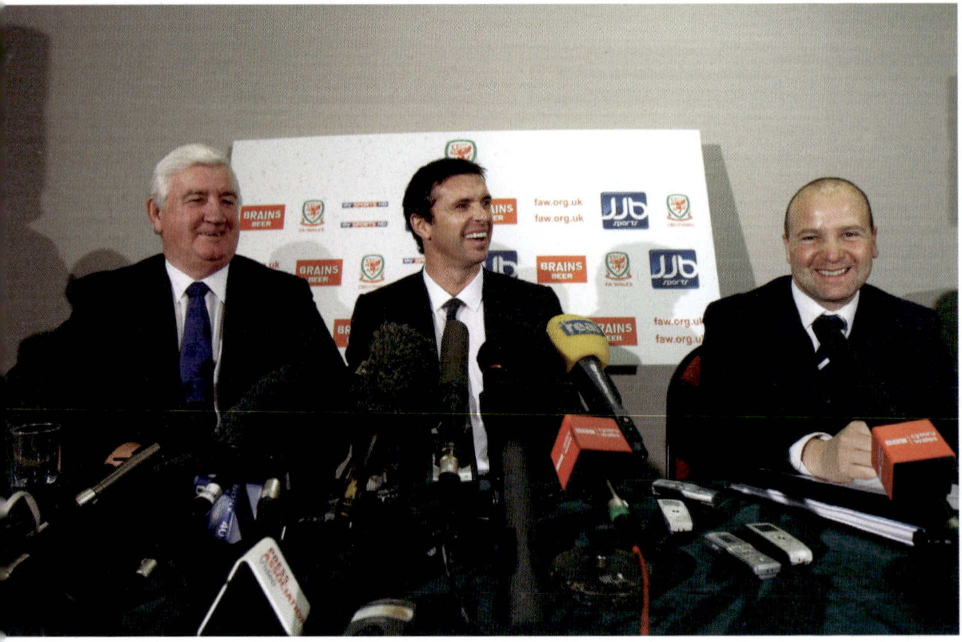

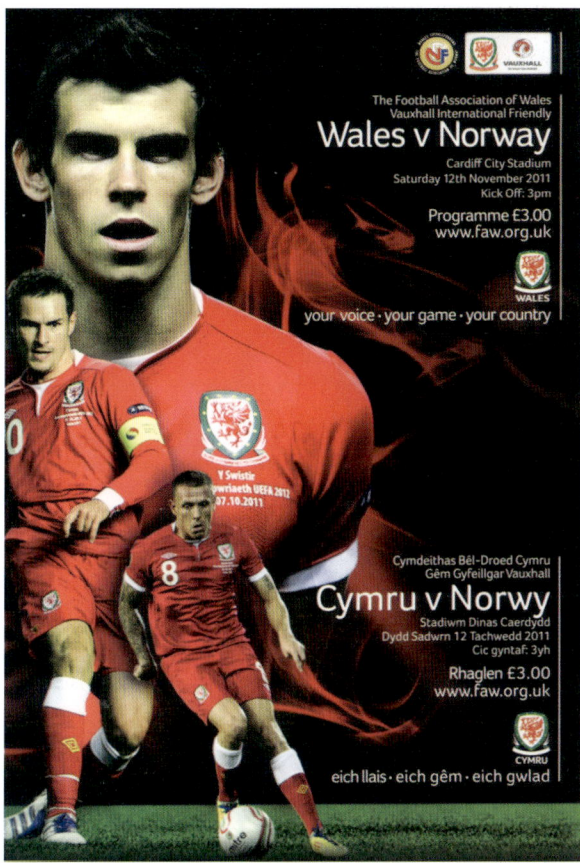

Star turns Gareth Bale, Aaron Ramsey and Craig Bellamy feature on the cover of the Wales v Norway programme in November 2011. Who would have believed this would be the last time they were to see their manager? Wales battered the Norwegians 4–1.

Such a sad night – skipper Craig Bellamy with Ed and Tom Speed at the Wales versus Costa Rica memorial match for Gary Speed in February 2012.

PA Images/Alamy

The match-day programme from that evening featuring Gary Speed on the cover as manager and inspirational player. Costa Rica were the same opponents Speedo made his debut against in 1990.

Chris Coleman and the Wales substitutes celebrate Ashley Williams' goal in a never-to-be-forgotten Euro 2016 win versus hot favourites Belgium. What a tournament that was.

Associated Press/Alamy

Ryan Giggs and his players celebrate reaching Euro 2020 after beating Hungary at Cardiff City Stadium. Sadly, it was soon to implode for the manager.

PA Images/Alamy

Would an experienced old hand like Terry Venables have erred in those circumstances? You'd like to think not.

Earnshaw was on fire for Cardiff City at the time, in the middle of a purple patch of form which saw him score 22 goals for club and country by the end of November. We will never know for certain what would have happened that night if, in the absence of the injured Craig Bellamy, Hughes had paired little Earnie with Hartson up front. But let's put it this way, Earnshaw began Wales' two subsequent games. He smashed a hat-trick in the first against Scotland. He scored the winner in the second against Hungary. Enough said, perhaps. If he could have his time again would Sparky pick the same XI? Only he can answer that, but Welsh fans I speak to tend to side with my viewpoint as they reflect on that squandered opportunity.

At the time, Hughes' team selection was quickly forgotten amid a flurry of fresh headlines surrounding Russian midfielder Yegor Titov, who had failed a drug test after taking banned substance Bromantane. That was the so-called 'secret' Russian drug which saw athletes stripped of their medals at the 1996 Olympic Games in Atlanta after positive results, only to have them reinstated because the then unknown stimulant had not been on the International Olympic Committee's official banned list. Hughes, who had noted how Russia grew stronger as the game went on while his own players wilted, was seething upon learning the Titov news. Demanding UEFA overturn the result, thus declaring a 3–0 win to Wales, Hughes claimed: 'If one player is guilty, then the whole team should be guilty.'

UEFA disagreed as they dealt with a formal protest from Wales, banning Titov for a year but ruling, 'in the case of a doping offence the punishment only applies to the player himself and not to the team'. Disappointed, but undaunted, Wales spent £100,000 on an appeal to the Court of Arbitration for Sport in Switzerland. The case wasn't heard until May, only a month before the 2004 Euros kicked off, but Hughes still wanted Russia thrown out and declared his players 'will be ready for the tournament,' noting how Denmark's stars had come off a beach to win the 1992 Championships after taking Yugoslavia's place at the last moment.

Sparky had the bit between his teeth here, which was to be commended, but politically I always feared it wasn't a fair fight. Little old Wales, with next to no clout inside UEFA's corridors of power, versus the might of Russia. When three judges in Lausanne threw out the case, decreeing Wales failed to prove that the Russian team were implicated in Titov's drug-taking, it prompted the FAW to maintain: 'The drug had a huge effect with regard to performance and relieving the tiredness that all players involved in the play-offs felt. It's disappointing to see that drugs cheating has prevailed.' The David versus Goliath battle had been lost.

A shame. There were some great sides at those 2004 Euros, Zidane's France; Sven's England golden generation; Ronaldo, Figo, Deco for hosts Portugal. But ultimately it was won by Greece, the biggest upset in European Championship history. Wales will feel they too could have made some sort of underdogs mark, just as Coleman's aces were to do 12 years later in France. Russia? They went out in the group stages, albeit they were the only side to defeat the eventual champions.

By now Hughes was being linked with Premier League jobs, but the lure of the 2006 World Cup in Germany also appealed, particularly after his Dragons were drawn with England. The two nations had not locked horns for 20 years, not since Hughes himself bagged the only goal in a 1–0 Wrexham win in the final Home International Championship match. Having got one over the old enemy as a player, now Hughes set his sights on doing so as a manager.

Trouble is, the campaign picked up where the Euro qualifiers had left off, in hugely disappointing fashion as Wales could only draw 1–1 with Azerbaijan and then 2–2 against Northern Ireland who had two players sent off early on a madcap Millennium Stadium night which also saw Robbie

Savage red-carded. This was further evidence for me the team had gone as far as it could under Hughes. Wales really should be beating a nine-man Northern Ireland side at home. As such no tears were particularly shed when Blackburn announced Sparky as their new boss, agreeing he could stay in charge for the looming double-header with England and Poland to give Wales breathing space to look for his successor.

There was already enormous hype building towards the England clash, but it was handed extra impetus because the game took place at Old Trafford, the Theatre of Dreams where Hughes established himself as a football legend with Manchester United. He was going home, albeit in the away dressing room. Much as we dreamed of a Welsh win, the realistic scenario was that they headed over the Cheshire border more in hope than expectation.

This was a star-studded England side, containing Wayne Rooney, Michael Owen, Rio Ferdinand, Sol Campbell, Ashley Cole, Frank Lampard and a captain by the name of David Beckham who was at his dazzling best. Thank goodness Steven Gerrard was injured! John Terry couldn't even get in the XI.

It turned into a day that started badly and didn't get any better. News filtered through in the morning that a British hostage had been beheaded in Iraq, which I'm told left everyone subdued. When Wales got to Old Trafford, veteran centre-back Andrew Melville injured himself during the warm-up, creating a state of panic. Hughes' plans were out of the window before a ball had even been kicked. Instead of making a like-for-like change, he shuffled the pack by bringing in Jason Koumas as a midfielder, moving Mark Delaney across to centre-half and shunting Simon Davies to right-back. The blend didn't look right from kick-off. Lampard scored after four minutes, Beckham added a second. After waiting two decades to meet the old enemy, Wales' biggest rivals, rather than breathing fire the somewhat cruel headlines were about 'Puff the Tragic Dragon'.

Nine competitive games without a win, Sparky's final match versus Poland, which Wales lost 2–3 in Cardiff, made it ten. By this stage some in the media were on the manager's back and I was very much part of that. Indeed, we had a robust exchange of views ahead of the Polish clash. Sparky felt I was over the top in my criticism; I believed the players were capable of achieving better results. We finished with a friendly enough handshake. I told Mark that earlier, golden 18 months under him was the best period I'd known covering the national team and that I would always be grateful for that, but clearly the end of the road had been reached between him and Wales.

In advance of kick-off I prepared a strongly worded editorial, to run as a back-page comment piece in the following morning's *Western Mail*, headlined, 'Save Our Soccer'. It was an appeal for Welsh powerbrokers to turn to John Toshack, by far the obvious candidate I felt to restructure this team and implement a much-needed youth revolution. Wales were hurtling backwards, fresh direction was required to look to the future and no-one else could match Tosh's know-how, gravitas, experience and willingness to make bold calls by starting anew. For 70 minutes I thought Wales, leading through an Earnshaw goal, played well, so called the office to say we should pull the piece for now. It didn't seem appropriate. My editor insisted we stick to our guns, and a one-two-three Polish whammy of goals in the final quarter justified his decision. I guess that's why he, as editor, was paid the big bucks! By the final whistle Wales were all at sea. They weren't even halfway through the group, but already the World Cup dream was over once again. Just like 2002 under Sparky.

Toshack, the man we were advocating to take over, was in the studio as a BBC Wales pundit and didn't hold back in his criticism. He demanded to know if it was really 'too much to expect Ryan Giggs to run past players down the wing like he does for Manchester United' and if the show's presenter should 'be happy we have gone two years and ten competitive games without a win, because I'm not.' The players, and Sparky, saw it as sniping from the sidelines, feeling a former international should be kinder in his comments. Tosh could see how badly things had gone wrong. He was paid to tell the truth, not sit on the fence. Given his track record as a manager at home and abroad, coupled with a willingness to speak his mind rather than hide behind diplomacy, he was the best pundit BBC Wales could have.

Not that Hughes views it that way, believing Toshack had gone too far and insisting that he managed to, 'Restore respectability to Welsh football, not just here but worldwide, too.' He went on to state: 'My legacy is for others to judge.'

So how do we definitively assess that legacy? As already indicated, it was so dramatically up and down that I'm probably still as unsure today as I was when penning that 'Hit or Myth' pros and cons article immediately after his departure.

In terms of facts and figures, Sparky was in charge for 41 games, with 12 victories, 15 draws and 14 losses for a win ratio of 29 per cent, exactly the same figure achieved by Bobby Gould. We had those wonderful 18 months sandwiched in between two record winless streaks. It was so perverse. Wales were so close to qualifying, yet so far away as well.

On the one hand, Sparky brought new-found pride and professionalism back into Welsh football, making the team highly competitive and indeed feared with those wins over Italy and Germany. The buzz and feel-good factor he helped to create should never be underestimated. The record crowds loved watching their team mix it with the best; robust, resilient and capable of producing some breathtaking moments of magic.

On the other hand, Hughes' overall tally of just six victories from 26 competitive matches is pretty woeful. Worryingly, his successor would be inheriting a team which not only hadn't won competitively for close on two years, but which also contained a whole plethora of players in their thirties, or fast approaching that age, who were much closer to the end of their international careers than the start. Indeed, of the main figures involved only four men – Craig Bellamy, Danny Gabbidon, Simon Davies and Rob Earnshaw – were aged 25 or younger, although at a push you could also put Jason Koumas in that category.

The age demographic was all wrong. The status quo couldn't continue. It was blindingly obvious a painstakingly difficult youth revolution, which would take time to come to fruition, was required.

There was only one man for that job. Wales had failed to land El Tel, more's the pity. Now it was the turn of El Tosh.

7

A load of Tosh
as the rebuild begins

THE FIRST TIME I met John Toshack, let's just say he wasn't exactly looking to win Charmer of the Year any time soon. I had been dispatched to Spain by my newspaper to write about how the boy from Cardiff ended up eclipsing managerial big beasts from Brazil, Argentina, Germany and Italy to become boss of Real Madrid, football's most pressurised job. Not too many people landed that gig. Tosh had the honour twice. He should have been in a good enough mood. His side had just thumped Real Zaragoza 7–2 in front of a packed Bernabéu Stadium crowd, part of a record-breaking first season in charge which saw Tosh's team win La Liga at a canter by scoring more goals than any other side in history. After making my way to the Bernabéu press room on the ground floor and waiting patiently for the Madrid media to finish with their post-match interviews, all performed in flawless Spanish by Tosh, I approached the big man.

'Hello John, I'm from the *Wales on Sunday* back home. Is it OK to have a quick word in English please about your time out here?'

'Let me see your ID,' came the curt response. Toshack, then at the absolute zenith of his managerial powers, had a lucrative contract to write an exclusive column for *The Sun* and, as such, was wary of speaking to anyone else in the British media. He looked at my credentials, noted they were genuine, but still barked: 'No, I'm not doing anything with you.' With that he turned his back and walked off.

'Oh come on John, I've just travelled a thousand miles from Cardiff to speak to you,' I tried in vain, the Spanish media wondering what this exchange of words was about. To no avail. Toshack continued walking away, right through a door into the Real Madrid inner sanctum where only players and senior club officials were permitted.

That was that then, I thought. Talk about a wasted journey.

Maybe something pricked in the big man's conscience because a couple of minutes later he popped his head back around the door and beckoned me inside, this time the Spanish press perplexed that I was being afforded this special privilege of entering what was a no-go area for them.

There we now were, just the two of us, right by the Real Madrid dressing room, Toshack politely explaining he couldn't say too much as other London-based titles, rivals of *The Sun*, would pick it up from my paper and report his words for themselves. There was a massive tabloid war going on at the time and the editor of *The Sun* wouldn't be best pleased. He did, however, give me a couple of Welsh specific lines I could use and a deep off-the-record briefing to provide insight for my article into what it was actually like to be in charge at the world's biggest football club. In newspaper parlance that meant that while I couldn't directly quote Tosh, I was still able to write in an informed manner about how he landed the job, what it entailed, and of the surreal experience of a Welshman going head-to-head every week with managerial giants from more traditional football powerhouses.

Unlike what had happened minutes earlier when he snubbed me, this Toshack could not have been more helpful, accommodating and pleasant. He chucked in a couple of lovely little anecdotes for good measure. I guess in those split moments you have John Toshack, bad cop, good cop, depending on your point of view. It's fair to say that during his six years in charge of Wales, from 2004 to 2010, he polarised opinion.

Toshack's supporters argue he inherited a right old mess from Mark Hughes, an ageing and losing squad that needed to be torn apart and shaken up amid a Wales Youth revolution that saw Gareth Bale, Aaron Ramsey and a clutch of other teens and early twenty-somethings burst onto the scene under his watch. Only Tosh, with more than 25 years of management behind him, possessed the know-how and courage to make those huge calls. He also tried to modernise the way Wales played, making the team more Continental with a patient pass and move approach after Hughes' more in your face British-style methods. Obviously, it didn't always work, but the more talented players in the side, Ryan Giggs, Craig Bellamy, Jason Koumas, had some of their finest hours in a Wales shirt under Toshack. He was happy to build a team around them – 'piano players', Tosh called them, while it was the job of the grafters to 'carry the piano'.

Most significantly, he fast-forwarded everything by giving debuts to so many of those youngsters. Euro 2016, that memorable march to the semi-finals, could never have happened without the solid foundations put in place by Toshack. Given those circumstances, with the young guns having to learn on the job against battle-hardened opponents in the harsh environment of international football, Toshack's record is to be commended: Played 53, Won 21, Drew 8, Lost 24, for a win ratio of 40 per cent. Only Ryan Giggs, of Wales managers who have taken charge of a significant number of games, boasts a superior figure.

Major plus-points there, then.

Toshack's detractors, on the other hand, point to the fact Wales never came close to qualifying under him. He failed to nail the big wins when they really mattered and that, while his record was decent in friendly internationals, out of the 29 competitive matches played a run of ten wins, three draws and 16 losses is nothing to shout about from the rooftops. They reckon his era can't be looked back upon too fondly, arguing it was defined by rows with senior stars, players retiring, crowds dipping amid a few awful performances, and squads depleted by withdrawals. Toshack was stuck in old-fashioned methods and it needed a more modern manager to kick-start everything again.

Some charge sheet against then, too.

In conducting research for this book I was told how one senior player asked an FA of Wales official what Toshack, aged 61 when he finished in the job, had actually achieved in football? The query was genuine, not flippant. When the somewhat perplexed official pointed out Toshack had won League, FA Cup and European medals as a player with Liverpool, taken Swansea City from the bottom of the Fourth Division to top of what is now the Premier League as manager, led Real Madrid to the La Liga title and won Cups in various other countries, it still didn't seem to particularly resonate. This was a different generation. Toshack was a wonderful orator, could tell brilliant stories about Brazilian, Spanish and Argentinian players he had managed at Real Madrid, but it was from a bygone age for some. Same with his assistant Roy Evans and any tales about the famed Liverpool boot room of the 1970s. To some that was decades ago, irrelevant in the modern age.

Toshack didn't even own a mobile phone, continue the critics, let alone have an understanding of the new world of social media and the internet. That said, FAW figures found him more reliable to deal with than one or two others. Toshack may have been based out in Spain, but if he arranged to take a call at an allotted time he would be by his landline waiting for it to ring several minutes before it actually did.

Judge as you see fit, I guess. Personally, I'm very much in the glass half-full Toshack camp. Were it not for his courage in giving youth its head, Wales would have been in the wilderness much longer than they actually were. Someone mentioned to me that you could put Toshack's managerial gongs on one side of the table, and the combined honours won by every other Wales boss in history on the other side, and it is still Toshack's which would be weighted down the most.

I also found claims Toshack was a football 'dinosaur' a little perplexing as, ironically and on the contrary, he was always a man ahead of his time. It was Toshack who introduced the sweeper system into British football with Swansea City back at the start of the 1980s, a tactic Bobby Robson mirrored and earned great plaudits for when taking England to the World Cup semi-finals a few years on at Italia '90. It was Toshack who invented a ploy which saw Real Madrid play with Mexican goal ace Hugo Sánchez as a lone striker, commonplace today but pretty unprecedented back then. 'Systemar Toshack', the Spanish media dubbed it. Real's success meant it quickly caught on.

It was another Toshack tactical first during his reign as Wales boss which actually led to us having sharp words. He played without a big centre-forward in a 1–3 Millennium Stadium World Cup qualifying defeat to Russia, utilising Craig Bellamy as a supposed striker but he spent half the game dropping deep or going out wide. I was heavily critical in my match report for the following morning's *Western Mail*, writing it was no wonder Wales lost because how on earth could they score any goals with such a negative approach. Toshack was straight on the blower, vehemently insisting my critique was harsh, arguing chances were created (it would be called XG, expected goals, in today's parlance) and that this would soon be the way forward in football. I stood my ground. Let's just say we agreed to disagree. Shortly afterwards Pep Guardiola adopted exactly the same blueprint with his brilliant and all-conquering Barcelona team. He used a guy by the name of Lionel Messi in the role. The false nine, as it became known, was the new vogue. Everyone began to mirror Pep – or maybe that should be Toshack? He had been ahead of the game again, I now concede. Tosh just didn't have the quality of Barcelona's superstars throughout the team to make a success of it with Wales.

Not that the somewhat fierce words we exchanged over Bellamy's role that night ruined our working rapport. Toshack wasn't the sort to bear grudges like that; he would have his say, then it would be forgotten about. Indeed, I've got on very well with him ever since that initial brush-off inside the Bernabéu press room. Whenever he was back in Wales we would meet up, either at Verdi's café on the Swansea seafront or an eatery in the trendy Pontcanna area of Cardiff, for what turned into compelling articles about what it was like to manage some of the greats of the game. Tosh would reel off tales about legends like Roberto Carlos, Gheorghe Hagi, Clarence Seedorf and Iker Casillas, talk of Real Madrid player-power, a critical Spanish media and what it was like trying to out-do leading managers, some of whom had won the World Cup or Euros.

He also agreed to write hugely popular and informative World Cup and European Championship columns for the *Wales on Sunday* and the *Western Mail*. Now normally how these things work is you interview the high-profile sporting figure, then ghost-write the column for them under their own name. Not with Tosh, he insisted upon doing it himself. Across the column would come from Spain in handwriting by Fax (why not email I hear the critics scorn?), offering fascinating tactical insight into what to expect from upcoming matches, brilliant analysis about what had just happened, or a lovely little anecdote about a star player he had invariably managed in the past.

Wales simply *had* to tap into that knowledge from one of their own, so once it became clear Mark Hughes was leaving, the *Western Mail* campaigned for Toshack to replace him. No-one else ticked as many boxes. After two decades of working in Spain, Portugal, Italy, France and Turkey, El Tosh was ready to bring home that vast experience to benefit his country. It would be a hugely exciting appointment, we felt. As well as being a tactical innovator, Toshack also happened to be a legend among fans of bitter rivals Cardiff City and Swansea City – some feat that, trust me – and would be able to open doors at UEFA simply because of who he was and what he had achieved in two spells as manager of Real Madrid. He also had a proven track record of developing young players for stardom, with teenagers Iker Casillas at Real Madrid and Xabi Alonso with Real Sociedad among the Toshack protégés. Given the Wales squad was full of players in their thirties, it was obvious a massive overhaul was required with a new emphasis upon youth. That would lead to short-term pain, which we saw, but also long-term gain, which we also so splendidly witnessed in due course.

Indeed, I was sitting in the office one Thursday afternoon when out of the blue the phone rang – with Xabi Alonso introducing himself to me on the other end of the line. Now, hands-up here, I didn't know too much about Alonso, even though he was playing for Liverpool. He won the UEFA Champions League with the Reds that season, went on to dazzle for eight years at Real Madrid and Bayern Munich, lifted the 2010 World Cup with Spain and more recently became the hottest young manager in the game after leading unfashionable Bayer Leverkusen to the German Bundesliga title. Real Madrid then came calling. So there was clearly somebody with a lot of kudos getting in touch with me here, even if, to my embarrassment today, I didn't realise it then.

Alonso was aware of the Wales vacancy and, Liverpool training finished for the day, he wished to push Toshack's cause via the Welsh media. 'He has the experience required for international football, a record of bringing through young players and making them into stars,' started Alonso. 'If Wales need a manager prepared to pick younger players and mould them for the top, then they couldn't have a better man. He changed my view of football. He picked me when I was just 18, made me believe in myself, made me think I was wanted and brought the best out of me. You need someone that first time to trust in you and to see something different that you might bring to the game. Not every manager has the ability to do that. If John hadn't put that trust in me, I don't know what would have happened. I feel he would be perfect for Wales.'

Well, that was some tribute. Given we also wished to push Toshack's cause, Alonso's words could only help our campaign as FAW bigwigs would clearly take note of what he had to say. They were also keen to speak to a couple of Frenchmen: Gérard Houllier, who had performed excellent work in his homeland, and Philippe Troussier, likewise with South Africa and Japan, plus Dutchman Dick Advocaat and Welsh legends Ian Rush and Dean Saunders. Houllier pulled out, realising the writing was on the wall with Toshack hot favourite for the job. Interviews took place at the Miskin Manor Hotel, just outside Cardiff, and very quickly a five-year deal was struck to make Toshack national team boss. That was an unprecedented length of time for a Wales contract, a firm indication of the scale of the task required for Toshack to totally revamp the team, settle Welsh football down and put the nation back on the right path again.

As he reflects upon it all today, Toshack says: 'The average age of the side was far too high. They had failed to qualify on a number of occasions, gone ten games without a competitive win and I just felt it was time to rebuild everything. Almost from scratch. When you do that you don't really expect to qualify for the next tournament, nor perhaps the one after that – remember, as an international manager you only get five or six games a season and that isn't much time to get your methods across. But my aim was to put in place the bedrock of a team to ensure that when they did eventually break that qualifying jinx, then they would do it two or three times in quick succession. That is exactly what happened. I'm obviously disappointed not to have qualified myself, but deep down I always knew somebody else would benefit from the painstaking changes we put in place, and at least there is the consolation of knowing we started it all off.'

Because Toshack and his ultra-loyal FAW bosses were looking at the bigger picture, specifically tasking him with such a major overhaul which would take time, they were never going to be distracted by senior players retiring or, in the case of Robbie Savage, also ensuring controversial headlines by being openly derisory about the new regime. The majority of the Welsh public seemed happy with the appointment of Toshack; his biggest obstacle in the short term was winning over the players, having been so openly critical of them as a BBC Wales pundit when Mark Hughes' empire fell down around him. Personally, I could never understand why a TV was on inside the dressing room immediately after games, enabling the players to hear Toshack's no-holds-barred views, but it was and they did.

Savage became a kind of dressing room shop-steward. Part of Toshack's first squad, a 2–0 Cardiff friendly win over Hungary in February 2005, he was dropped for the following month's back-to-back World Cup qualifiers with Austria. Toys out of the pram, Savage responded by telling Toshack he could 'stick it up your arse' and he was retiring from international football anyway. A savage (pun intended) blast followed in the London tabloids, Robbie pretty much slating everything from Toshack's training methods through to the fact players had to eat fried bananas. I'm told they had been accustomed to lavish food options under Hughes – chicken, lasagne, Sunday roast, puddings – but let's just say the menu was now rather more limited. As it happens, a dietician reckoned fried bananas were extremely nutritious and good for sportsmen ahead of a game, but Savage wasn't necessarily viewing it that way.

The problem for Savage was that he became something of a lone voice in his public criticism. Other players kept their own counsel, as by and large did Welsh veterans Gary Speed, Andrew Melville and Mark Pembridge who had chosen to hang up their international boots because of age by the time Toshack was appointed. Savage didn't really want to join them in retirement; at 30 he still had plenty to offer and his impish personality was important for morale inside the dressing room where team-mates would laugh along at the pranks played and jokes told by him. However, Savage had played into Toshack's hands by quitting. He said he didn't want to be 'humiliated'. The manager argued he couldn't adapt to the more patient passing style he wanted from his Welsh midfield, where ball retention was key. Nor did he score goals. Nor was he disciplined enough.

Savage versus Toshack was dubbed one of football's top-ten feuds, with Mick McCarthy versus Roy Keane listed at number one, and there was to be no way back for Robbie. Toshack had dealt with proper player power inside the Real Madrid dressing room, where groups of major stars possessing influence among fans and with high-ranking friends in the Bernabéu boardroom could gang up together against him, so a sole spat with Savage was hardly going to perturb him, however unwanted the headlines.

As the row rumbled on, it led to one of the most riveting 15 minutes of broadcasting ever heard in British sport whereby Savage went on the Wales-based *Real Radio* phone-in show to have a right old ding-dong with Leighton James, one of his arch-critics. Leighton, capped 54 times as a team-mate of Toshack's in the 1970s and '80s, was the greatest Wales player of his generation and had forged a new career for himself as a pundit prepared to speak his mind. Savage saw the show as an opportunity to get all the hurt and frustration off his chest, meaning the two men went hammer and tongs at one another during an epic showdown where Sav insisted he should be playing for Wales and James outlined why he wasn't.

I almost had to do a double take at one point when Savage

decided to bring my name into it. As emotions reached fever pitch, he told James: 'You're best mates with John Toshack. You and Paul Abbandonato and the Welsh press are all over him like a rash.'

It then got a little unnecessarily personal. James wasn't much of a tackler in his day, Savage asserted, adding: 'You wouldn't go in for 50–50s. And if I played against you these days, oh dear, dear.'

'You wouldn't catch me,' retorted James, who went on to say: 'One day, when you have got a command of the English language Robbie, you will perhaps become a pundit.'

Savage bit back by claiming he 'wouldn't want to be one' when he finished playing, reckoning: 'I wouldn't want to slaughter my ex-team-mates to earn a few quid. I would be in a fortunate position to have enough money to retire.' Ironic comments, given Savage went on to write a column for *The Mirror*, hosted the BBC's flagship *606* Saturday night phone-in show and regularly appeared for BT Sport to voice his opinions. Just like James! Albeit Robbie will argue he is constructive.

The *Real Radio* show was compelling listening, Savage's exasperation at not being able to increase his tally of 39 caps for his country was palpable, but it altered nothing. The stand-off continued, although Savage did at least inject some humour into proceedings when he subsequently stated: 'John Toshack said it was his way or the highway – well I guess I'm on the M56 then!' Amid what I felt were unnecessary previous barbs and sordid headlines, that was more like the real Robbie Savage speaking. He has always been good for a quip or two to lighten the mood. It brought a smile to my face, anyway.

Reflecting upon it all today, Toshack prefers not to individually name Savage, but he explains: 'I just felt the team had grown old together. They hadn't been able to qualify, we needed to start afresh, do things differently, play a different way. These players had had a few attempts at it, we needed to move on from that.'

Privately Toshack conceded that of the senior stars who retired, the only ones he wished he could have kept were Gary Speed and Ryan Giggs. Speed, who at the age of 35 announced he was departing a full month before Toshack was appointed, was the leader on the pitch, a huge character in the dressing room. When he went the team lost its rudder. 'I just felt Gary could have handed the younger players the benefit of his wisdom and wished he'd given us a few more years. He could have played a key role. They would have looked up to him, his experience would have been hugely beneficial,' says Toshack.

An even bigger loss was that of Giggs, who midway through Toshack's reign called it a day after 16 years, 64 caps and 12 goals in a Wales shirt. Soon to be 34, Giggs announced he wanted to focus upon his club career and felt his decision was justified as he went on to play for Manchester United until he was 40. If he had carried on playing for Wales, Giggs reckons his longevity in the game wouldn't have been so great. Toshack had made Giggs his captain for three years and Wales' more liberated Continental style suited him. However, Giggs was not for turning and duly bowed out to a rapturous ovation from the 30,000 Millennium Stadium crowd when he was substituted in the final minute of a 0–0 European Championship draw with the Czech Republic in June 2007.

'I wasn't surprised when Ryan told me of his decision,' reflects Toshack. 'To keep to the standard Manchester United wanted, he felt he needed to rest during international breaks. And, as we know, Fergie was always a bit hesitant when players went off on international duty. We were in a moment of changing everything and, much as I would clearly have liked Ryan to stay on, this was part of that whole process.'

Giggs was always an exemplary professional when on Wales duty. He would meet charity groups or FAW commercial partners for photographs, embraced the responsibilities of captaincy and was well schooled in what to say and perhaps, more importantly, what not to say at pre-match and post-match press conferences. Ryan was rarely anecdotal, funny, or spoke out of class. He ensured there were no negative headlines, even when regularly asked to respond to Savage's own headline-making remarks. Giggs would simply give an Alastair Cook-style flat-batted response, emphasising the players were merely focusing on the game and the outside noise was for others. The Manchester United way of doing things, I guess.

Plenty is written about Giggs elsewhere in this book, but this really was the end of a magical era. There are some who will have you believe he never played well for his country. I don't know whether that's the memory playing tricks, or selective amnesia in wishing that to be the case. The truth is that he produced some of the finest individual performances we have witnessed from any player in history in the red of Wales, and against a wide range of opponents too. The 'twisted blood' defenders of Germany, Italy, Belgium, Finland, Azerbaijan and others are among those who will testify to Giggs' dazzling brilliance down the wing. In one game, a 2–3 Windsor Park World Cup qualifying win away to Northern Ireland under Toshack, I gave Giggs ten out of ten in my player ratings. That pretty much never happens, but he was simply unplayable that afternoon, and scored the winning goal. As he was on many other occasions, too. He wasn't quite Gareth Bale for Wales, but he was very much the next-best thing.

That doesn't mean everything was brilliant, because it clearly wasn't. Giggs should have won double his number of caps and scored double his number of goals, even though opposition teams would often put two or three men to mark him. Stop Giggs, Stop Wales was their motto. 'The pressure is always on Ryan's shoulders and it's unfair,' reckoned Craig Bellamy. 'If we don't win it's always Ryan who gets the blame.' There were huge games when he under-performed and did indeed receive stick, notably the win-or-bust qualifiers with Romania in 1993 and Russia in 2003. An anonymous showing during a desperately disappointing 1–0 loss to the Republic of Ireland at Croke Park under Toshack also stands out. The critics will argue that when it really mattered Giggs didn't deliver for Wales whereas Bale did.

It's a fair point. However, when Giggs was good, like Bale he was truly exceptional and his departure added to the problems for Toshack who only four games afterwards also found himself on the brink of quitting, just halfway through his reign. It is a story that has never been made public until now. In the end FAW officials persuaded him not to go and Toshack took the helm for a further three years and 28 matches, in doing so making up his mind to fast-track the Welsh Youth revolution with even greater haste.

There had been a mixed set of results from his first 25 matches in charge, nine wins, six draws and ten defeats, incorporating much of the Euro 2008 qualifying campaign which went from the ridiculous to the sublime – a 1–5 home thrashing by Slovakia, that desperately disappointing 1–0 Croke Park loss to the Irish when Giggs was poor, a commendable 0–0 draw in Germany, a stunning 2–5 slaughter of Slovakia in the return match. That night in Trnava was Craig Bellamy's greatest display as a Wales player, with Toshack's new captain scoring twice, forcing an own goal, running Slovakia ragged, and for 90 minutes producing an individual wondershow to match anything we saw from Giggs or Bale.

'Craig was either outstanding, as he was that night – or he'd give you the biggest dilemma possible,' smiles Toshack. 'There was no in-between. He was either the best player on the park, or you almost wished you didn't pick him! I don't mean that in a detrimental way. It's just I felt sometimes the problems he could bring with him took things out of you as manager. That night he was inspirational, I couldn't recall when I'd last seen one player have such an impact on the outcome of a game. Normally you have 22 evenly-matched players battling away; this one was 21 players – and one who was just unbelievable.'

Yet despite the Bellamy masterclass, there were rumblings

of discontent behind the scenes and it all came to a head in the next match, a 13 October 2007 Euro qualifier away to Cyprus which was to be followed four days later by a trip to San Marino. That thumping win in Slovakia a month earlier gave Wales hope of a decent enough third-placed finish behind runaway group leaders Germany and the Czech Republic, with six points there for the taking against Cyprus and San Marino. Instead, it turned into a Nicosia nightmare for Toshack as his side produced a terrible performance, throwing away an early lead given to them by defender James Collins, to crumble to three second-half Cypriot goals.

The manager was furious. He'd had enough. This was a lamentable display too far, the straw that broke the camel's back. He couldn't get a tune out of these players. He ripped into them for 20 minutes at full-time, then stormed out of the dressing room where he spotted the FAW's head of international affairs Mark Evans, and their media chief Ceri Stennett. 'That's it, I'm done,' he immediately told them. 'I can't do anything with this lot.' Alarmed at what they were hearing, and fully aware Toshack wasn't even halfway through a rebuilding process, the FAW officials sat him down in a chair in the corridor outside the dressing room. They had ten minutes to change his mind before he announced to the press that he was going. Toshack was drained, exhausted by the horrendous 90 minutes he had just witnessed and also by the warts and all dressing-down he had just given to his players. There was nothing left in the tank. His very recently appointed number two, Dean Saunders, would have to step in for the game in San Marino in four days' time.

It was pointed out to Toshack that he needed to be stronger than this, that he must have been through similar crises during his managerial career in Spain and that surely he could do the same with Wales as well. If there was a battle of wills with the players, as manager he had to win that. Toshack eventually relented. 'OK, we'll go to San Marino and see what happens there,' he grudgingly accepted, heading into the press conference and choosing to take defeat on the chin in public. Bad loss, pride hurts, we have to bounce back versus San Marino. He knew what to say in those circumstances.

Inside the Welsh camp it was a very different story. Toshack was still seething. And he wasn't in the mood for any moaning from his players after a performance as appalling as that. Wales were staying at a beautiful hotel in Larnaca and, anticipating three points, a day off had been arranged on the Sunday to enable everyone to wind down and relax by the swimming pool. At short notice that was cancelled as Toshack held the most monumental of post-mortems, giving every player the chance to speak privately in a bid to work out what had gone so badly wrong. The following day they flew to the lovely resort of Rimini to prepare for the game in nearby San Marino, another beautiful hotel overlooking the Adriatic Sea. Toshack now reached the end of his tether again. He lanced the boil by going public, accusing the players of being too pampered and saying they had even complained about the waves keeping them awake at night. It defied belief for him.

'I don't like some of the things I'm seeing,' he fumed. 'There are people who have paid to come to Cyprus and have to go back home and do a shift. They're paying money again to come to San Marino and watch the game. Sometimes you just have to remind players that those fans are not as fortunate as we have been. We travel around, get paid for doing it and it doesn't cost them a penny. Maybe after the Cyprus game all those things came to me and, I'm sorry, I just needed to let a few of them know how I felt.'

Perhaps it was Toshack's way of trying to tell the press 'What am I supposed to do with this lot?' Either way, it made San Marino a lose-lose situation. Wales managed to scrape a 1–2 victory, courtesy of Rob Earnshaw and Joe Ledley goals, but it was a soulless night, a turgid game, a crowd of just 1,182, in effect a large portacabin for a dressing room and not a great occasion for motivational purposes. Skipper Bellamy described it as 'one of the worst atmospheres I've been in', and went on to say the chanting from the Welsh fans 'was vicious and took its toll on the players as well. It wasn't nice.'

However, Wales had just about got away with it. Toshack was able to fight another day and eyes started to turn to the qualifying campaign for the 2010 World Cup in South Africa. Just Toshack's luck to be drawn with the Germans again, as well as Euro 2008 semi-finalists Russia, with Finland, Azerbaijan and Lichtenstein making up the group. It wasn't a stellar campaign. Wales played well in falling to late goals in Germany and Russia, but a new nadir came in the spring of 2009 with a 0–2 Millennium Stadium defeat to Finland in front of just 22,000 fans. That was the game when Jonatan Johansson, a journeyman forward with St Johnstone, Hibernian and Charlton Athletic, opened the scoring which led to the 'I don't know how, he's not good enough' barb from Welsh captain Bellamy.

It was also a match where I again had words with Toshack afterwards, arguing in print that he should have played Aaron Ramsey, a teen sensation who had burst through at Cardiff City and just joined Arsenal. Knowing he had already picked a host of young players, Toshack fired back: 'What do you want me to do, put yet another one in there?' My answer to that was yes – Ramsey was the midfield future for Wales. However much we admired the silky skills of Jason Koumas and Simon Davies, as senior players they were desperately disappointing against the Finns and I felt, even at his terribly tender age, Ramsey was too good a player to be overlooked.

And so we saw one of the massive plus-points of the Toshack reign. He had already handed a full debut to a young superstar in the making by the name of Gareth Bale. Even in the 1–5 Millennium Stadium horror show versus Slovakia, Bale stood out like a beacon and scored a cracking free-kick goal – the first of many we were to witness with Wales. As well as Bale and Ramsey, others Toshack gave Wales debuts to included Wayne Hennessey, Chris Gunter, Neil Taylor, Joe Ledley, Joe Allen, Sam Vokes, plus Ashley Williams. This was very much the core of the team who went on to dazzle at Euro 2016, young players thrown in at the deep end and needing to grow up very quickly in international football. As we saw with Manchester United and their famed Class of '92, there is nothing quite like a group of talented home-grown youngsters coming through at the same time to create a special team spirit, resolve, buzz and camaraderie. Now Wales had that. The future looked bright, the future was red. Toshack wanted this new group to end the age-old issue of players pulling out of Wales duty and to go on to win 100 caps for their country. No-one had achieved that landmark. As Toshack hoped for, Bale, Hennessey and Gunter each went on to smash through the barrier, while Ramsey and Williams had more than 80 internationals to their name.

'When I managed in Spain players would head off all over the world to play for Brazil, Mexico, Argentina. There was never any question of them not going. Sometimes I wouldn't see them again until the morning of our next game. So it used to drive me crazy when so many pulled out of Wales squads,' says Toshack. 'We needed to change that narrative. And we did. This group didn't pull out. They were always there together, enjoying one another's company.'

A key part of Toshack's shake-up was putting his former Wales team-mate Brian Flynn, the ex-Wrexham and Swansea manager, in charge of all the age grade sides. Instead of the under-17s, under-19s and under-21s having separate managers and understandably wanting the best players for their own teams, Flynn took overall control and fast-tracked youngsters through the system as he saw fit.

'Flynnie was brilliant at spotting talent and telling me when these players should step up into the senior side,' says Toshack. 'He knew I was never averse to picking teenagers – if you're good enough, you're old enough for me. The key thing was Cardiff City manager Jimmy Scoular giving me my own debut at the age of 16. That influenced my thinking. I had to start somewhere, so too did these Welsh youngsters. That is why I had no hesitation in giving Bale his debut at 16 against Trinidad & Tobago. He was clearly the brightest talent, you didn't need to be a rocket scientist to realise he was going to reach the highest level.

'I could have stuck with older players, given them more caps, possibly even had one or two better short-term results, but it would have been at the expense of developing these younger ones for the future. I knew we would take a couple of beatings here and there, like 1–5 at home to Slovakia, because that's what happens with inexperience. Ups and downs, inconsistency. But I felt the older ones had had enough chances, that these youngsters couldn't do any worse, and I remember saying, in time someone else would reap the benefit from this work. By then I would be retired, sitting up in the stand enjoying watching these players purvey the ball. It was no surprise to me they went on to achieve what they did. We take pride in the fact we started it off.'

If Bale was the jewel in Toshack's crown, Ramsey wasn't too far behind. Flynn picked him at the tender age of 17 in a Welsh under-21s win over Italy in Swansea, when Ramsey was man of the match, and did the same in a European Championship play-off tie with England at Villa Park. England's side contained stars of the future, including Joe Hart, James Milner and Adam Lallana, but Ramsey, three years younger than others on show, was the best player on the park and scored in a 2–2 draw.

Flynn tells a superb story of how England boss Stuart Pearce made a substitution with only half an hour gone, taking off Lee Cattermole and sending on Bolton's Fabrice Muamba.

'My assistant Alan Curtis turned to me and said, "There's something going on over there, Brian. England are putting a substitute on",' says Flynn. 'We hadn't noticed any injury. Pearce wanted Cattermole to, in effect, man-mark Aaron, but it didn't work. So he put Muamba on – and that failed too! Funnily enough, I saw Fabrice recently at a Burnley match and he mentioned what had happened that night.

'Aaron was just so special, even at that age and against older players. I first picked him for the under-21s for a game against Sweden in Halmstad. He was 16 at the time and I wanted him and Joe Allen to come along just for the experience of travelling and to see what training and preparation was like. I had no intention of playing either of them, but we were 3–1 down at half-time, being battered and over-run in midfield, so I chose to send the pair of them on. Aaron ran the game and Joe got the winner as we won 3–4!

'Tosh kept saying to me "What type of midfielder is Ramsey?" My response was "What do you want him to be?" He could play 6 or 8, but I invented the 10 role for him. I needed to fit Ramsey, Allen, Andy King and Jack Collison into the same under-21s starting XI. The only way I could do that was to play Aaron really advanced as a 10, just behind the striker. He never looked back from there. That became his position for club and country.'

Wales finished their World Cup qualifying group in a disappointing fourth place, miles behind top two Germany and Russia. The abject defeat at home to Finland was followed by more misery in the Helsinki return when, not only did Wales lose 2–1, Toshack was so short of numbers he could only name four players on the bench instead of the customary seven. This was akin to a Sunday League pub side turning up with only nine men, certainly not befitting of an international set-up. The substitutes that night were Sam Vokes and Neal Eardley, who both came on, and the unused duo of goalkeeper Boaz Myhill and centre-half Craig Morgan.

Yet, despite the woes, the emergence of Bale, Ramsey and the other young guns lifted the mood. A new dawn was about to emerge and the fresh optimism and hope appeared fully justified when a team made up almost entirely of players barely out of the under-21 side thumped Scotland 3–0 in a friendly at Cardiff City Stadium towards the end of 2009. From here on in, and for Euro 2012 qualifying, this was the way forward Toshack determined. Wales weren't even supposed to have a game that day in late autumn, but the FAW were contractually obliged to hold their annual awards evening that week, a black-tie event their commercial partners always attended, and thus needed to get the players together anyway. Negotiations were done in double-quick time to play the Scots, and in front of a raucous crowd Ramsey was utterly sublime, scoring a stunning goal of his own and setting up the other two. Suddenly, after years of watching the hard-working but very limited Barry Horne, Robbie Savage, Mark Pembridge, Carl Fletcher and Carl Robinson in midfield, Welsh fans had a glimpse into what could be a golden and creative future. Ramsey and Bale were the way forward.

By that stage even Toshack's arch-critic Savage had done something of a U-turn, conceding after an earlier match: 'Those youngsters ran their hearts out, covered every blade of grass and I thought fair play to John and Brian Flynn. They have got them playing with some style and self-belief and that's fantastic. It's no good being bitter about the whole thing and I'm man enough to say I was wrong and John is right. He's taking Welsh football in the right direction with the kids and I can see that now. I didn't back then. I admit that I was too quick to have my say. He stuck to his guns, is his own man and things are looking a lot brighter for Welsh football.'

Tosh probably had to sit down in a state of shock when he read that!

The other big change the manager wanted was a move away from the Millennium Stadium, which was a fabulous venue when Wales were playing in front of 74,000 crowds, but cavernous, soulless and lacking in atmosphere when gates were as small as they had started to become. This wasn't as straightforward as just upping sticks from one ground to another, because the FAW had signed a 21-year deal with the Welsh Rugby Union, had put money into the building of the venue, and were aware of contractual obligations which meant they were required to appear there three times a year. They were loath to change, hesitancy which was understandable as that contract wasn't even halfway through yet.

However, aware of behind-the-scenes disquiet from Tosh and the players I spoke to, the *Western Mail* chose to help out by leading a campaign calling for a permanent switch to the newly built 33,000-seater Cardiff City Stadium instead. To me, it just seemed the logical thing to do. Thus, over a period of weeks, we ran a number of strongly worded comment pieces outlining the reasons why the move needed to be made. While conceding the Millennium Stadium had been the scene of many magical occasions, I argued it had started to become more of a hindrance than a help to a young Wales team very much in transition. Opposition stars loved appearing at the venue: big, swanky, fabulous, the close proximity of the steep stands to the pitch almost creating an amphitheatre vibe. What wasn't to like for them? The huge swathes of empty seats played into their hands. What Wales needed was a new fortress, proper home advantage, a partisan, hostile crowd creating real fervour and passion that reverberated around a much smaller venue.

I had seen how Cardiff City's own passionate fans, many of whom also made up numbers at Wales games, really galvanised their team in the Championship back then, making an incredible noise, creating a special buzz and often influencing 50-50 refereeing calls. That is what home advantage is about. We argued a crowd approaching 30,000 inside Cardiff City Stadium was almost a sell-out, generating a feel-good vibe the players could feed off. Inside the Millennium Stadium, it was close to two-thirds empty, a totally different atmosphere.

The final straw for me was a World Cup game against Germany on 1 April 2009. The date is appropriate. Early on, the ball cannoned off a German midfielder and ballooned into touch for a clear Welsh throw-in. The officials hesitated, the fans were quiet, there was a delay and inexplicably Germany were awarded the throw-in. Several yards away, stand-in Welsh skipper for the night Simon Davies threw his hands into the air in protest, but too late. The throw was taken and Michael Ballack whacked the ball from 30 yards over Wayne Hennessey's head and into the net. Talk about an April Fool's joke. That simply would never be allowed to happen at Cardiff City Stadium with the noise from the fans, who would have demanded the referee and linesman make the correct call, and whose fervour has always rubbed off on the players.

We also outlined concerns the Welsh players had at not being made to feel welcome at the venue, whether that was actually reality or not, and over the state of the pitch, which was built on pallets, meaning it moved and thus could lead to injuries. Eventually, grudgingly, the FAW relented. Cardiff City Stadium became Wales' official new home and before too long, amid a *TogetherStronger* mantra, results started to significantly improve.

'The Millennium just wasn't for us, it wasn't like when 70,000 screaming rugby fans are watching Wales beat England,' says Toshack. 'It's obviously a fantastic stadium, but for some people who went there it was more like a day out. They probably didn't know who some of the players even were. They weren't always as interested as those who used to go to Ninian Park, The Vetch or The Racecourse. I would rather have 15,000 who are proper football fans and create a real atmosphere than double that number when a lot of them aren't.'

Finally seeing a clear path forward, most of the old guard now gone, Toshack was re-energised and threw himself into preparations for the 2012 European Championship qualifiers where Wales would lock horns again with England, keen to make amends for the dismal showing versus the old enemy under Mark Hughes a few years earlier. Yet, almost typical of Welsh football, just as there was newfound optimism came the dreadful news that Ramsey had broken his leg following a horror Ryan Shawcross tackle while playing for Arsenal against Stoke. This hugely gifted 19-year-old playmaker, who had produced his man-of-the-match showing versus Scotland just weeks earlier, was now out of football for more than a year. One step forward, three back. The Welsh players wore 'Thinking of you Aaron' T-shirts at their next game, a 0–1 friendly defeat to Sweden.

Toshack was devastated by the news, which threw his planning up in the air, and in early autumn 2010 his tenure came to an end. Just one game into the new qualifying group. Montenegro away was the sort of match Wales should have been able to win with something to spare, but there was an early sense things were not right when Toshack, standing in his technical area, had to barge away a TV cameraman who got too close while he was singing the national anthem. The manager was worked up about that before a ball had even been kicked and, by the time a Mirko Vučinić goal gave Montenegro a 1–0 win, the writing seemed to be on the wall.

By this point the FAW had a new chief executive, the dynamic Jonathan Ford having taken over from the more conservative David Collins. 'Well that wasn't very good, was it?' Ford said to Toshack on the flight home. The manager, who got on well with Collins, decided it was time to go. On this occasion, unlike after the loss in Cyprus, there was to be no stepping back from the brink. His time was up.

The Toshack years will continue to divide opinion, but his backers will staunchly argue that, without his belief in youth, the magical Euro 2016 journey simply wouldn't have been possible. The team he built, and finished with, was entirely different to the ageing one he had inherited six years earlier. His successor was being dealt a much better hand. The future here really could be bright. Brian Flynn, desperate for the job, was put in temporary charge for the next two matches, but defeats to Bulgaria and Switzerland were hardly the best of applications. Three games in, Wales were pretty much already out of Euro qualifying. Again.

There was one final fixture to play at the Millennium Stadium, a sell-out clash with England the following spring, before the permanent switch to Cardiff City Stadium that Toshack had demanded. What Wales needed now was a younger man to build upon the excellent foundations Tosh had put in place, someone with modern methods the players would more closely identify with.

Enter Gary Andrew Speed MBE.

8

The hope… and the tragedy

WALES ARE LOSING 0–2 to England in front of a capacity Millennium Stadium crowd. There are barely 14 minutes gone on the clock and, with Wayne Rooney, Frank Lampard, Ashley Cole and John Terry among the stardust names in the Three Lions line-up, a heavy defeat in front of their own fans against their biggest rivals is on the cards.

This is not what close on 70,000 fervent Welsh supporters were anticipating from the European Championship qualifier as they flocked into Cardiff that sunny Saturday afternoon in March 2011, but with 76 minutes still to go, and England already rampant, they are fearing the worst.

Down on the touchline, it represents the first major test for Gary Speed as manager. How does he get his team out of this mess?

Speed was the iconic figure the FA of Wales turned to, somewhat surprisingly, after John Toshack's six years at the helm came to an end. If Tosh was seen as a little old school in his thinking, then Speed, much closer to the young Welsh players in terms of age, was considered more contemporary in his approach.

Not the best of beginnings for the new man, though. A 3–0 hammering by the Republic of Ireland in Speed's first game is now being followed by Rooney and his mob looking to run riot in the Welsh capital. This could get embarrassing – but Speed is not for turning. He has instructed his team to play in a style that is somewhat alien to them. They don't appear comfortable with it against England, but Speed tells his players to keep following his methods because, in the end, Wales will be better for it. Even if they end up losing to the old enemy by four or five today...

Upon being appointed 15 weeks earlier, Speed had given those players a PowerPoint presentation. Called 'Mission Statement, Brazil 2014', it was a forensic analysis of how they could finally get to a World Cup. Most pertinently, it centred around the style of play Speed wanted Wales to adopt in order to achieve the Brazil goal. The rookie manager knew exactly where the end point was; he then had to work backwards from there in order to reach the destination.

Thus, with the help of his assistant coaches, the highly respected Osian Roberts and the outspoken Dutchman Raymond Verheijen, Speed drew up a six-phase plan which Wales would slowly build upon, bit by bit, during training sessions and games at each international camp, until what the new manager wanted became second nature. This was a mix of tiki-taka, which may be all the rage nowadays but certainly wasn't back then, coupled with the explosive power, pace and creativity from star trio Gareth Bale, Craig Bellamy and Aaron Ramsey further forward. Speed's predecessor John Toshack always insisted upon stylish football from his various teams down the decades, but for differing issues he struggled to make a success of that consistently with Wales.

Speed knew it would take a lot of painstaking work to achieve the final result. Patience was key. One step at a time. The first phase, introduced for those initial Republic of Ireland and England games, was focused upon build-up play from the goalkeeper through the back four and into midfield. The second phase, for the next couple of matches, was how to integrate the midfield players better into the system. The third phase centred around differing patterns of play involving Bale, Bellamy and Ramsey, designed to get Wales through opposition defences.

Phases four, five and six were further tactical enhancements on the above, including implementing the high press. Tragically, losing Speedo meant that Wales never got beyond phase three. But he felt the plan was the correct one and was determined to stick by it through thick and thin, even when the going got tough. Like versus England.

Osian Roberts recalls that particular match, saying: 'We knew if we were to implement this properly over time we would have to take some early hits. None of these had played this way together before, nor did their clubs back then. It was new to them. I remember saying to Gary, "You do realise that doing this against England may mean we could concede four or five?" He replied, "Yes, but if we have to take some short-term blows in order for us to take the team forward the way I want, so be it."

'Now Gary saying it, and actually doing it when you're two goals down at home to your biggest rivals after just a quarter of an hour, are two entirely different things. OK, here comes the acid test, if you like. We spoke about this in a meeting, but England have already scored twice, so do we stop trying to play out from the back because Rooney, Lampard and others are pressing. We can't get out and are inviting trouble? Do we carry on with this and risk conceding more goals, or do we change approach and go for damage limitation instead?

'Gary stuck to his guns, insisted we had to keep playing the way he wanted because, in time, Wales would benefit. So rather than rip it up, amid fears of a heavy drubbing, the message at half-time was, "How can we do what Gary wants better?" Results to us internally early on didn't matter, although we obviously didn't say that to the players, or in public. Building up the style of play and eventually perfecting it was what counted. It was very much about the longer-term gain for Gary. This England match was part of the big learning curve.

'Afterwards, as a squad, we watched a tape of that game...

and then compared it with a video we'd put together during training of where the players should have been positioned. By looking at the two videos together, Gary was able to show the midfield men they were way too close to the defenders, inviting trouble and making it easy for England. The training video, on the other hand, showed how it was supposed to work. "Oh yes, but we were only trying to help out," was the reaction of the players. "Yes, but you are actually making it worse," we were able to demonstrate, indicating exactly why. As a team we learned so much from that one and Gary demonstrated real courage and conviction in standing by his beliefs.'

As it happens, Wales rallied against England, didn't concede any more goals and finished the stronger of the two teams despite the 0–2 loss. Speed saw gains and continued to do so, even though there was none of the new manager bounce you traditionally associate with a fresh appointment, as Wales lost four of his first five matches in charge. For Speed, though, it was a means to an end. He knew it would come good. It did. Suddenly, and very quickly, Wales embarked upon a run which saw them win Euro qualifiers against Switzerland, Bulgaria and Montenegro and unluckily lose the return game with England 1–0 at Wembley. The run culminated with a 4–1 thumping of Norway at a Cardiff City Stadium friendly on 12 November 2011. Wales, becoming more accustomed to Speed's wishes, and with Bale, Ramsey and Bellamy providing an unstoppable cocktail up-front, were now running rampant.

Two weeks later, Gary Speed was with us no more, a tragedy in every sense. Welsh football would never be quite the same again.

It is fair to say that the modern Wales, the team which suddenly started qualifying for major tournaments, was borne from three key appointments which came in close proximity to one another.

Jonathan Ford arrived as the new chief executive of the FAW, joining from world renowned soft drinks brand Coca-

Cola where he'd held down a top executive role in their European operations. Ford's predecessor, David Collins, was a secure enough pair of hands, not the sort of individual to upset the applecart, but the new younger man breezed in with dynamism, ambition and a can-do attitude which meant he was prepared to push boundaries. Ford was bringing the FAW more in tune with the 21st century. Not before time, cynics might suggest.

Osian Roberts was appointed as technical director of the FAW Trust, the charitable body encouraging youngsters to take up football and develop their skills. He revolutionised things behind the scenes and introduced the 'Welsh Way', which saw players at age grade level learn the national anthem, buy into the history of the country, create a special bond with one another and eventually bring that ethos with them into the senior side.

The third appointment, of course, was the more high-profile one of Speed, brought on board by Ford just before Christmas 2010. Ford says that if Toshack put down the foundations for the future with his courage in picking younger players, 'Gary very much built the first floor.' Speed's more modern approach included a heavy focus upon sports science, something he was big into as a player himself – the extra one per cents, if you like, which stars like Bale and Ramsey were accustomed to at Premier League clubs

Indeed, the trio of Speed, Ford and Roberts came together with a joint vision to set Wales on a new path that was eventually to come to fruition in spectacular style as they became one of the rising forces of world football, even if the manager wasn't around to see it unfold. It was Speed's stated aim that, following years of boom-or-bust heart-break as a player, he wanted Wales to not only finally qualify for a major tournament, but to be in a position to do it again and again. He didn't get to witness what he'd started to implement, but he would have been proud of the eventual outcome as Welsh football blossomed in such a manner that an entire country became enthralled and fell in love with its national team.

When Ford, taking the first steps into his FAW job, started the hunt for a new manager post-Toshack, the name of Speed wasn't even in the public domain. In any case, he had recently put pen to paper on a three-year contract to become boss of Sheffield United. Instead, a trio of other Welsh favourites, Brian Flynn, Dean Saunders and John Hartson, were interviewed for the role at the Feathers Hotel in Ludlow, Shropshire. Twenty-four hours later the seven-man FAW delegation conducting the process headed south to the Taplow House Hotel in Buckinghamshire to speak to Chris Coleman and veteran boss Lars Lagerbäck, who had impressive pedigree in charge of Sweden and Iceland. Former Northern Ireland manager Lawrie Sanchez was also in the frame.

The front runner, it seemed, was bound to come from those six, probably one of the latter three. However Ford, determined to get his first managerial appointment spot on, was keeping a secret ace up his sleeve.

'We had all and sundry expressing an interest, people who felt they could build upon the good work Tosh had done over a period of time,' reflects Ford. 'We did a lot of prep work on the candidates, held interviews over two days, but the pack I put together and gave to the FAW sub-committee didn't include Gary. I just told them, "I've got somebody else to bring to the table too."

'Annoyingly, he'd just signed his Sheffield United contract. He was employed by them and I knew our interest in him couldn't be kept quiet. But I also felt if we could persuade Gary Speed to come for an interview, we'd be in a situation where those FAW members would go for him. I always believed he was probably our number-one target.

'We had a scoring system out of five, asking candidates to talk about a range of subjects on how they saw Welsh football's future. They knew the questions beforehand, so were given plenty of time to prepare. It doesn't make the decision for you, but perhaps it discounts one or two who aren't really in the running and you then have a proper discussion over those who remain. Gary fared very well, systematically going through what he wanted, from backroom staff to choice of team hotel, training facilities, everything. We held the interviews during the week. By the Sunday morning I was meeting Gary at a Chester hotel to sign heads of terms on the contract. It was a unanimous decision to choose him.'

In rushing north, Ford says he even picked up a speeding ticket while heading over the Brecon Beacons. Ah well, a price worth paying, as it turned out.

Speed, in so many ways, fitted the bill perfectly. He was a standout professional, a natural leader as captain of his country, hugely respected everywhere. He had always been a wonderful ambassador for Welsh football, fronted up at press conferences, albeit careful with what he said in public. The ultimate diplomat. He and I got on well. At times, Speedo did confide in me certain views he held on players, managers, issues, his helpful way of steering me in an informed direction when writing stories, but they were not always for general consumption and it would be wrong of me to betray those confidences now.

The one drawback with Speed was the obvious one – he lacked experience. As such, it was a gamble. Yet, appointing Welsh legends as their rookie manager was a well-trodden path for the FAW, from Mike England back in the 1980s through Terry Yorath, Mark Hughes, Speed himself and subsequently Ryan Giggs and Craig Bellamy.

Ford believed Speed would be more in tune with the exciting brand he wanted Welsh football to become. He was very much a marketing kingpin, having overseen multi-million pound Coca-Cola deals for the World Cup, European Championships and Olympics. As a visionary he intended to throw off the shackles, walk the walk, not just talk the talk, and take the Welsh game in a new direction.

He even delivered the biggest annual club match on the planet for Wales, bringing to the Millennium Stadium the 2017 UEFA Champions League final contested by the Galacticos of Real Madrid – Cristiano Ronaldo, Luka Modrić, Gareth Bale, Sergio Ramos and all – versus a star-studded Juventus side. There were many major issues holding Cardiff back as the Welsh capital vied for the showpiece game against giant European cities boasting a much more powerful football tradition. Complications included finance, infrastructure, transport links and even hotel accommodation, but Ford's determination, with a little bit of ingenuity, was to win the day.

He cites a story of the moment UEFA president Michel Platini, the legendary French captain and talisman of the 1980s, was persuaded to throw his full weight behind Cardiff, given the Millennium Stadium's superb location right in the middle of the city centre.

'We knew there were accommodation shortages, but part of our pitch involved fans staying in London hotels and coming by train, or car, on the day of the game and being able to walk a few yards to the ground. The two cities are 150 miles apart, but I told Platini it could sometimes take as long to get by car from a central London hotel to Wembley as it would to travel by train to the Millennium Stadium,' says Ford.

Platini raised eyebrows, but Ford goes on: 'That night he was heading to Arsenal for a Champions League game – and rush-hour traffic meant he didn't get there until half-time! Maybe my suggestion of us needing to look at a bigger geographical pool for hotels and transport links made sense. We bought up hotel rooms in Wales and across the border and sold them back to the sponsors, so that money was able to come back into Welsh football. We seamlessly moved 10,000 people back on trains from Cardiff to London on the night. I'd also point out that, since Cardiff, the final has had various issues. Cardiff was the last unequivocal success.'

Upon becoming FAW chief, Ford set himself five goals as he reinvented the playbook. He wanted to double the turnover, bolster fan engagement, improve public relations, see Wales qualify for a major tournament and bring the Champions League final to Cardiff. That was all achieved within seven years. He also helped lead the talks that will see Euro 2028 matches being hosted in Wales and the other UK countries, albeit Ford's plan was a little more grandiose, as the original intention was to bring the 2030 World Cup to Britain.

Perhaps it is typical of Welsh football that the FAW ruling council subsequently passed a no-confidence motion in Ford, forcing him to depart in controversial circumstances. He had already been rapped over the knuckles after a tongue-in-cheek comment about why Chris Coleman's successor as manager should be 'Welsh most definitely, foreign possibly, but definitely not English'. Ford eventually left amid a rumpus over appointing Angela van den Bogerd as the FAW's head of people. She was a Post Office director criticised by a judge in the case emanating from the wrongful imprisonment of a group of sub-postmasters, a miscarriage of justice brought into sharp focus by the *Mr Bates vs The Post Office* TV drama.

Her appointment was evidently a blunder on Ford's part, but that he was a force for good, turning the FAW into a more dynamic, diverse and modern organisation, is beyond question. Ford's mission statement was to have the FAW crest on the bedroom wall of every youngster in Wales. While that was never likely to happen in such a rugby-mad nation, he intended to give it his best shot. Bringing Speed on board to help sell that dream, both as manager of the team and by attending Q&A forums at local football clubs throughout Wales, was key to the vision.

Speed wasn't coming home to Wales for the money. The £250,000 salary on offer was half of what he was on at Sheffield

United, the FAW needing to be mindful of their financial responsibility to the governance of football at all levels in Wales. Ford points to other pulls though, arguing: 'There are only 200-odd international manager jobs in the world, and only one available to Wales. I get how powerful club football has become, but I like to think the international game has fantastic elements to it as well. Where did Pelé play his club football, I ask? He is remembered far more for what he did with Brazil in World Cups than anything achieved at club level. Gary was aware of the financial constraints, but his attitude was "I'm taking the job because I believe in what I'm doing".'

That belief involved what can perhaps be viewed as something of a contradiction. Speed hugely respected the work Toshack had done in bringing through so many young players who now had a number of international caps to their name. At the same time, though, he wanted to change everything – from the way the team prepared, to even leaving the Vale of Glamorgan hotel base on the outskirts of Cardiff which had become Wales' home for more than a decade. If he didn't exactly associate everything from the previous regime with failure, Speed felt the optics of a complete changing of the guard were important to get the players to buy into his new way of doing things. So Wales switched to the five-star St David's Hotel in Cardiff Bay, then to the Celtic Manor Resort in Newport, which had just housed the 2010 Ryder Cup won so splendidly by Colin Montgomerie's European team.

'There was a financial penalty to leave the Vale as we had a contract with them, but Gary's plan was to tear things up and start again. He wanted X, Y and Z and I got the board to nod it through,' says Ford. 'He felt we needed to create a different environment, put his own stamp upon things, move forward together. Gary wanted the team to operate as a group of friends, with the passion needed to play for your country.'

Because of the major shake-up, Speed felt he needed to be hands-on to get it to work properly. Thus, while the family home remained up north – a big gated property just over the Welsh-English border in Cheshire – Speed rented a posh apartment in the beautiful Cardiff Bay waterfront area and regularly sauntered into the FAW's offices just a couple of miles away to prepare and plan with staff.

'He was a popular figure, would come in and speak to everyone,' says Ford. 'We used to have a birthday club, where people would put in £3 to buy a gift to whoever's birthday it was. Gary was part of that, wasn't aloof in any way despite his fame. If the staff spontaneously decided they were going out for a Friday night beer, Gary would be there in the pub with them, putting money behind the bar for drinks for everyone.'

Far more significant than switching hotels was a complete alteration to the backroom coaching set-up. Gone were Toshack's three lieutenants, Roy Evans, Dean Saunders and Spanish fitness guru Salva Iriarte. In came Ray Verheijen, and, crucially, Osian Roberts. It was a completely different age demographic with Roberts something of a visionary, big into sports science preparation methods and proving to be the perfect foil for front man Speed.

Roberts, of course, has since gone on to make a significant name for himself as a leading coach, many viewing him as the real power behind the throne to Wales' stunning Euro 2016 success under Chris Coleman. He did an impressive job as overall boss of Moroccan football and also had a decent spell as Patrick Vieira's number two in the Premier League with Crystal Palace. More recently he took little Como into Serie A, their first promotion to the top flight of Italian football in 21 years. Some CV then, we can agree.

Back in the early days though, when results weren't great under Speed and perhaps more particularly Coleman, I questioned Roberts' role in the Welsh set-up in a strongly worded *Western Mail* article. 'World-class players like Gareth Bale and Aaron Ramsey deserve a world-class coach with Wales,' I stated, knowing that was also a view shared among some FAW powerbrokers. Time proved I should never have doubted Roberts. Thus, in the age-old spirit of holding your hands up when you have got something wrong, I apologised to him in private. His response was typical of the genial guy Osh is. 'Don't worry about it Abbo, you were right,' he responded. 'I hadn't proved myself as a coach at that level and it was my job to do so.'

Perhaps he was being a little modest there because Roberts' role in the new Wales post-2010 cannot be overstated enough. In many ways, looking at the whole picture, arguably he has had a bigger influence upon Welsh football for the best part of two decades than anybody else, even including Bale, Coleman, Toshack and Speed. As such, it is worth briefly charting his story and how it led to such a resounding impact upon the senior Wales team.

Roberts was player-manager of US side New Mexico Chiles when he received a telephone call in 1992 that was to change everything. At the time, because of severe financial restrictions, the FAW didn't always appear to be overly supportive of age grade teams or player development, but Roberts was asked to come home to start a football development scheme financed by Anglesey County Council. It was the first role of its kind in Wales – very shortly, realising this was win-win, every local authority followed suit by creating similar positions. A Welsh football explosion was beginning.

Roberts jokes that he only signed a three-year contract, 'Yet 15 years later I was still doing the job!' He then landed a much more significant position, in 2007 becoming technical director of the FAW Trust, the body set up to promote and protect youth football. Suddenly Roberts was the main man, in effect responsible for overseeing the game in Wales. He didn't for one second expect to be given the job, feeling a figurehead such as Ian Rush or former Wales captain Barry Horne, whose names would resonate better with the public, were the inevitable options to generate greater interest and publicity. However, by this stage, Roberts had also managed the Wales under-16s and under-18s, he'd been asked to mentor the great Neville Southall who wanted to become a coach, and had experienced successful, but contrasting, spells in charge of League of Wales sides. At cash-strapped Bangor City he could only use local players while winning three trophies; at money-laden Rhyl he had his pick of personnel and broke records in leading them to the League of Wales title and other Cups. Roberts explains those differing 'have and have not' experiences gave him first-hand knowledge of alternative ways to play in order to achieve good results – very much tactical with Bangor, more free-flowing at Rhyl.

'Having worked in virtually every environment in the Welsh game, I knew I owed it to myself to go for the technical director job because I didn't feel there was anybody better equipped,' says Roberts. 'Even if they went for a bigger name, at least I'd go in there and tell them what I believed needed to happen, so the new man could work towards ensuring that, even when the first team had lean years, youth development and our age grade sides would always be protected.'

Having won over the FAW interviewing panel, Roberts himself was able to set about implementing the changes he knew would benefit Welsh football. On top of that, he also introduced a world-class coach education system which saw future managers take their badges under him at courses held in Newport and Aberystwyth. Among Roberts' star-studded pupils were Mikel Arteta, who went on to lead Arsenal to the Premier League summit, and Roberto Martinez, who guided Belgium to number one ranked side in the world. They evidently had an excellent tutor! Also coming under Roberts' guidance were French legends Thierry Henry, Patrick Vieira and David Ginola, plus of course Speed, who simultaneously noted the special things starting to happen with Roberts' Welsh under-16s side.

As well as good results, which included historic wins over

England and France, what Speed was particularly impressed by was the special camaraderie within the dressing room as a result of Roberts implementing that 'Welsh Way' of doing things. This involved an easy on the eye passing style of play, but players also had to sing the anthem, buy in to the past and present culture of Wales and be made aware of the immense pride they should feel upon pulling on the red shirt.

This included many Anglos, dual-qualified players, after Roberts had drawn up a database to tap into any available talent throughout the United Kingdom, and indeed the world, to bolster Wales' options. England invariably came calling to try to tempt some of the better ones away. Instead of being defensive about it, Roberts encouraged the teenagers to 'go with England, sample the experience, and then make up their own minds'.

'But every single one of them came back to us – and stayed,' he smiles. 'I like to think that was because of the culture we were creating. Gary had noticed this and I will never forget him coming to do a caps presentation for my under-16s after a Welsh Cup final in Llanelli. "We want to do with the first team what Osh has already been doing with you at this level," he told them. My ears pricked up. Suddenly we would have complete consistency in Welsh football. Gary comes in... and the world changes.'

Speed and Roberts set about creating a similar team spirit with the senior side, trying to resolve what had become something of a disconnect between the players and public. Attendances weren't exactly brilliant at the time. When it came to popularity and publicity, Wales football was very much fourth-best in the pecking order behind Warren Gatland's Six Nations Grand Slam-winning rugby team and resurgent club duo, Cardiff City and Swansea City.

Speed vowed to change that, saying the players needed the fans fully behind them to win matches, but they needed to win matches in order to bring the fans back! It was classic chicken

189

and the egg. As an absolute minimum though, he insisted every player had to belt out the anthem, link arms while doing so, and demonstrably display a togetherness the supporters demanded.

'We knew we had to meet our fans halfway, engage much better if they were to come and support us,' explains Roberts. 'We had to show how much we cared, just as they did. Players learning and singing our anthem was a part of that. Pride and passion for the country has always been innate for me, but it was important we passed that on. One of my proudest moments came when Scotland asked me for a video of our under-16s singing the anthem ahead of one game. A kind of "just look at them" feeling. Nobody does it quite like us, wherever we went, was my view. It doesn't mean we win or lose games, but it has to be part of our nature.'

At age grade level, a former head teacher called Cledwyn Ashford, himself something of a bigwig in north Wales football coaching, taught the anthem to any of the teenagers or Anglos who didn't know the words. Speed realised something different was required with his senior stars.

'It wasn't going to be easy for players to stand up with a piece of paper, no piano, and start singing in front of a school master,' points out Roberts. 'So one day we told them "Look, we have to sing it. So we've brought in someone famous today to help you out." At that point Courtenay Hamilton, who was Miss Wales, walks in. She is a trained classical singer and had led the anthem on the pitch ahead of the home game against England. Suddenly they all perk up in that room. Yes, I will learn it; yes, I will learn it!'

This was just part of the process, Roberts explaining: 'When we came in we felt there wasn't enough interaction among the players. In international football you can't just have two hours of training, come down for an evening meal, and players then head back to their rooms. There have to be social activities too because Gary wanted everyone looking forward to joining up as a squad and for each player to feel as valued as the next one.

'How do we change that? How do we create team spirit? What even is real "team spirit"? So we brought a magician on board. Over the evening meal, he'd tap a player on the shoulder. Pick a card. Suddenly he's played a magic trick and pulls the same card from his back pocket! Then he moves to the next table, and the next. Same magic trick. "How's he done that?" the players were asking one another. Suddenly they are talking, together as one. This helps the bond, on and off the pitch.

'Next we'd get a comedian in, make sure the players were laughing and interacting again. We had quiz competitions. We'd show episodes of *Only Fools and Horses* or Billy Connolly on the big screen during meal time. With my under-16s, we'd already sought to get rid of inhibitions with the Connect Four board game or *X Factor* competitions, with the coaching staff as judges. We'd choose the *X Factor* groups and they would go off and sing their bit. So when we're teaching some of them the national anthem, and they're having to stand up and practise it in front of everyone else, they're not in the slightest bit embarrassed because two days before they've done *X Factor*.'

This new-found spirit was supplemented by the hi-tech sports science approach Speed brought in with Wales. He had been heavily influenced by anything that could give an extra edge when playing under Sam Allardyce for four years at Bolton. Big Sam, the former England manager, may be viewed as old school in terms of the route one tactics his teams employed, but his preparation methods were ahead of his time as Allardyce scrutinised top American Football sides and New Zealand rugby to find out what made them tick and what he could bring from their training routines into the Premier League.

Allardyce always had an army of backroom staff to assist with his plans and Speed now brought in extra medics, masseurs and nutritionists to try to ensure his Wales players were in tip-top shape come match day. Daily saliva and urine tests were introduced, the results used as part of a 'traffic light' system. If a player's results were viewed as 'green' at the start of the week, he would be held back in training to ensure he didn't peak too early. 'Orange' or 'red' meant players needed to be worked harder. The idea was for everyone to be on 'green' by match-day morning. This was certainly cutting-edge stuff.

Another significant change was the appointment of Aaron Ramsey as captain, something that personally delighted me as I'd penned articles in the *Western Mail* calling for precisely that to happen. I'm not sure too many other journalists followed my lead; to be fair, it seemed a preposterous suggestion to put forward given Aaron was just 20 years of age at the time. There were more experienced candidates. However, I just saw leadership credentials in Ramsey and an intelligence, on and of the field, that I felt would serve this new regime well over time. Whether he was influenced by my articles or not, Speedo evidently agreed with me. He knew deep down Ramsey wasn't ready for the captaincy just yet, but felt he would quickly grow into the role as part of the longer-term thinking. Will Carling did it with England rugby, now Ramsey was doing it with Wales football.

Of course, you can have all the sports science, vision, ideas and gimmicks in the world, but ultimately managers will always be judged by results, and early on things were pretty poor, to put it mildly, under Speed. A run of four defeats in his first five matches saw Wales hit rock bottom with a home loss to Australia and an alarming dip down to an all-time low of 117th in the FIFA rankings. A proud nation which had produced true greats of the game, like John Charles, Ryan Giggs, Ian Rush, Mark Hughes and more recently Gareth Bale, was now sandwiched in between those footballing superpowers of Haiti and Grenada. Only five European teams were ranked lower. It meant that, come the Brazil 2014 World Cup qualifying campaign, Speed's 'Mission Statement', Wales would be placed in the bottom group of seeds next to Andorra, San Marino, Malta, Liechtenstein and Kazakhstan. As if the task wasn't going to be hard enough, anyway.

Immediately after those rankings were published I telephoned Speed to gauge his take on them, what he intended to do about it and, indeed, when he saw it coming good for him as manager. He was driving at the time, but didn't want to hide away. Speed wasn't the type to duck interviews with me, anyway.

'It's embarrassing,' Speedo said straightaway. 'It's embarrassing for me, it's embarrassing for the players, it's embarrassing for the FAW and the fans... there's no getting away from that, no point trying to bury our heads in the sand.' Candid assessment out of the way, Speed continued: 'There's only one way we can do anything about this and that is to start winning football matches. Then we'll quickly rise again to a position where you and I know we deserve to be in.'

That is precisely what happened, and with incredible haste. Wales overcame Montenegro (2–1), Switzerland (2–0), Bulgaria (0–1) in the remaining Euro 2012 qualifiers and then hammered Norway 4–1 in that final match under Speed's command. In the space of just 11 weeks they rose in those FIFA rankings, as Speed predicted they would, from a lowly 117th up to 42nd, winning FIFA's 'Best Mover of the Year' award.

The way they were playing, and given the youthful exuberance in the team, Wales were bound to keep rising, too. The players, now brimful with confidence and seeing the future for themselves, were loving their football under Speed. Little did they know, as the manager said his goodbyes to them after thrashing Norway, that would be the last time they would see him. The devastating news on 27 November 2011 jolted us to the core. He was just 42 years of age. He is still missed by a Welsh nation.

Early that Sunday morning, the FAW's president Phil Pritchard was at home in the mid Wales town of Welshpool when his mobile rang. At the tenth time of trying, FAW chief executive Jonathan Ford, who discovered it wasn't easy to raise people at that time on a Sunday, had eventually managed to get through. 'He started with the words "Phil, are you sitting down? I'm sorry to say Gary has passed away",' recalls Pritchard. 'Like everybody else, I was numb with shock. Jonathan asked if I could come down to help him take questions at a press conference in Cardiff. I'd just taken ownership of a brand-new car and was nursing it carefully. Suddenly I was trashing it in order to get to Cardiff in double-quick time, loads of questions still going around in my mind. Why, Gary?'

Although Ford was the go-ahead new chief executive the FAW needed and responsible for day-to-day operations, back then Pritchard was also a real kingmaker. He wielded enormous power in various FAW roles for well over a decade. If Pritchard pushed for something it tended to happen, and he was heavily responsible for the managerial appointments of Speed, Chris Coleman, John Toshack and Mark Hughes.

'They were each successful in their own differing ways. I've so much time for them all, but for me Gary and Tosh were the best of the lot,' Pritchard reflects. 'Tosh takes enormous credit for giving younger players their chance. We wouldn't have got to where we did without him. Gary was the perfect man to build on that work, as man manager and people arranger. If Gary said jump, people jumped. He made his presence known, but not in an aggressive manner; it was just that everyone had such huge respect for him they automatically did what he asked. He possessed no real managerial experience when we appointed him, but I felt he ticked so many boxes of what we required and that, with the right backing from ourselves, he would definitely lead Wales to success.'

Just 11 months previously, Pritchard and Ford had proudly sat either side of Speed to announce him as new Wales manager at a Cardiff press conference. The three of them, grinning like proverbial Cheshire cats on the top table, could scarcely contain their delight as they looked ahead to the future.

Now Pritchard and Ford had to sit together on the top table once again, this time without Speed, at a far more hastily arranged media briefing held at St David's Hotel in Cardiff Bay to field questions about the shocking news of his death. It was a desperately sad situation, but Ford realised that, as Speed's employers, the eye of the storm would very quickly fall upon the FAW. Amid an outpouring of grief which transcended way beyond football, Pritchard and Ford handled the tragedy as well as they could, dealing with the myriad of questions being thrown their way with patience, dignity and diplomacy. The only one they couldn't answer, of course, was why? That remains as much of a mystery to this day as it was back on that dark Sunday morning. It will always be the case, of course.

Six days earlier, Brazil 2014 at the forefront of his mind, Speed had flown to Brussels to attend a fixtures' meeting with his rival managers after Wales were drawn in a World Cup qualifying group containing Croatia, Serbia, Belgium, Scotland and Macedonia. Ironically, the new manager of Macedonia was one John Toshack, who was about to lock horns with Speed and the very young guns he himself had brought through with Wales.

The two men had a relaxing lunch together, discussing the pros and cons of the Wales players and what was in store in the battle to reach Brazil. Speed knew he was benefiting from the hard yards Toshack had put in to give so many of these Wales then-teenagers their international bows.

'Gary seemed fine that day. We talked about Wales, what he saw as the way forward. We had a joke about various things,' says Toshack. 'Everything appeared OK on the surface. I was sitting there with him and honestly there didn't appear to be anything whatsoever troubling him. The news that was then to reach us a few days after simply defied belief.'

It still does, but in time everyone had to move on and in order

195

for Wales to do so that meant organising a special memorial match at Cardiff City Stadium three months later against Costa Rica, the opponents in the same city when Speed had made his Wales debut back in 1990. It was a highly emotionally-charged evening, Wales lost 0–1 to an early Joel Campbell goal, but the result was utterly irrelevant. This was about a nation paying tribute to Speed and ensuring that his family members present – who included wife Louise, two sons, Ed and Tom, and mum and dad Carole and Roger – were left with a feeling of immense pride to go with the understandable sorrow.

Ed and Tom, aged just 14 and 13 at the time, led the team out of the tunnel, each wearing red Wales jerseys bearing the name Speed on the back, one with number 11, the other number six. They stood next to the players as a minute's applause for their dad started well before the referee's whistle was blown, and went on and on... and on and on. It was a beautiful moment amid such sadness.

'My only wish was that Roger, Carole, Louise and the whole family felt everything was done correctly, that whatever they wanted from the evening was fully respected,' says Roberts of that terribly difficult night when he was put in charge of the team.

Roberts and the FAW rightly received a lot of plaudits for organising it so sensitively, but Gary could not be forgotten. A few months later Wales lost a friendly against Bosnia which was attended by barely 6,000 fans at Parc y Scarlets in Llanelli.

'Everyone was still struggling to overcome his loss,' accepts Roberts. 'That night was the worst-case scenario – we were beaten 0–2, there was no atmosphere, small crowd, we couldn't cope. I remember Craig Bellamy saying in the dressing room, "Lads I know it's hard, it's difficult for each of us. I'm struggling badly myself. But we have to get out of this mental trap that we're in, move on and win games again."'

By this point, Chris Coleman, one of Speed's close friends and his Wales room-mate for many years, had been named as the new manager. Coleman had decent pedigree, and in the circumstances seemed a really good appointment to me. Trouble was, this was close on mission impossible. How on earth do you replace Gary Speed in the eyes of the players who adored him? Or the fans, for that matter?

Poor Cookie, the nickname he is known by, had a really tough beginning amid what I believed to be an unfair clamour for his head. Results were awful, but he needed a bit of time and latitude. Given it, suddenly everything just bloomed. The exciting days Speed confidently predicted were just around the corner were to come to fruition – in truly spectacular fashion.

9

Real story behind Euro 2016 fairytale

I was literally about to open the door to the gents on the second floor of our Media Wales offices (don't need to go into that any more!) when my mobile buzzed in the top pocket of my suit. The name Chris Coleman came up on the screen; thought I'd better answer.

Less than a couple of minutes earlier, I had pinged a text to the Wales manager, who was coming under fierce criticism after losing his first four matches in charge. I was supportive of Coleman from the off, but he wasn't a popular choice for some. Now bad results were increasing the angst.

The night before, Coleman's team had been crushed 6–1 by Serbia in a World Cup qualifier, Wales' heaviest defeat in 16 years. For the avoidance of doubt, that was pretty abysmal, but I believed Coleman was being his own worst enemy and it was remediable. He was treading on eggshells, I felt, hesitant to change things for fear of upsetting dressing room harmony post-Gary Speed. In other words Coleman, who had done a decent job with Fulham in the Premier League for four years, wasn't being true to himself because of the desperately difficult situation he had inherited.

'Chris you've got to stop trying to mirror Gary and start managing the team your own way, not how you think he would have wanted it done,' was the gist of my message. Followed by, he shouldn't let the FAW make a decision on his future 'without being comfortable how you've gone about things. Don't leave yourself wondering what might have been.' That kind of thing.

Coleman, clearly grateful for the message, was on the phone straightaway. 'You're absolutely right Paul, one or two others have told me this as well. I've already decided changes need to be made and I have to start being my own man,' he said, before going on to explain some of those differences we would begin to see.

This was 12 September 2012, Coleman's lowest point in football. Four years later, but only after a few more hardships amid loud calls for him to go, he became the most successful manager in Wales' history, leading his country to the semi-finals of Euro 2016. The mother of all turnarounds.

Now, given my affection for the Wales football team, I'd love to be able to say that in the most infinitesimal of miniscule ways possible, I played a teeny-weeny part in that success by helping to encourage Coleman to change tack! But, of course, that would be nonsense. He'd already come to that conclusion, as any good manager should. Nonetheless, given I had got to know Coleman from when he first burst through as a young defender with Swansea City at the start of the 1990s by standing outside the Vetch Field to interview him, liked him and indeed backed him for the Wales job, I felt compelled to provide some reassuring words at the worst moment of his managerial career. By that stage I was schooled well enough in Welsh international football, the workings of the FA of Wales hierarchy and, as a sports journalist, to be confident enough to offer encouragement and outline what I thought needed to happen.

Coleman, demoralised by the slaughter in Serbia, appreciated our chat, agreed things couldn't carry on like this and spoke of the need to tinker, making Wales more defensively resilient and learning to win matches in ugly fashion. In time I was given the go-ahead to run a back-page story on the most contentious part of the change, which was young Aaron Ramsey, the bold choice as captain for the future under Speed, being replaced in the job by Ashley Williams. The rationale, I pointed out in the article, was Coleman wanted a more experienced skipper and for Ramsey to be freed up so he could focus upon his own midfield mastery and become the hub of the team moving forward.

In hindsight, Coleman concedes he should have stamped his own authority on the team from the start. 'However, Gary was such a presence, such a great man, I thought it best to carry on doing the things he wanted. I decided after a while to do it my way, come what may,' he was to explain publicly.

These were completely unique circumstances anywhere in world sport and for context we should rewind to what was happening as FAW bosses, slowly recovering from the Speed shock, started to look for their new manager. An initial move was made for Ryan Giggs. A marketing man's dream at the time – if anyone could carry on selling the Wales vision Speed had started, then fellow Welsh legend Giggsy was the man. However, he was quickly ruled out after signing a new Manchester United playing contract which would take him through to the age of 40.

High-ranking FAW sources were telling me they didn't plan to go through an interview process and that Coleman, who had lost out to Speed a year earlier, was the man they planned to go after. They were working, however, against a backdrop of emotional public pressure being applied by Dutchman Ray Verheijen, who along with Osian Roberts had been a key member of Speed's backroom team. Dutch Ray, as he became known, went public with a number of messages, claiming there was no need for a new manager, that he and Roberts should run things in conjunction with a 'figurehead' and that the FAW would 'turn their back' on Speed and not 'respect Gary's legacy' if they appointed a new man with his own ideas.

As if Gary Speed was just 'a figurehead'? Nonsense, of course, Wales powerbrokers and pundits pointed out.

While unwelcome, those outbursts from Verheijen could be dismissed. More worrying for the FAW was Speed's skipper Aaron Ramsey expressing similar views about retaining the status quo. Ramsey has never been the type of individual to court controversy, it must be stressed. That approach simply isn't in his DNA. However, in an early-morning interview with BBC Five Live, Ramsey spoke from the soul by stating the players didn't want major change and he was disappointed their views had not been canvassed. Gareth Bale, another who tends to avoid headline-making drama off the field, upped the ante further by saying he hoped Wales would 'come to their senses and stick with what we've got'. Any change would be 'absolutely ridiculous', he reckoned.

The FAW, however, weren't for bending. I was contacted by a leading powerbroker who told me in no uncertain terms that they had firmly set their sights on Coleman and no amount of public statements or dressing room pressure would deter them from that path. It would be very easy for them to do the simple thing and leave well alone, it was explained to me, but that wouldn't be the right thing for Welsh football. Thus, armed with this top-level information, in the following day's *Western Mail* we splashed the newspaper with a banner headline stating 'Wales step up move for Coleman as they ignore Ramsey's no change plea'. We reported talks would begin at once and that Coleman would be bringing his former Wales defensive partner, Kit Symons, on board as number two, in effect spelling the end for Verheijen. A few days later, Coleman was announced as the new manager. Although Dutch Ray was to go, more importantly Osian Roberts would remain as a key member of the backroom team.

Personally, and professionally, I was delighted with the choice of Coleman. By then I'd known him on and off for more than 20 years. Indeed, two of the more emotional articles I have written during my sports journalism career were centred around Cookie. The first outlined how the world of football was losing a true warrior of the game when he had to quit playing following a horrific car crash. The second was of my delight at Mark Hughes handing Cookie a swansong with a 30-second cameo appearance in Wales' 1–0 Millennium Stadium win over Germany in 2002. The rapturous ovation Coleman received that night was wonderful as he came on for his 32nd cap deep into injury time as a substitute for Rob Earnshaw. I'm not sure Coleman even touched the ball, but much better to bow out that way in front of his own people in a showpiece match, I stated, than playing a few minutes for Fulham reserves before one man and his dog.

They were touching articles which went down well. More importantly, Coleman had decent pedigree from taking Fulham to a top-ten Premier League finish and also did reasonably well with Real Sociedad in Spain, which meant he would be a good choice for Wales, I felt.

Reflecting upon the appointment, then FAW boss Jonathan Ford says: 'This time we didn't feel it appropriate to go through an open recruitment process. Chris was in effect runner-up when we chose Gary, so he was the natural fit in extremely difficult circumstances. In fact, back then I'm not sure Chris even knew Gary was going for the job too. They were big mates and, I'm told, one day Chris rang Gary to ask where he was. "Sitting in that big chair at the FAW," was Gary's response! I think that might have been the first he knew of it. They shared a good laugh.

'After what happened with Gary, one or two others picked up the phone about the job. "It's a tragic situation, but I'm here if you need me." But we'd already determined Chris was the obvious candidate. I met him at a hotel around Christmas time to go through everything. On the one hand he was delighted, on the other he was gutted. Chris had been a room-mate of Gary's, remember. He knew the enormity of the task, but I feel he handled an emotional situation with diplomacy and sensitivity.'

Starting with a mentality of, if it ain't broke, don't try to fix it, Coleman was wary of imposing his own methods on the team. Trouble is, early results were woeful. Wales lost to Mexico, Bosnia, Belgium and Serbia at the start of his reign, scoring just one goal and conceding 12, and in all Coleman won just five out of 17 internationals before the Euro 2016 qualifiers kicked in. The Brazil World Cup 'Mission Statement' drawn up by Speed had been blown to smithereens.

There was plenty of hostility against Coleman and, as mentioned, rock bottom was hit with that hammering away to Serbia in Novi Sad. His assistant Osian Roberts recalls Wales being booed off the pitch that night by their own fans. 'There was a track around the pitch and our dressing room was underneath where our supporters were housed,' he says. 'As we walked off to the jeers I remember thinking, "I recognise some of these!" I suppose it doesn't get any lower than being booed by your own fans, but to compound matters the dressing room was old, there was no window, just a hole in the wall and no lights. When we got back in there it was dark. This just about caps it all off, I thought.'

Another low point came away to minnows North Macedonia, when Coleman lost his passport, missed the team's flight and training session in Skopje – and Wales humiliatingly went down 2–1. Uncharacteristically, having obtained an emergency passport to make the game on time, Coleman snapped at the media afterwards, saying he had nothing to apologise about, all the main preparation had already been done back home and us journalists could just 'write what you want'. That wasn't like Coleman, normally so engaging at press conferences and, if anything, sometimes too honest for his own good. This unnecessary and unusual outburst was a clear sign of the pressure getting to him.

Amid mounting talk his Wales future would be determined

by the final two matches in the failed World Cup qualifying group, a Cardiff return clash with the North Macedonians and an away game in Belgium, I felt the time was right for a supportive article in print – stating that if the FAW saw Coleman as the right man previously, then they needed to stick by him. Thankfully Welsh powerbrokers saw it that way, too.

One of the reasons for my optimism had been a clash against a battle-hardened Scotland up at Hampden Park a few months earlier when Wales lost Gareth Bale at half-time, but produced an excellent performance in horrible conditions, freezing, miserable, driving snow, and emerged as 1–2 victors thanks to goals from Aaron Ramsey and Hal Robson-Kanu. That night, you could see the method behind what Coleman was attempting to achieve; his team just had to produce it far more consistently.

At times in the first half, Scotland couldn't get close to Wales, yet perversely Coleman's men trailed 1–0 at the interval. The manager was so frustrated, I'm told he punched a locker in the dressing room. Osian Roberts reflects: 'I remember Craig Bellamy saying, "Lads, we just need to keep doing what we're doing. I'd rather lose playing how we do than win the other way. But it'll come good." That was a more powerful message, coming from a senior player like Craig than it could have been from us as coaches. It showed they were buying into what we wanted.'

That cold night at Hampden, Coleman had controversially dropped James Collins to the bench, a regular Premier League centre-half, and instead paired Ashley Williams with the unsung Sam Ricketts, more of a full-back who played much of his football in the lower divisions. Collins, known as 'Ginge', was understandably disappointed, but the theory went that Ricketts was better in possession of the ball and thus more likely to give Wales what they required in terms of build-up play from the back.

Roberts smiles: 'Ginge was sitting just behind me in the

dugout. We'd put a few passes together at the back, but now Scotland were closing us down. As the ball came to Ricketts, Ginge shouted spontaneously, "Stick it up-field, Sam." Instead, Ricketts calmly kept control, played it out to the wing, we launched a counter-attack to almost score. "And that's why I'm on the bench!" Ginge laughed.'

There was to be one more hugely significant change which enabled those seeds of hope spotted against Scotland to bloom in the most beautiful of fashions as Wales not only finally broke their decades-old qualifying jinx, they then gave Welsh folk everywhere the summer of their lives by rampaging to the semi-finals at Euro 2016. At a FIFA coaching conference held in Warsaw, Coleman told his number two Roberts, 'We need to do something different. we have to change to five at the back.' To the tune of the Beach Boys' iconic hit 'Sloop John B' the fans made up a song about the new tactics:

'Chrissie Coleman had a dream,

To save the national team,

He's got no defenders, so he plays five at the back,

Five at the back;

With Bale in attack,

With Bale in att-aaack,

So watch out Europe,

We're on our way back.'

The ditty became one of Wales' signature songs at matches. However, the changes Coleman made were obviously way more nuanced than that, with everything centred around: a) tightening up the defence, and b) getting the best out of superstars Bale and Ramsey, who were now coming towards the peak of their hugely impressive powers.

To do so, Wales struck upon the novel idea of using them both as No. 10s in the same team, in effect two playmakers, after first being alerted to the innovative tactic from a UEFA Champions League game played between Liverpool and FC Basel in December 2014. A star-studded Liverpool team containing Steven Gerrard, Raheem Sterling, Philippe Coutinho and Jordan Henderson were expected to comfortably win at their own Anfield lair, but the Swiss side's novel approach completely threw them and they drew 1–1. FC Basel went through, Brendan Rodgers' Reds were surprisingly out. This was just before the Jürgen Klopp era kicked in.

Osian Roberts explains that Welshman Chris Davies, who was Rodgers' lead analyst with Liverpool and more recently worked as Ange Postecoglou's Tottenham assistant, was conducting a study on Paulo Sousa's Basel team as part of his Pro Licence coaching badges. He passed on the snippet of information that was to change everything for Wales.

'Chris explained Liverpool didn't have a clue what Basel were doing, which is saying a lot when you have a tactician as astute as Brendan,' starts Roberts. 'So they watched a video back of the game and noted how Sousa had played with a square midfield box – two holding players at the base, two 10s right in front of them. It enables you to have an extra man, an overload, against the usual three that play against you in midfield.

'I thought that's interesting, nobody else was doing it at the time. I think Sousa tried it for about six games when he was manager of Swansea, but they started losing, it didn't last and nobody picked up on it. Cookie wanted us to play differently at the back, which was fine, we had the personnel to do that. How would the rest of the team then look, we wondered. I said I'd show him clips of that FC Basel side at Anfield. We quickly decided a similar approach would enable us to get the best out of Bale and Ramsey. We could use them as two 10s, get them into places on the pitch where they could do the most damage to the opposition.'

After narrow, but most welcome Euro qualifying wins over Andorra and Cyprus, and scoreless draws with Bosnia and Belgium, Wales used the new tactics for the first time away to Israel on 28 March 2015 – with stunning results. The five at the back were supplemented by a midfield box of four – Joe Allen and Joe Ledley lying deep, Bale and Ramsey further forward in front of them. It was the best Welsh performance for years, Bale and Ramsey handed freedom to run riot and scoring the goals in a 0–3 thumping that could have been much heavier for Israel. We had lift-off. This is the line-up that day, and how the new-look midfield box worked, as drawn for me by Roberts:

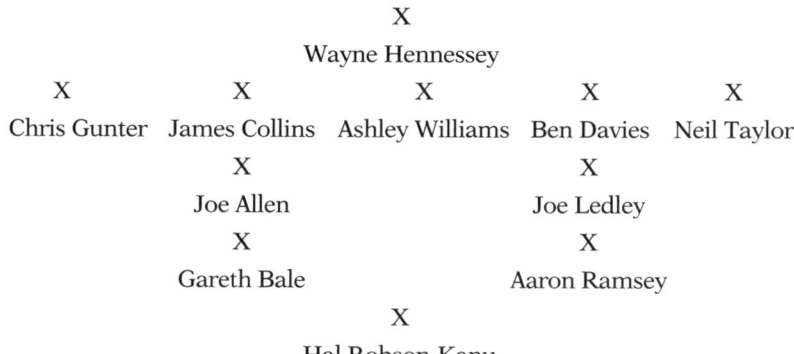

X
Wayne Hennessey

X   X   X   X   X
Chris Gunter   James Collins   Ashley Williams   Ben Davies   Neil Taylor

X   X
Joe Allen   Joe Ledley

X   X
Gareth Bale   Aaron Ramsey

X
Hal Robson-Kanu

Roberts says: 'We didn't feel we were perhaps getting the best out of Gareth and Aaron before that game. Now, as two No. 10s for the first time, we definitely were. This was to be the way forward. Remember, at the time Israel were flying, a real threat in that group, they were in the ascendancy going into the match, but we absolutely battered them. The new approach worked perfectly.

'After we'd first explained the idea in a team meeting, messages filtered back that players were talking. I don't think they were too happy, or understood it fully. As coaches you have to remove any lingering doubts about the game plan, need total clarity, so we held another meeting. We'd already explained how it would work, now we had to do the why.

'We always had our midfield box of four versus three, which gave us an extra number and enabled us to play either side of the opposition. When Israel had the ball, we explained Gareth and Aaron needed to go wider to help defend in those areas and we became a solid 5–4–1. But when we had the ball, the idea was to put Gareth and Aaron in the best positions further forward, get it to them in central roles, and that's where they would damage the opposition.

'It started in Israel, but we used the ploy thereafter with tremendous success. The great Italian manager Fabio Capello has a famous quote about all coaches being thieves when it comes to nicking the best ideas from others. Well we make no bones about it, we took the two 10s from Paulo Sousa and FC Basel because it perfectly suited the players that we had.

'It was a bold decision from Cookie to change everything. He was under pressure, back up against the wall, but still had the clarity of mind to know what was required to take us to the next level. The decision could have led to things going the other way, but instead we flew.'

Bale was at it again three months later as Wales beat world number one ranked team Belgium 1–0 at Cardiff City Stadium, the evening when a capacity Welsh crowd realised their team was really up against it in the closing minutes and spontaneously burst into a wonderful rendition of the national anthem to spur the players over the line. If there was ever an example of the clichéd so-called 12th man at a football match, then this was it. Feeding off the passion of the crowd, Wales' players, out on their feet, suddenly found newfound energy and metaphorically grew a foot taller and a yard quicker. Kevin De Bruyne, Eden Hazard, Romelu Lukaku and their team-mates realised they weren't just playing against 11 Welshmen, they were up against an entire nation. A few more good results and finally it had happened – after close on 60 years of hurt Wales had qualified for a major tournament, runners-up to Group B winners Belgium. They had sealed their place at Euro 2016.

Any initial dressing room doubts about Coleman coming in as their new manager had well and truly evaporated as jubilant Welsh players threw the boss up in the air amid wild celebrations on the night qualifying was made official, away to Bosnia and Herzegovina in Zenica. As Wales subsequently rampaged through those finals in France, most of the earlier question marks among the fans towards Coleman also disappeared.

Again a little context is required, I feel, because the reservations from the public were totally understandable and not to be so readily dismissed. I was fully behind Coleman's appointment, but even firm backers like myself have to accept that sometimes it is a matter of timing. Coleman knows he was fortunate in so many ways, benefiting greatly from the work started by Toshack and Speed. It meant that by the time those Euros kicked off, Coleman possessed Welsh gold-dust – the rare mix of players with all the athleticism and energy that went with still being in their mid-twenties, but who were also seasoned international campaigners of 50 caps or more, having been thrown in the deep end as teenagers by Tosh. Sink or swim time. They swam.

It represented a truly potent combination, one which was enhanced further by the fact that Coleman could call upon a host of Premier League regulars. Not always the case for whoever is manager of Wales. The stars aligned perfectly. Come Euro 2016, these players were ready – battle-hardened, in their prime, full of energy and with one genuine world-beater in the mix, Gareth Bale, and another who wasn't too far behind, Aaron Ramsey. There was also a special team spirit, a dressing room bond forged by coming through the age grade system together and from sticking as one after the tragedy surrounding their previous manager.

For Coleman, it was a case of being in the right place at the right time and he never once underplayed the work done by his two predecessors in the job. However, he still had to put the game plan together, manage the situation, relax the players, deal with the pressures of having an entire nation, indeed a whole continent, suddenly looking at his team. Wales hadn't been in a major finals since 1958. The world was a very different place back then; the scrutiny was far more intense in the modern age. With the expert assistance of Roberts, Coleman did all of the above wonderfully well.

The goal was now for Wales to rampage at these Euros and turn the football world on its head. To that end, no stone was left unturned. FAW chief executive Jonathan Ford worked closely with Coleman and Roberts to set up a state-of-the art training HQ in the Brittany coastal town of Dinard, 260 miles west of Paris. UEFA offered various base camps to competing countries, including one on the beautiful Mediterranean island of Corsica, but Ford quickly ruled out that option.

'We are NOT going there,' I said. 'We're not on holiday, we're at this tournament to do well.' A little ironic, really, given Bale said on a number of occasions during those Euros that, 'We're having such a great time it just feels like we're on holiday with our mates,' a legacy of the special camaraderie built up in camp.

Wales spent a fortune turning their Dinard base into a home from home. Team room and hotel facilities were first class; grass pitches were installed to mirror the ones they would come across during their group matches; £100,000 even went on installing a Wi-Fi signal.

'The last thing we needed was players complaining because they couldn't contact people back home,' explains Ford, who was in charge of the finances and logistics. His attitude was spend, spend, spend. 'Bank the team' was Ford's motto. As Wales progressed deeper and deeper into the tournament, huge prize money kept rolling in. But so did the expense. As a general rule of thumb, a third went on the cost of Dinard, a third went to the players and management, and the remaining third was invested into Welsh football.

'I told the FAW board we couldn't necessarily expect to bring lots of money back. Anything we were getting I needed to invest in the team to give them the best chance,' reflects

Ford. 'I banked the Wales team. The three-way split remained in place as we made our way through the knockout rounds. Northern Ireland went out much earlier than us, yet brought back as much money from the tournament as we did – but they didn't have the semi-final legacy. That was greater than anything for us.

'As I look back, this was the moment when everything we'd built towards from the early days with Gary Speed came together. A massive part of that was the *TogetherStronger* hashtag we'd built up. None of us can remember how that first came about. We had regular brainstorming meetings and we were messing around with ideas at one of these. It was an amalgamation of group work. I don't think any of the staff can definitively say "It was totally my idea". *TogetherStronger* just summed us up perfectly, encapsulated everything we were doing, on and off the pitch. It just cottoned on, the players and fans bought into it. I guess when Hillary Clinton then used the words, albeit turned around, for her US presidential election bid later that year, it demonstrates the power of them.'

The painstaking planning also involved Osian Roberts tapping into the expertise of veterans from past World Cup and Euros tournaments – after all, this was unchartered territory for Wales. Leading figures Roberts knew well after taking them through their coaching badges in Newport were sought out for their opinions. French legends Thierry Henry and Patrick Vieira, both Euros winners, offered expert insight of what to do, and perhaps more importantly what not to do, when the tournament kicked off to give Wales the best chance of success. Sol Campbell, who had experienced penalty-kicks anguish with England, gave an alternative perspective. Former Scotland manager Craig Brown supplied the manager's viewpoint; ex-English Football Association director and communications chief Adrian Bevington advised, 'Look after the Welsh media, make them feel a part of it.'

All of this helped make Wales perhaps the happiest team

at the tournament. Smiles invariably on their faces, Bale turning on the charm by grinning his way through daily press conferences, their demeanour was certainly in stark contrast to that of England's players who, with Roy Hodgson and Gary Neville at the helm, often appeared to cut distrusting and evasive figures during those finals.

As for the greatest summer Welsh folk everywhere have known, so much has already been said and written about it, but here, game by game, are some largely unknown dressing room stories of what actually happened in Euro 2016. As told by Osian Roberts...

Wales 2 Slovakia 1
(Group game 1, Bordeaux, 11 June)

With Bale opening the scoring, and Ramsey setting up the winner for Hal Robson-Kanu, Coleman's two No. 10s master move is now working a treat, just when it matters most. But Wales have to overcome a morning-of-the-match shock when Wayne Hennessey, their undisputed number one goalkeeper, suddenly pulls out with a bad back and Danny Ward has to hastily take his place.

Osian Roberts' tale: 'Cookie and I had done so much homework ahead of the tournament. In fact, we started going around France looking at facilities before we had even qualified, something we weren't exactly comfortable with. We didn't want to be photographed booking hotels when we weren't even certain of reaching the finals – although I'm sure England, Spain, the Netherlands probably do it about four years in advance!

'The intensive planning involved putting our Dinard training base together. It was perfect. Small village, the airport was only a 10-minute drive to the hotel, no traffic. We weren't going into Paris and then making connections. One thing Thierry Henry advised was, "Decrease your travelling time. Finish a match," he said, "get to the airport, board the flight and at the other end players just want to get back to the hotel room to sleep. The killer for players is to have another hour or more on the bus once you land." We deliberately made sure we avoided that trap.

'Then, after all those months and months of painstaking planning, we land in Bordeaux the day before our opener – and the pilot goes past our arrivals gate! You can't just reverse the plane, you have to be pushed back. Other flights are coming in, so he can't just turn back around on the runway. It means we're stuck waiting on the plane for 45 minutes before it is pushed back. Only then can we get off and go in. This throws our schedule. Instead of going to the hotel first to check-in as planned, we have to head straight to the ground for training at our allotted time.

'Because Wayne Hennessey has been left seated on the plane, then the bus to training, we learn that his back has gone. It's the first message we get when we come down for breakfast on the morning of the game. Not the greatest of starts!

'The first ten minutes are then something of a whirl. Slovakia put us under pressure, Marek Hamšík sticks the ball past Danny Ward – and Ben Davies gets back to make that incredible clearance off the line. We weather the storm, Gareth Bale gives us the lead, runs over to celebrate with us. That wasn't pre-planned, Gareth just wanted everybody to join in the moment. *TogetherStronger* working perfectly.

'Our message ahead of the game was let's take small steps as the tournament unfolds. Can we get our first goal, our first clean sheet, our first point, our first win? Other than the clean sheet, everything happened on that very first day.'

Wales 1 England 2
(Group game 2, Lens, 16 June)

Gareth Bale, who else, puts Wales ahead once again, but this time they are pegged back with Jamie Vardy and Daniel Sturridge goals handing Roy Hodgson's men their only win of the tournament. Despite the pre-match hype that goes with Wales versus England, Coleman is in a relaxed mood ahead of kick-off, as demonstrated by a spoof team-sheet containing icons of the game who become Welsh for one day!

Osian Roberts' tale: 'The English media spotted Roy Hodgson had a notepad in his hand during training. When they zoomed in, it contained his starting team on it, which invariably made plenty of pre-match headlines. We saw the story over breakfast and I said to Cookie, "We should do this ourselves in training today, make sure the media can see it – but let's put a team together with Eusébio, Maradona and George Best. Heck, let's put Pelé in there too!" We also had Bobby Moore and Zico, for good measure.

'Cookie holds the team-sheet in his hand so it's visible to the TV cameras and photographers, and we have a good laugh afterwards. When the pressure is on, and it gets no bigger than Wales v England at a major tournament, having a bit of fun to relax and lift spirits is important.

'In the game we are so good without the ball. I think Wayne Rooney has a chance early on, but by and large we nullify them. Vardy equalises when the ball comes to him in an offside position off one of our own players, then Sturridge scores in the last minute, but it's more after a ricochet bounces their way than a goal that carves us open through dexterity. With the ball, however, we are useless. We are so focused upon stopping England that we don't play or show what we know we're capable of.

'A mix of that, and England's last-minute winner, means we are devastated as we head back into the dressing room. Cookie knows some man-management is required here. "OK, that's a tough one, but we just have to take it on the chin. We've all been together in each others' company for four weeks. Let's have a break. Everyone have some time off; we don't want to see you. Go to the beach, spend time with your families, whatever. We'll meet back up again in a couple of days."

'Back at the hotel, nursing our wounds from the loss, we're in the staff room when there is a knock on the door. Gareth Bale comes in. "We've just had a chat out there and we don't want to go off in different directions," he tells us. "Yes, let's have a change of scenery, but the players and staff have to stay as one. We win together, we lose together."

'Well this is music to our ears. Instead of training, we head en bloc to the coast for a relaxing three hours over a meal, talking about anything other than football, sharing jokes, having a bit of fun. But we stay as one, as the players wish. It does the trick. This is *TogetherStronger* in action.'

Wales 3 Russia 0
(Group game 3, Toulouse, 20 June)

The most controlled and exhilarating performance of the Coleman era to date. Ninety minutes of Welsh football poetry in which the two 10s tactic works beautifully with joint playmakers Bale and Ramsey running the show and scoring. Full-back Neil Taylor nets Wales' other goal, his only one in 43 appearances for his country. I'm not sure who is the more bewildered – Tayls himself as he wonders how to celebrate, or a Russian side utterly shell-shocked by the result? Wales top Group B, ahead of hot favourites England.

Osian Roberts' tale: 'What a night, particularly when you consider this is must-win if we are to go through to the knockout stages. The pressure is on after the manner of the defeat to England, but our message to the players in the dressing room is, "Whatever happens, let's prove to the world how well we can play. Let's show Wales at our best."

'Midway through the second half, three goals to the good, I stand up next to Cookie in the technical area and say, "Enjoy this mate, because you don't get these type of situations very often." You don't either – big game, major finals, must-win, and we're absolutely cruising it.

'Taylor's goal sums up everything good about us at those

Euros. It comes from a counter-attack where, at the beginning, Tayls and Chris Gunter are defending in our own box. As we go upfield at pace, and Tayls ends up scoring, the other player inside the Russian penalty area is Gunter. That's our system working at its best. Yes, it centres around the two 10s, but gives a chance for others to bomb forward, too.

'The following day we hold a feedback session, the usual pros and cons from the 90 minutes. At the end, Cookie is showing Tayls' goal on the big screen, then suddenly stops the video. "But lads," he starts, "The one area we've got to improve upon is your goal celebrations. Look at Tayls here, he's in shock!"

'They all fall about laughing. That's our togetherness, again.'

Wales 1 Northern Ireland 0
(Last 16, Paris, 25 June)

Because of the complicated nature of the draw, Wales don't know their first knockout opponents until the final possible moment. In the end they discover they are to meet Northern Ireland, one of the best third-placed teams, who come behind Germany and Poland in Group C. This is where painstaking work conducted behind the scenes by Roberts and his own backroom staff pays dividends. Welsh analysts have been exhaustively poring over detailed data of every team in the competition. It means that whoever Wales face, Coleman's players will know everything about every member of the opposition, including which foot they prefer to use, which way they turn, what happens at set-pieces and weak points to be exposed.

Nothing is left to chance. As it happens, Wales obviously know the Northern Ireland players anyway. They edge through a tense Battle of Britain showdown in the French capital, Gareth Bale producing the match-winning moment by forcing Gareth McAuley into an own goal.

Osian Roberts' tale: 'I had lots of FAW Trust staff

working for me at the finals and they were going to every game to study potential opposition we could be meeting at any stage. Major planning was involved. We worked three-day cycles – game, report, travel. The analysts supplied us with every report of every team from every game because we simply had no idea who we would be playing through the knockout stages. Once we did know, we sat down with the analyst, picked out the most important things and put them together for the team. Players would have details on their iPads of how their direct opponent operated. You can't feed them too much information 24 hours before a match, but it's there if they want to take a look.

'We know everything changes for us in this one. Suddenly, we're expected to win and we aren't always at our best in those situations. Again, I feel our togetherness gets us through it. This is the type of match we'd typically have lost 1–0 from a set-piece in the past, but our team spirit and resolve ensures no-one switches off at a key moment. We're not punished, we keep a clean sheet. Then up pops Gareth and we win the game.

'One of my abiding memories is what happened afterwards. We are given the PSG home dressing room which must be one of the biggest in the world. You've got venues in the United States where the locker rooms are larger, New York, Pasadena, one or two others, but they tend to be American Football grounds. PSG is among football's biggest and right in the middle of this enormous room is a huge table.

'Joe Ledley decides to get up on it and start dancing away. Others join in. Now the whole team is rocking away. If you had walked into our dressing room that day you'd have seen what togetherness and team spirit really is about. It gives me extra satisfaction because I was there at the very start when we didn't have that. To come from that point, to this, is so incredibly rewarding.'

Wales 3 Belgium 1
(Quarter-final, Lille, 1 July)

The result which sends shockwaves through the football world. Belgium, FIFA's number one ranked side and favourites to win the Euros, take an early lead and are expected to run away with it, but are left stunned as Ashley Williams, Hal Robson-Kanu and Sam Vokes reply with the greatest wham-bam-slam riposte in Welsh football history. The game is played just ten miles from the Belgian border, it is akin to a home match for Kevin De Bruyne and Co., but Welsh passion and team spirit wins the day.

Thousands of fans, who had returned home after the group stages, decide to make spontaneous trips by car back out to France, defying delays in the Channel Tunnel which means they almost miss kick-off. One close friend, Andrew Morgan of Cardiff, tries to persuade me to join him. 'It's win-win Abbo,' he says. 'We're either going to be there to celebrate the end of a wonderful journey – or to see the greatest result in Welsh history.'

Osian Roberts' tale: 'Everyone writes us off, but we'd beaten and drawn with Belgium so that gives us confidence. You still have to do it again, though. This is the stage when it all happens, the eyes of the world are upon you, and we know we need everything to go our way.

'When Radja Nainggolan scores for them early on, many will have been fearing the worst, but we aren't overly concerned on the bench. In fact, his goal, struck from 30 yards out, demonstrates our very strength of togetherness. Joe Allen and Aaron Ramsey, in wanting to help out the defence early on, are too deep. In this case our strength becomes our weakness because they can't close down the shot. It's a nice weakness to have, they wish to help their mates, they just don't need to go quite that far back.

'That collective nature of the whole team is key. The starting point for us is that even our best players are ready to give everything for the cause. Aaron Ramsey covered more ground than any other player in the tournament. Gareth Bale never stopped. Because they do it, everyone else naturally follows. Belgium have the individuals, we have the team.

'Actually, that early Belgium goal relaxes us in a way to just play as we know we can. Again, the attitude was if we're going to go out, let's go out showing people everywhere just how good Wales are at football. Belgium throw everything at us, but we withstand it and score three crackers of our own. When Ashley Williams gets our first he runs straight to the halfway line to celebrate with us. Once again, this is what *TogetherStronger* means. It's not a strapline, they have these values every single day. Ash just wants to share the moment with everybody in the whole group.

'The following day we hear stories of families meeting up at the team hotel; who was in the swimming pool at 3am and so forth? Wonderful celebrations. But the players not involved against Belgium are up early for a really hard training session, which must have been difficult physically and psychologically. Yet they give it everything – and the coaching staff are out there with them. Those who played against Belgium gave everything in front of millions. These guys, like James Collins and David Cotterill, are doing it in front of nobody, so to speak. But crucially, the ones who played the night before are there watching on, supporting and doing a warm down on their bikes in the marquee. They see the effort and appreciate it. This is what team spirit is about.'

Wales 0 Portugal 2
(Semi-final, Lyon, 6 July)

The Monday morning after the victory over Belgium, yours truly is asked to go on BBC Radio Wales' breakfast show – someone who has covered the highs and lows of Welsh football in the media for so many years trying to put into context what is happening to the country. Before reading out that morning's news bulletin, and then canvassing my own views, presenter Oliver Hides tells a Welsh nation: 'It's Wales in the semi-finals of Euro 2016 week... and these are your headlines.' It's a surreal moment, one that has an impact on even a hard-bitten football writing hack like me. Wales really are in the last four, headlines no-one envisaged reading out on air, or writing in the newspapers.

OK, goals from Cristiano Ronaldo and Nani ensure Portugal prevail. Indeed, they go on to lift the trophy. But Wales return two days later to a heroes' ovation, an open-top bus tour and a civic reception.

Given this is all being arranged at extremely short notice, I am taken into the FAW's confidence beforehand to help publicise and promote the planned celebrations around the streets of Cardiff. Obviously, we can't print anything until we know the result of the game. It's hush-hush for now, but a card marked just in case. This is unknown territory for the Wales football team and I detect concern among some about whether many members of the public will bother turning up. They have no need to worry, the people come in their hundreds of thousands to celebrate with Coleman's side.

Osian Roberts' tale: 'We'd had a settled team, so losing Aaron Ramsey and Ben Davies through suspension is a blow for us. Physically, the tournament has taken its toll by this stage, perhaps one match too far for us.

'The first goal is always going to decide the game. Portugal are quite cautious really, but Ronaldo changes everything with a wonderful header from a corner. We've looked back at it and James Chester, who is marking Ronaldo, does nothing wrong. Ronaldo doesn't make a movement, doesn't get away from Chessy, he is marked as tightly as is humanly possible. Chessy is high in the air when the corner comes in, yet Ronaldo is a foot above him. It's unstoppable. Sometimes you just have to tip your hat to a special moment from a special player.

Cristiano Ronaldo is that good. James Chester can have done no more.

'Once Ronaldo scored, we don't have the energy to turn this one around. We'd run our race. Everybody tried their best, but physically we are a notch lower than we'd been against Belgium. When the final whistle blows there is a sense of despondency – but also one of immense pride, too.

'Since the Russia group game, and through the knockout stages, there was a little bit of a strange process. The players knew they could be going home the next day, might be heading to Florida by the weekend, so what do you do with your hotel room? Do you pack everything, knowing you could go back to the room after the game and need to be out of it very quickly? Fortunately, each and every time we kept extending our stay by another four days. Ahead of Portugal it was a case of let's get the barber back!

'The deeper we went into the tournament, the more it became clear the players couldn't just go straight off on their holidays from France. The FAW wanted to do a function at the Welsh Senedd. The plans seemed to get bigger and bigger and ended with Cardiff Castle, an open-top bus tour, and Cardiff City Stadium. It was amazing, fantastic scenes. Finally, after all that, having spent weeks away together on this special journey, we separated and went our different ways.'

Piers Morgan was highly critical of those celebrations around the streets of Cardiff, telling his five million Twitter followers: 'The Wales football team do realise they didn't even make the Euro 2016 final, right? So the Welsh rugby team will also get an open-top bus for coming third in next Six Nations?' Piers went on to claim an Andy Murray win at Wimbledon 'would be ten times bigger' and announced he would sort the parade himself for the tennis star.

Amid a huge kickback from Welsh folk everywhere, he continued in derisory fashion: 'Sport is about coming first. What will you do if they actually win something? Throw a party on the Moon? Love the Welsh, but these open-top bus parades for losing, coming third or fourth, are not really my bag.'

It prompted me to respond with a *Wales Online* article headlined '200,000 reasons why Piers Morgan is WRONG to criticise Wales' brilliant homecoming parade'. This, I pointed out, was a once-in-two-generations event at best. Crikey, didn't England's cricketers have a parade for winning the Ashes in 2005, a regular contest with Australia. Fair play to Michael Vaughan's team, but the Euros was a much bigger event than that. OK, Wales may not have lifted the trophy, but they were winners in every other sense, evoking pride and passion in a nation which poured onto the streets of Cardiff during that parade. There was joy, there were tears of emotion. This was *TogetherStronger* in action, players and the people as one.

'Good article,' conceded Piers on Twitter… 'but you're still wrong!' Ha, let's just say we agreed to disagree. For many, those Euros will always be remembered as Wales' tournament.

Here was another example of the huge contradiction the Wales football team could be. From biggest under-achievers in the world – given the failure of dazzling talent to qualify down the decades – suddenly they were perhaps the biggest over-achievers. Coleman's side now soared into the top ten of FIFA's rankings, reaching a high spot of eighth and finding themselves above England, Italy and Spain and one place behind Brazil.

Things had changed so dramatically. From being among the bottom seeds for the previous World Cup qualifying campaign, they were now top seeds in the race for Russia 2018 as Wales were placed with the Republic of Ireland, Serbia, Austria, Georgia and Moldova. If the Euros were a one-off, a fairytale which could never be repeated, the World Cup was the ultimate goal and this Wales team, with Bale and Ramsey still very much in their prime, were ready to go again.

Which is why failure to get to those finals in Russia ranks for me with the 1993 World Cup setback against Romania as among the most disappointing moments I've known covering the team. At least the Romanians were a dazzling outfit, boosted by the great Gheorghe Hagi, who went on to beat Argentina and shine at USA '94. No games are easy at international level of course, as the old cliché goes, but if Coleman could have handpicked a qualifying group then it would have been close to the one fate dealt him.

Five beatable teams standing in Wales' way. Unfortunately, they found themselves on the backfoot right from the start, disappointingly drawing three of their first four games, including a costly 1–1 stalemate with Georgia in Cardiff. It meant that heading to Dublin for their next clash away to the Republic of Ireland, Wales were already being roundly written off by all and sundry. The Irish, managed masterfully by Martin O'Neill, were soaring clear at the top of the table, with Serbia also ahead of Wales. Dublin was supposedly where the World Cup dream would disappear.

I wasn't buying any of that doom and gloom. Not for one second. Not with this Wales team. They hadn't suddenly become ordinary overnight. In an attempt to alter the narrative, and present a more positive mood, I penned an article for *Wales Online* arguing it was ridiculous for so many to be writing them off so readily. While heading to Ireland's Aviva Stadium lair to play against a battle-hardened team with momentum, belief and confidence would be a daunting challenge, Coleman's men had nothing to fear, I stated. To demonstrate the point, I picked a composite XI from the two countries – and, as I recall, only two Irish players made the cut. Séamus Coleman, captain of Everton, won the nod over Chris Gunter at right-back, and Shane Long was better than Hal Robson-Kanu up top. Other than that it was Wales, Wales and more Wales. There were a couple of 50–50 calls, Wayne Hennessey versus West Ham's Darren Randolph in goal, Joe Ledley up against Glenn Whelan in midfield, but I sided with the men in red given what they had so recently achieved during the Euros.

The article certainly provoked plenty of debate, not least

across the Irish Sea, and I was asked by their media outlets to justify my choices. I found it reasonably easy to stick to my guns – Wales had the superior players, I insisted, even if results were currently suggesting otherwise.

Perhaps there was some kind of Euro 2016 hangover for Coleman's side, but personally I felt they had become victims of their own success. Other teams were so wary of the Bale–Ramsey joint 10s axis that they had begun to work out Wales, were sitting deeper and not allowing themselves to be counter-attacked at breathtaking speed. As such I argued that, while the wing-backs system with Chris Gunter and Neil Taylor had worked brilliantly up to that point, it now required evolving with Coleman needing to find extra craft in the wide positions further forward.

Wales duly drew 0–0 in Dublin, then away to Serbia, and finally got on the front foot with a hat-trick of victories over Austria, Moldova and in the return game with Georgia as Coleman did, indeed, alter his tactics and approach by utilising fresh blood. It meant that by the time the Irish headed to a capacity Cardiff City Stadium for the group finale in the autumn of 2017, Wales had turned it completely around and merely needed a draw on home soil to guarantee a World Cup play-off spot.

That was the night I maintain Coleman got everything wrong, which proved costly. To me, Wales shot themselves in the foot. The Republic had to win to have any hope of getting to the World Cup so, in what was bound to be a cagey affair, Wales just needed to sit in, then hit the visitors on the break in the closing 20 minutes when they threw men forward to chase victory. The first error for me was Coleman starting Hal Robson-Kanu ahead of Sam Vokes up top, when the former's pace would have been far more threatening as a substitute against tiring and isolated Irish defenders in that final quarter. The bigger mistake came when Coleman replaced the concussed Joe Allen with Jonny Williams early on. The manager had other options on the bench, but instead chose to move Aaron Ramsey back into Allen's more defensive role and put Williams as his 10 playmaker. In doing so, I was of the view Coleman weakened two positions instead of just one and, at the same time, negated Ramsey's very strength, which was probing and creating further forward – even more important in this game given the injured Gareth Bale was absent.

When James McClean subsequently scored the only goal of the game near the end, I was annoyed because I felt Coleman's decision-making had blown a golden World Cup opportunity. I immediately made my views known on Twitter, never a good thing to write in anger, then in more measured tones in a comment piece for the *Western Mail*, outlining where Coleman had gone wrong in my eyes. Some FAW figures weren't overly pleased. On the other hand, I felt their attitude of 'We've lost, we just go again' was naive. It was evident to me that Wales had reached a crossroads under Coleman. For all the excellent work he had done as manager, on this occasion he was out-thought by the wily O'Neill who got his own game plan and selection spot on.

Osian Roberts defends what happened that night by arguing: 'When Gary Speed came in, our vision was to qualify not just once, but to do it with regularity. To aim for three tournaments out of four, or at least take it to the final game of qualifying. Going from zero over many decades to three out of four is a massive jump, but remember we were unbeaten in the group heading into that Republic of Ireland game.'

Fair point Osh, but the inevitable intense speculation over Coleman's future quickly followed. Quite rightly, Cookie had a lot of credit in the bank and many wanted to see him carry on. Others were of the view that a change of manager was required. Speaking to sources close to the dressing room, I was being told it was getting to the stage where a new voice was needed to run the team.

Within a handful of weeks, Coleman contacted FAW chief

executive Jonathan Ford to tell him he was leaving to take over as boss of Sunderland, third from bottom in the Championship and staring League One in the face.

Ford recalls: 'I'm at home one night relaxing, iPad open, phone by my side when it starts ringing. Chris tells me his news – I almost spat my wine across the table. Even I knew how difficult the task would be up there.

'Chris was linked with clubs. Did we fight as much as we could have to keep him? No, perhaps it was the right time for each of us to move on. The Wales job tends to suit people just starting out in their managerial careers, or in Toshack's case coming towards the end. Cookie was in the middle, which was something of a rarity, and he wanted to take up another challenge.'

There were some suggestions Coleman was close to trebling his salary by joining Sunderland. Whatever the precise truth of that, the FAW knew they simply couldn't compete financially. One leading source telephoned me on the night the news broke to say they would have had to make swingeing cutbacks – including pretty much wiping out planned growth for the women's game – to match the money Coleman was being offered at club level.

Coleman wasn't in it for the cash, let me stress. He loved being manager of his country. However, Sunderland are a massive football club and he felt this was a fabulous new challenge. Deep down, he also must have known he had taken Wales as far as he could. For clarity, that was incredibly far.

For some, there remains an element of doubt when judgement is made on Coleman. On the one hand, he gave us the golden days we dreamed of and, as such, his name is well and truly etched into Welsh football folklore. On the other hand, right time, right place, he certainly benefited from the rock-solid foundations put in place by Toshack and Speed and from inheriting maestros like Bale and Ramsey at their peak. The critics will point to the fact Sunderland dropped into

League One under Coleman, that he was dismissed within five months, and immediately afterwards only managed in China, Greece and Cyprus, rather than landing another top job.

Will the real Chris Coleman stand up? Judge as you see fit, I guess.

What can never be taken away is the incredible journey this Wales team embarked upon under a manager many didn't want from day one. As someone who had backed Coleman from the start, yes that meant his success was extra special for me – but all good things come to an end. I knew after the Republic of Ireland loss that Cookie's era was over.

It was now time to get behind another Wales manager, even if an *#anyonebutGiggs* hashtag was about to reverberate around social media.

10

Rise and fall of Ryan

I'm RELAXING AT home on a Sunday tea-time in early January 2018 when a message comes through on my phone that is to trigger a manic few hours ahead.

'Ryan Giggs is the new manager,' I'm told.

This is *major* news, indeed it would become the biggest Welsh sports story of the year. I knew Giggs was part of the interview process as FA of Wales bosses started their hunt for Chris Coleman's successor, but this was happening a tad quicker than I'd anticipated. Very few people knew at this stage Giggs was getting the job, but I couldn't sit on something as significant as this. Welsh sport can be a village when it comes to gossip. In an era of social media and fan messageboards, the news wouldn't remain secret for too long.

My highly-placed source couldn't have been more reliable, yet this was too important a story to splash as the lead item on *Wales Online* based upon one tip-off. For peace of mind, I needed to check it out with others who might be in the know, fully aware that only a small number of individuals would be actually in the loop.

Yes, Giggs was the chosen one, it was confirmed to me again. But it was an incredibly tight call. Apparently, the six-man FAW sub-committee tasked with making the appointment were split right down the middle. Giggs impressed, but so too did Craig Bellamy, another Welsh legend who was also spoken to and who gave what was being called a 'Hollywood'

PowerPoint presentation about his vision for Welsh football. These were Bellamy's own ideas, he delivered them expertly and with authority, but they had been partly put together for him in an inspiring glossy package by technical gurus at Sky Sports. At the time Bellamy was working as a pundit for them. Knowledgeable and prepared to speak his mind, he made a good fist of it too, before becoming Vincent Kompany's number two with Belgium giants Anderlecht and then Burnley in the Premier League. Those Welsh bosses were quite taken aback by the powerful message Bellamy delivered.

Osian Roberts, assistant to Coleman during the Euro 2016 march, and Mark Bowen, who had worked next to Mark Hughes, were also interviewed, but in the end it boiled down to a straight choice between the two stellar names. Three committee members voted for Giggs, the other three plumped for Bellamy. They could only be separated, I was informed, because crucially the FAW's president David Griffiths, handed the casting vote in these circumstances, threw his support behind Giggs.

Thus, shortly after 7.30pm on that supposedly quiet Sunday evening, the headline 'Ryan Giggs to be named Wales manager despite "Hollywood interview" by hugely impressive Craig Bellamy' was emblazoned across *Wales Online*. The sub-title underneath read, 'FAW boss in negotiations with Giggs, but Bellamy pushed him to brink for Wales job'.

Cue a social media outcry. An *#anyonebutgiggs* hashtag had already been doing the rounds on Twitter since it became apparent Ryan was among the favourites, but now the condemnation went into positive meltdown mode. A whole series of accusations were thrown Giggs' way amid suggestions the FAW didn't have a clue what they were doing and were letting down an entire nation with this decision. One or two, oblivious to the truth, simply refused to believe what we were reporting, claiming it was 'typical newspaper nonsense', would not be happening, and that only Welsh FA bosses knew the truth. Yawn, yawn, like respectable local media outlets just make up this kind of thing without checks and balances.

Anyway, while the hoo-hah was erupting, I received another message, this one telling me Giggs had just travelled down from his Manchester home to the five-star St David's Hotel in the waterfront area of Cardiff to finalise terms on a four-year contract. The £500,000 salary said to be on offer was small beer compared to the sums of money Giggs was accustomed to as a playing superstar with Manchester United, but it still made him the best paid manager in Wales' history. With the breaking news now also appearing in media outlets everywhere, the FAW had to hastily arrange a press conference for the following afternoon to make the announcement. Technically, the decision to appoint Giggs needed to be rubber-stamped by their full 34-person ruling council, but they weren't due to meet for another month. There was no time to wait, thus plenary powers were used which entitled the small FAW sub-committee to go with the decision, tasking chief executive Jonathan Ford to ring Giggs with the good news.

'Hello Ryan. How would you like to start a new chapter… as national team manager?' Ford began the conversation.

Giggs, of course, had no hesitation in saying yes, thanking Ford for the opportunity.

It quickly became clear that while much of Wales was excited by the appointment, plenty of others were, shall we say, disappointed at best, incandescent with rage at worst. There remained a lot of angst towards Giggs for not appearing in exactly 75 per cent of the friendly internationals staged during his Wales playing days. There were further grumblings about him quitting international football midway through 2007 while continuing to perform so excellently for Manchester United for a further seven years. Club before country was the feeling from many, the opposite to Gareth Bale.

Ahead of the unveiling press conference, and trying to put some context on the many charges being thrown his way, I ran a lengthy article headlined, 'The furious Ryan Giggs backlash from Wales fans; the accusations, the truth and the fiction.' The opening sentence to the story read, 'So Ryan Giggs is Wales' Chosen One. For some, Public Enemy Number One might seem a more appropriate phrase,' which pretty much summed the hostility.

Now it was neither my job to defend Giggs, nor to justify the FAW's decision for them. They were each big enough and ugly enough to do that on their own. Supporters were perfectly entitled to their opinion – and many were making their views known in rather robust fashion.

That said, I also felt the majority of assertions being thrown Giggs' way didn't stack up as being credible and, for the sake of balance, were worth examining properly. They included concerns that Giggs was 'English, not Welsh'; he wasn't committed to his country as demonstrated by those constant withdrawals as a player; he never performed well, or tried hard enough, in the red of Wales; he appeared for Team GB. There was even dismay expressed that he was a regular commentator on rivals England for ITV.

For good measure Giggsy also lacked personality, the players wouldn't respect him, he was merely a corporate appointment… and no-one wanted him.

Ouch, quite a lot of disquiet there, then! Most of which, of course, was easily shot down as being either untrue, conjecture, or, in the case of the Team GB accusation, totally irrelevant. Craig Bellamy also played in those London 2012 Olympics. So too Aaron Ramsey, Joe Allen and Neil Taylor, quite rightly feted as idols during Euro 2016. In fact, Giggs and Bellamy reckoned the chance to experience tournament football for the first time in the Olympics would hold those then Welsh youngsters in good stead when matches came thick and fast in the real thing of the Euros or World Cup.

Be that as it may, or not, there certainly more appropriate anti-Giggs sentiments to put forward than 'He played for Team GB'. Same with the silly claim that nobody wanted him as manager, which clearly wasn't the case. On the contrary, amid the #anyonebutgiggs consternation I was aware there were also lots of supporters, plus former players, who were hugely enthused by the prospect of him becoming Wales boss. They, too, were pretty vocal about it. Perhaps best to say he was a choice who divided opinion.

Two of the claims made against Giggs did hold much greater credence in my eyes. One was that he lacked any managerial experience and there were better candidates out there. Fair enough, that was entirely true. Trouble is, even that one became weakened when a few of those critics putting it forward stated in the next breath that they wanted Bellamy. Much as I personally would have loved to see Craig in charge, and was delighted when that subsequently happened several years down the line, his CV was hardly one full of managerial gravitas either. The FAW often give a Welsh legend his first managerial job, it's just their way of doing things. Given a need to keep a close watch on the purse strings, Pep Guardiola, Jürgen Klopp and José Mourinho were hardly options, were they?

The other credible concern over Giggs were claims being made about his off-the-field behaviour. Indeed, I know one or two on the FAW were wary about tawdry headlines surrounding his private life. In attempting to censor one kiss-and-tell story, Giggs even ended up on the front pages of every national newspaper after being named in the House of Commons where absolute privilege is afforded to MPs. He had taken out a court injunction to stop the publicity; it couldn't have backfired in a worse manner. Other unsavoury headlines didn't make for particularly pretty reading, either. These were entirely justifiable concerns being raised by his critics.

I wrote the following at the time: 'You could, of course, argue this has nothing to do with football. But it is something the FAW should have at least considered because the manager of Wales is a role model. As figurehead of your country, there are different criteria to any club job. Perhaps Giggs is simply a victim of being so famous his private affairs have been pored over. Either way, he will want only Wales' football to grab the headlines from here on in. More pertinently, that's what the FAW will want.'

Ironic then, or prophetic perhaps, that almost three years down the line it was to end in the manner that it did. Maybe the detractors putting that particular argument forward were proven correct after all in fearing something else unpalatable would hit the newspapers and cause this to go wrong.

At the time, Wales' hierarchy certainly didn't see it as an area of worry as they proudly introduced Giggs at a packed out Cardiff press conference that was rammed with TV cameras, broadcast journalists and written scribes from Welsh newspapers, London-based nationals and indeed foreign media outlets. Only John Toshack, when he was appointed Wales manager, had created this amount of media hullabaloo at home and abroad.

Evidence for chief executive Ford that this was a marketing dream. Moving forward, he could envisage the mouth-watering prospect of Ryan Giggs and Gareth Bale, manager and captain, sitting side by side at press conferences, corporate branding of the FAW's commercial partners behind them, to broadcast Wales to the world. With the greatest of respect to their predecessors, Chris Coleman and Ashley Williams, the gravitas Giggs and Bale held meant this was in another galaxy from a promotional perspective when it came to opportunities to sell the Welsh dream.

Giggs was put through the wringer at that hour-long media briefing, quizzed constantly, and in differing ways, about the many concerns being put forward by Welsh fans. He appeared irritated at one point, even saying to me, 'You're asking a lot of questions aren't you, Paul?' as I pressed the point once more. Giggs insisted he had received nothing but well-wishes and had been snowed under with good luck messages since the news broke, including from staff and guests at the hotel where he had stayed overnight. Perhaps this was the more silent majority. Who knows? It's impossible to give a percentage breakdown of how many were pro-Giggs and how many were anti. What we can say is that while the cynicism continued to bubble under the surface, Giggs was to disarm most of the knockers – for a while anyway, until his implosion – by establishing the best win, draw and losses ratio of any Wales manager in history.

Three days before the press conference unveiling, Ford and the FAW sub-committee had convened in the private room of a swish Birmingham hotel to conduct the interview process. Timings were arranged to ensure Giggs, Bellamy, Roberts and Bowen didn't bump into one another, two of them spoken to in the morning, the other pair in the afternoon. They had each been asked to produce a presentation on the way forward for Wales, their vision for the future and how they would get the team to qualify for Euro 2020 and the World Cup in Qatar two years later. All impressed. Bellamy blew away the panel with his bubbly enthusiasm and the positivity of his delivery. Many of the suggestions he put forward then were to be repeated six years down the line when he did eventually land the job. Roberts came across as the most knowledgeable and experienced, which he was, but you always sensed Giggs would need to do just enough, so to speak, to win the day. He was the one the FAW really wanted, albeit Bellamy gave him a right old run for his money. As it happens, Giggs too wowed with his ideas, professionalism and the Manchester United-like winning mentality he said he wished to bring to the Wales fold.

Ford reflects on what happened by saying: 'Of all the jobs within a national governing body, getting the manager's appointment right is the most important one. I put an awful lot of effort into driving the process, whittling down a very longlist to a shortlist, spending half a day with the candidates beforehand to talk them through our philosophy, what the FAW wanted to achieve, why it was such a great opportunity, what the finances would be. Ryan, for example, was accustomed to a big salary, but we had to tell him what we could afford before he even came to the interview.

'The reality is the Wales job is for someone wanting to do it for the right reasons. Part of a career choice, but ultimately someone who is passionate about the Wales football team, sees it as an honour. That, in truth, probably means someone who is Welsh. Given where he was in his own career at the time, keen to break into management, Ryan was the ideal type of person. He, and we, knew this was a perfect opportunity to work with star players, bring through younger ones, craft his skills, look and learn. The best training ground for would-be managers I guess, as it was for Mark Hughes and Gary Speed.

'Ryan and the other candidates already knew the financial package and bonus structure on offer. So once we made our final choice, while the agent might tinker around the edges a little bit, in effect a handshake on a contract had already been agreed.

'At the interview Ryan put his speaking volume up a couple of notches. He even said, "My agent told me to turn up the volume." Something as simple as that made him come across more forcefully. He was honest, and enthused, about the way he saw the future of Welsh football and we were very impressed.'

While the candidates each drove home after their talks, the FAW members stayed overnight at the Birmingham hotel and the following day went through the pros and cons of each of them. Eventually, after a robust debate and the tightest of votes, they settled on Giggs ahead of Bellamy.

'We knew there was a bit of a battle against some of our hard-core fans, but Ryan was the consummate professional. He'd learned from the best in Sir Alex Ferguson and we could foresee definite improvements in the team with him at the helm,' says Ford. 'He knew where his weaknesses were and he wasn't stubborn enough to think he could do everything. He made sure other coaches were empowered to do their jobs, if that was their strength. This is all part of being a good people's person when it comes to managing.

'Ryan qualified us for Euro 2020 and I honestly believe he'd have got Wales to the World Cup too. As such, he would almost certainly have gone on to become a very decent club manager, either with a Premier League team or a club right towards the top of the Championship.'

One of the things Giggs had stressed to Ford and his colleagues was the hurt he still felt at missing out as a player on the 1994 World Cup and the 2004 Euros, when Wales were just 90 minutes away from qualifying on each occasion. That was the missing element to his CV – the fire still burned within and he was determined to make up for it now as manager of Wales.

The start of the Giggs reign, it is fair to say, was mixed at best. Wales were suddenly playing in far more swashbuckling fashion at times, thumping China 6–0 and the Republic of Ireland 4–1, but the record from his first 13 matches in charge read won five, drew one, lost seven. Back-to-back Euro qualifying defeats in Croatia and Hungary, where I argued in print Giggs had made selection errors by not picking a proper centre-forward, led to his critics among the fan base finding their voices again. Giggs was spending too much time in his role as co-owner of Salford City, or with a coaching academy in Vietnam, we were told, all at the expense of doing the Wales job properly. There were even reports about Giggs losing the dressing room, rumours I was asked about at the time but certainly could not stack up as being true. More nonsense, in fact.

Results needed to improve though – and how dramatically they did. Giggs resolved his centre-forward issue by discovering a new Welsh cult hero from the lower leagues in the 6ft 5in frame of Kieffer Moore. To outsiders, Kieffer may look ungainly; to Welsh fans the team was better balanced with him in it.

Wales won seven and drew three of their next 11 games, their solitary loss coming in a friendly versus England at Wembley. The run ensured they thrillingly qualified for Euro 2020 by beating Hungary 2–0 at Cardiff City Stadium, while Giggs also took them to the verge of joining Europe's superpowers via promotion to the top tier of the UEFA Nations League.

Defeating Hungary at home to reach the Euros may not sound much, but this was exactly the kind of win-or-bust final qualifying fixture in front of their own fans that Wales had failed in, time and again, down the decades, and were to do post the Giggs era too. Some of his predecessors in the job, Terry Yorath (Romania, 1993), Mark Hughes (Russia, 2003), and Chris Coleman (Republic of Ireland, 2017), would testify to the pressures involved and the hurt caused by such all-or-nothing occasions, as would Giggs' successor, Rob Page. He got Wales through a Cardiff play-off final versus Ukraine to reach the World Cup, but then saw his side fall to Poland in similar circumstances in their bid to reach Euro 2024.

Giggs had not only banished those demons, he did so with a team in transition, having ruthlessly ripped up the side under Coleman which achieved so much to bring through a new crop of international rookies with skill, energy, effervescence and a fearless approach. Out went most of the old guard; into their places came young guns like Harry Wilson, Dan James, David Brooks, Neco Williams, Ethan Ampadu and Joe Rodon to usher in a new era for Welsh football. Giggs wanted a more vibrant, adventurous team, almost Sir Alex Ferguson Manchester United-like in their pass and move at pace approach. A bit of zip and swagger – which meant bold alterations needed to be made.

Of the many Coleman shoo-ins approaching 30 years of age or above, only Gareth Bale, Aaron Ramsey, Joe Allen and Wayne Hennessey remained in Giggs' starting XI. If anything, those four appeared re-energised by the plethora of new talent around them who could now do most of the running.

It really was a changing of the guard. Giggs had been through this himself as a player, part of the famous Manchester United Class of '92 of home-grown youngsters who totally helped transform Old Trafford fortunes, so he was falling back upon first-hand experience of how it worked. Nonetheless, when Giggs afforded me an hour-long Zoom interview during Covid (trust me, one-to-ones with Ryan could be as rare as Halley's Comet, so he must have been bored!), he opened up on the 'difficult conversations' required with those senior Welsh players who had become part of the furniture but were now being dropped.

'It's not easy. These can be hard conversations to have. You're leaving out players who are big characters and who have done so much for their country. Sometimes I don't even have an excuse,' Giggs told me. 'But you just have to be as honest as you can. Players will not like it, some have been regulars, might expect to play, that's totally understandable. I get that, but decisions have to be made. There are younger players whose form I just could not ignore.

'I saw the two sides of this myself as a Man Utd player. First, when that group of us came through together in the '90s. You play without fear, but you also quickly improve because you're suddenly next to senior stars who can guide you in the right direction. Then I also saw it years later as one of the older players in the United dressing room. I tell a story of how for a decade I was up against Gary Neville in training. I'm not saying either of us got stale, but we became familiar with one another's style. Suddenly Sir Alex Ferguson brought in Rafa da Silva, a young Brazilian right-back. He was running back at me non-stop, doing different things. My attitude and focus had to change. He made me step up my own game. That's how it happens, the young players energise you.'

It would have been easier, but wrong, for Giggs to stick with Coleman's tried and trusted. He didn't. Tough calls out of the way, Wales' future was suddenly looking very rosy again. Even

Giggs' old boss and mentor Sir Alex was impressed. 'Ryan is intelligent, has great drive about him and is doing a great job – and giving young players a chance too. It is fantastic to see,' said the great man. This team was on the up, going places and could only get better and better as the manager, himself still a rookie remember, gained greater knowledge and experience.

Who on earth could have possibly forecast what was to happen next? By the time Euro 2020 took place, postponed for a year because of the pandemic, Giggs was in the middle of an extended stay of gardening leave, kicking his heels in frustration on the outside while his FAW bosses had no idea what the future held – for Ryan, the team or themselves.

Giggs had continued his good run in the autumn of 2020 with impressive UEFA Nations League results against Bulgaria (twice), Republic of Ireland and Finland. On 14 October, having led Wales to a 0–1 win in Sofia, he spoke excitedly about the future by saying: 'I'm really pleased. We're a young team, we can improve and we will.'

Just 18 days later, Giggs' world fell in amid the incident involving his partner Kate Greville which was to lead to the subsequent court case. The news broke just as Giggs was due to meet the Welsh media to name his squad for the next batch of games. That scheduled press conference was hastily cancelled. Instead, it was announced he was temporarily standing down as Wales manager.

It was totally unclear at that stage, of course, what 'temporary' meant and just how long Giggs would remain on the sidelines, but the more the legal process dragged on and on, the less and less it made the likelihood of him stepping back into his role. The FAW were placed in an unenviable position. They didn't want to get rid of their manager, nor did they have legal grounds to do so. They were fully aware of the fundamental principle of British justice – innocent until proven guilty. Giggs was fighting for his reputation and his football future here. His employers couldn't just ditch him completely.

However, given the nature of the accusations and subsequent charges, it became clear he could not manage Wales while the prospect of a court case was hanging over him. Thus Giggs' deputy Robert Page stepped-up as caretaker manager and took the team to those delayed Euros in 2021, without particularly setting the world on fire. Wales got through their group, a 2–0 win over Turkey the high spot, but were then hammered 4–0 by Denmark at the first stage of the knockout rounds. The extravagant success of France four years earlier was not to be repeated. Would Wales have fared better with Giggs at the helm? Yes, many felt.

Still there was no sign of an end to the impasse. Page, as the stand-in boss, took charge of more and more matches as Giggs remained absent. In total, Page was Wales' caretaker manager for 26 internationals and more than a year and a half, an unfathomable number of games for a temp! His first match was a 0–0 draw with the USA on 12 November 2020. His last, before officially being appointed full-time, was a 3–2 loss to the Netherlands on 14 June 2022. Under his watch the brilliance of Gareth Bale drove Wales to the winter World Cup in Qatar with splendid Cardiff play-off wins over Austria and Ukraine. It was at that point the FAW's new chief executive Noel Mooney, who had replaced Jon Ford in the role, and Giggs agreed this stalemate simply couldn't carry on indefinitely amid no indication of when the legal process would be concluded. It had already gone on way too long.

Giggs' reaction to Mooney's telephone call was brilliant, I'm told. 'He was good as gold' is the description used. Ryan chose to take the bull by the horns to announce that he was resigning. 'While I am confident in our judicial process, I had hoped that the case would have been heard earlier to enable me to resume my managerial responsibilities,' read his statement. 'Through nobody's fault the case has been delayed. I do not want the country's preparations for the World Cup to be affected, destabilised or jeopardised in any way by the continued interest around this case. I am sad that we cannot continue this journey together because I believe that this extraordinary group will make the country proud. I have been fortunate enough to have enjoyed some unforgettable moments. I am proud of my record and will cherish those special times.'

Giggs' trial started two months later amid an inevitable media scrum outside Manchester Crown Court. This was an even bigger story than anything he had achieved with Manchester United or Wales, the interest worldwide enormous. He pleaded not guilty to the charges against him and the jury was eventually discharged after failing to reach verdicts on whether he assaulted and controlled his ex-girlfriend Kate Greville and assaulted her sister. Giggs had to wait another year for the retrial and was 'deeply relieved' when Judge Hilary Manley formally entered not guilty verdicts. In a ten-minute court hearing in July 2023 prosecutors said they would not be pursuing the case. Giggs' former girlfriend did not wish to give evidence again.

Giggs' barrister, Chris Daw KC, maintained: 'The position is that he has always been innocent of these charges and there have been very many lies told about him. Going forward he will seek to rebuild his career as an innocent man.'

The case had taken a heavy toll – and price – on Giggs, however. Admitting, 'I loved managing Wales, I do miss it,' he would have been hoping to see his Dragons dazzle first at the Euros, then the World Cup, perhaps putting his name well and truly in the frame for the Manchester United manager's job. There has been a revolving door at Old Trafford since Ferguson left, with David Moyes, Louis van Gaal, José Mourinho, Ole Gunnar Solskjær, Ralf Rangnick, Erik ten Hag and Ruben Amorim employed.

Solskjær held down the role for three years and 168 matches, despite being an unequivocal flop in his only other UK management job when he relegated Cardiff City from the Premier League in 2014. Given Giggs' legendary status with the Reds, it is not a massive leap of faith to think the Man Utd hierarchy would have considered him if Wales had continued on the upward journey he was taking them on. That isn't likely to happen now. Indeed, we wait to see just how high a level Giggs ends up managing at again.

He is bound to have a deep sense of unfinished business with Wales. A case of what might have been in his eyes, and indeed those of Welsh fans who felt the team were on the verge of something special with him at the helm. Giggs' 50 per cent winning record from 24 internationals in charge was the best ratio of any manager in the country's history. Gary Speed also had the same impressive figure, but he also had a 50 per cent loss ratio. Ten matches is not a fair number upon which to judge Speed.

For comparison, John Toshack's win ratio was 40 per cent (21 victories from 53 games), followed by Chris Coleman 39 per cent (19 wins from 49), Terry Yorath 39 per cent (16 wins from 41), Bobby Gould 29 per cent (7 wins from 24) and Mark Hughes 29 per cent (12 wins from 41).

Rob Page, previously elevated from the Welsh under-21s to Ryan's number two with the senior team, took over the reins on a permanent basis as the FAW sought much-needed stability amid the chaotic situation they found themselves in. Under any other circumstances, Page would not even have had the remotest of look-ins for the Wales job. Port Vale and Northampton in the lower leagues were the high spots on his management CV, and he had left the Cobblers under a cloud after saying it was like 'men against girls' when his side lost 5–0 to Bristol Rovers. The comment caused an outcry, Page apologised, but given it was his team's eighth defeat in ten matches the writing was on the wall and he vacated his post.

There was always the sense Page was merely a short-term appointment until Wales went for a bigger name boss, or even saw Giggs return to the fray. Yet as well as those 26 matches in charge as caretaker, Page was also at the helm for a further 19 games. His final record read, played 45, won 15, drew 16, lost 14, for an underwhelming win ratio of 33 per cent. That put him below Giggs, Speed, Toshack, Coleman and Yorath, but ahead of Gould and Hughes. More significantly, it was also an awful lot of matches for a guy who was only supposed to be standing in on a temporary basis.

Page has his backers. Whether down to Bale brilliance or not, he was the manager in situ when Wales finally qualified for a World Cup for the first time in 64 years and deserves credit for that, yet there always remained large elements of the fan base who questioned Page and who raised baffled eyebrows at the FAW's decision to reward him with a four-year contract. Many were never really sold on Page from day one, feeling he was promoted way above his station only as a result of the unique circumstances. Indeed, having waited six long decades for the big moment on the global stage, Page's team unfortunately bowed out with a whimper in Qatar, scraping a 1–1 draw with the USA, being humiliated 2–0 by Iran, and then barely throwing a punch in anger while losing 3–0 to the old enemy England. They were on the first plane home. A shame, when you've waited that long.

Things didn't really get too much better as Page then had to deal with what was the nigh-on football impossible – Wales post the Bale era, as Gareth the Great, team talisman and inspiration for more than a decade, hung up his boots. Wales didn't win a single game in their next UEFA Nations League campaign, losing five of six, and then failed to make the top-two in the qualifying battle for Euro 2024 in Germany. That one was a mix of the sublime and the ridiculous – a 2–1 win over Croatia which was their best performance under Page; an abject 2–4 home loss to Armenia which was their worst.

Courtesy of the work performed earlier by Giggs in pretty much securing promotion to the top tier of the UEFA Nations League, Page was handed a back door route to the Euros via the play-offs. As with the World Cup games against Austria and

Ukraine, again the draw was kind, with Page handed home advantage, this time versus Finland and Poland. Amid questions raised over his team selection, substitutions and tactics, Wales lost the final in the most agonising fashion possible, knocked out on penalties by the Poles.

The previous time Wales had missed a penalty in a win-or-bust Cardiff qualifier was in 1993 against Romania when Terry Yorath controversially found himself out of a job. This time the FAW declared they were staunchly backing their manager – naive comments from their president Steve Williams amid growing disquiet among the Welsh public. Even without Bale, the fans believed a team containing a clutch of young talents, Brennan Johnson, Neco Williams, David Brooks, Harry Wilson among them, would have seen off Poland at home with a better manager at the helm.

I've known and got on well with Steve Williams for more than two decades. He tended to be a voice of reason amid some questionable FAW decisions down the years, thus I always respected his views. On this occasion, however, the president called it badly wrong. I simply couldn't understand why Williams left himself hostage to fortune by backing Page so staunchly when it was becoming abundantly clear from conversations I was having with his colleagues that others didn't exactly share his confidence. The Welsh public certainly didn't.

Surprise, surprise, just two matches later, Page was dismissed after a horror summer which saw Wales embarrassingly draw 0–0 with that football superpower of Gibraltar and smashed 4–0 in Slovakia. Football's dreaded vote of confidence had struck again! In the FAW's case, this was a rarity as they have tended to be fully supportive of their managers. Page was actually only their sixth full-time appointment this century and two of his predecessors, Giggs and Speed, needed to be replaced years earlier than anyone anticipated. For perspective, over the same period of time,

Wales' top three club sides, Cardiff, Swansea and Wrexham, had 63 different managers between them.

By the end, the calls for change from so many fans had turned into a crescendo, meaning poor Steve Williams had no option but to make a massive, and rather humiliating U-turn.

Like many supporters I always had major misgivings over Page and even World Cup qualification didn't dissuade me from that view, but one thing that can never be questioned is his passion and utter determination to do his best for Wales. I'd witnessed first-hand experience of that when Page was a player back during Mark Hughes' tenure as manager. At the time I led a campaign in the *Western Mail* for Danny Gabbidon, then bursting through as a classy new centre-back sensation with Cardiff City, to be chosen as a kingpin of Sparky's defence. 'Dan the Man' was simply too good to overlook, I argued. Someone, of course, would have to make way. Unfortunately, that meant Page.

One Thursday morning, directly after a Wales game when I'd pushed Gabbidon's cause again, the telephone rang on the sports desk with an unhappy Page wanting to know why I kept running him down. I tried to explain it wasn't an anti-Page thing, it was just pro-Gabbidon. We had to agree to disagree, there was a reasonably amicable ending to the conversation as I recall. However, very quickly Gabbidon did emerge as Hughes' number one defender, one of the rocks upon which the historic 2002 Euro victory over Italy was built, perhaps Wales' greatest ever result at the time. Were it not for a persistent back injury, which affected his movement and ability to train and play, Gabbidon would have become one of the greats, probably going from Cardiff to West Ham to one of the Premier League's really big clubs. So I think I was proven right in my judgement. At the same time I also had no issue whatsoever with Page forcefully having his say. Awkward conversations go with the territory as a sports journalist when you're prepared to voice strongly-held opinions. This discussion demonstrated how keen Page was to play for his country, something I fully understood. Not that I was for budging on my Gabbidon stance, mind.

Indeed, Page went on to become Wales captain, albeit briefly, and then manager, two roles that he could never have envisaged fulfilling but which left him brimming with pride. It is a little ironic that he, rather than the likes of Yorath, Hughes, Toshack, Coleman or Giggs, should be the one to have finally taken Wales to a World Cup. For that, some reckon Page deserves a place in folklore, of sorts. The suspicion is that Giggs would not only have qualified Wales, but also ensured they shone much brighter out in Qatar, too, before going on to bigger things himself.

Instead, after such a promising beginning, everyone was left with a sense of what might have been. The bombshell telephone call FAW boss Jonathan Ford received from Giggs informing him of his original arrest triggered a chain of events which led to yet another of those somewhat disbelieving happenings that were by now a well-trodden path for Welsh football.

Mind, 'one man's misfortune...' as the old saying goes. While there was a dramatic downward spiral for Giggs, the career trajectory of the person he had only just pipped for the job was heading in an entirely different direction.

11

Bell of the ball

'You know that giant mural of Gary Speed as you head towards Cardiff City Stadium?' started Craig Bellamy.

'Well, it gets me every single damn time. That's why I have to do this. I'm really proud of being Welsh, but preserving Speedo's legacy is really important to me.'

Perhaps it won't surprise you then to learn that a photograph of Speed was placed on the wall above Bellamy's desk in his office at Dragon Park, the Welsh National Football Development Centre in Newport, where he based himself after being named Wales manager in July 2024.

The photo is obviously not as big as the mural Bellamy speaks of, which features Speed in red national kit and is painted on the side of a house on the approach to the ground where Wales play. However, the very fact Bellamy felt a need for Speed to be there next to him is just one indicator of the enormous esteem in which he holds his number one international football mentor.

There is lots of history between the two men. When playing at Newcastle they would travel together for the 650-mile round car journey to Wales matches, Bellamy listening intently to every word uttered by his travelling companion. Speed, he felt, was the ultimate professional, thus his methods on what to do as a footballer – and what not to do – were worth following. Bellamy was even a pall-bearer at Speed's funeral, with close club team-mates Alan Shearer, Shay Given and Kevin Nolan among others carrying the coffin.

Fair to say then that Wales under Bellamy was always going to be shaped by what he believed Wales under Speed would have become, albeit the task was always going to be harder with real stardust like Gareth Bale gone.

'Gary had a huge impact upon me, not just as a footballer but also as a human being,' Bellamy recounts of Speed. 'His professionalism, the high standards he set, were second to none, but he was always very humble with it. He had such good habits; eat on schedule, wear the correct clothing, train hard. Speedo was never at the back of the group when we did running drills, he was always at the front. These may seem tiny little details, but they matter. I clung on to him. The best pros are often the best players. Speedo never looked for the easy way out, nor men like Steven Gerrard, Luis Suàrez when I was at Liverpool. They never missed a day's training. They wouldn't just jog halfway to a cone, then back. They'd go full tilt, the whole way. If you want to be the best, these are the kind of people you need to follow. Another thing I learned off Speedo is if you've got something to say, then do it in the dressing room when everyone is there to hear. Don't bitch about it in the showers afterwards. Do things the right way.'

Bellamy might have been talking there about that infamous dressing room blast Speed directed the way of Bobby Gould after Wales' 4–0 humiliation in Tunisia back in 1996. He could have moaned in private. He preferred to tell the manager to his face. Either way, having been handed his own opportunity to lead his country into battle, Bellamy's intention was to go about the job in the same way he felt Speed would have continued on the path of were it not for the tragedy which rocked the football world.

Now, given what happened with Speed and Giggs in reasonably close proximity, you might have thought the last thing Wales needed was a combustible character like Bellamy as their new manager after some of the high profile off-the-field incidents surrounding him down the years. They made banner headlines. Golf clubs, court cases, spats with managers and team-mates, leaving his job as Cardiff City Academy chief under a cloud. Those have been well documented, no need to go into them again here. Even something as simple as Bellamy's post-match interview after Wales lost a Euro qualifier to Finland in 2009 would raise eyebrows. The Finns' opening goal that day came from Jonatan Johansson, an unsung forward with Charlton Athletic, Hibernian and St Johnstone, prompting Bellamy to scorn: 'I don't know how. He's not good enough to score against us.'

No holding back there then, Craig! Repeating anything akin to that as manager of his country almost two decades on would probably lead to football's version of an international incident.

Yet, there was a feeling in the minds of the top FAW officials leading the hunt for the new man post-Rob Page that they were dealing with a different Craig Bellamy. The fire and brimstone clearly still burned deep, they wanted that ambition to drive Wales to greater heights. But there was also a new calm, smooth, relaxed manner about Bellamy which was in no small part due to him working as number two to the great Vincent Kompany with Burnley in the Premier League and Anderlecht. Kompany, of course, is the embodiment of a winner who can also be Mr Laid Back personified. He was Manchester City's inspirational captain as they gobbled up major trophies and was capped nearly 100 times by Belgium. Kompany doesn't do controversy. He is the ultimate diplomat, a football figure who commands respect everywhere. His traits, how to conduct yourself, don't go overboard about the highs, don't get too deflated at the lows, had rubbed off on Bellamy, felt FAW bosses.

Their new chief executive Noel Mooney, himself a bundle of enthusiasm, energy and ideas – just like Bellamy – explains:

'I obviously had to look after the image of the FAW, but when I first met Craig I was struck by how zen he was. I discovered someone who was obsessive, who would take things to the edge to win, but who was structured, confident, incredibly knowledgeable and possessed the huge ambition we shared to go forward as a football country.

'Of course, I spoke to a lot of people who'd had interactions with Craig. I have to say the vast majority talked of a great guy. One or two might have been a little jaundiced by how Craig used to act as a player. But we weren't hiring a 25-year-old Craig Bellamy, we were taking him as he is today, in his mid-40s. Vincent Kompany is a really bright person who wouldn't have bad people around him, people who couldn't handle the Premier League. That made it easy for us. If Kompany bought into Craig, enjoyed working with him, then we could too.

'There is a saying about risk tolerance in business; how much risk are you prepared to take in order to get rewards? This fell well into our risk tolerance for me. Look, if at some point Craig plays to the old stereotype, gets into a row with someone, critics will doubtless say "I told you so". But it's genuinely my belief we have hired a football genius, someone who knows how to react to situations now, someone who I believe will cast an enormous legacy over the Welsh game and who will go on a journey to manage one of the biggest clubs in the world. I really do get that sense with Craig. He has everything needed to be a top global manager one day.'

Some testimony, that. Wales were clearly happy with their appointment. For Mooney, who himself wanted a dynamic, light-on-its-feet FAW organisation able to take Welsh football into a fast-moving future, there was clearly a meeting of minds with Bellamy who shared those ideals with the national team and the various age grade sides he planned to keep a close eye upon.

Bellamy concurs with Mooney's take on his more relaxed demeanour these days. I was the one member of the mainstream media to attend his first public Q&A as Welsh boss, held at Splott Conservative Club in his home city of Cardiff. As well as explaining the impact Speed had on him, as outlined earlier, Bellamy told the audience: 'Look, my standards are ones I will always have. If I believed someone fell below that and was taking liberties, you won't get to like me because I will call you out. I could have turned a blind eye, but that's not me. Do well though, and I was the first there to offer encouragement.

'Looking back, I burned up loads of energy arguing over stuff that couldn't be changed. But as you get older you become smarter, wiser and understand the triggers more. Working next to Vinny was such an education. We enjoyed the highs, but he never got too upset at the lows. That enables me to be more balanced in my own outlook. If a player seems to be struggling during training, instead of nudging them with "Come on, try harder", my first instinct these days is to ask "What's up?" You can't just perform at your best if something is wrong. I've learned the human side of it is so important. I wouldn't have thought like that 20 years ago because back then football was everything to me.'

For time immemorial, the search for a Wales manager was led by the old four-man FAW officers' committee comprising of president, two vice-presidents and treasurer. These were the top positions and tended to be held by time-serving individuals who were well into their sixties and beyond. Viewed as an anachronistic set-up or not, to be fair more often than not their appointments were shrewd ones. This time around the task was placed in the hands of the younger Mooney and Dave Adams, the FAW's new chief football officer who helps develop Welsh coaches and who brought a greater sports science, analytical and data-driven approach to the process.

Adams drew up a shortlist of potential targets, with tentative soundings made. They included Rob Edwards, then in charge of Premier League Luton Town. He was quickly handed a new four-year deal by the Hatters. So he was out. Fellow Welshman

Steve Cooper, the England Youth World Cup winning manager, was considered. He was about to take over at Leicester City in the top flight. He too was out. Adams even threw in the left-field name of the largely unknown Des Buckingham at little Oxford United. Surely not? That one couldn't proceed. A Welsh nation would never wear such an underwhelming appointment. Nor the dressing room.

At the other end of the spectrum was the glitz and glamour of Arsenal and France superstar Thierry Henry, who took his coaching badges in Wales and retains an affection for the country. He returned to a FAW seminar held at the Celtic Manor in Newport where he spoke at length to would-be Welsh bosses about playing with Lionel Messi and the impact Pep Guardiola had on his own career at Barcelona. The sight of Henry wearing Wales branded kit for those three days was a sight to behold. If only, those of us present thought!

Well, if not possible as a player, why not as manager? If there was a candidate to galvanise a nation, a figurehead who would appeal beyond just a football audience, it was right there. Henry would cost a fortune, but it was speculated that his image would bring in that sum, and a lot more on top, through sponsorship deals with companies desperate to be associated with his name. With Henry at the helm Wales matches would be guaranteed global appeal, British and foreign TV companies and press outlets not able to get enough of him. His old Arsenal boss Arsène Wenger was canvassed for his views. Would Wales be able to land Henry? Would he have the right drive and tempo required to lead the team to new heights? Did he possess a strong enough coaching CV to take on the role? There were lots of question marks. Henry was viewed as the right person, and the wrong person, at the same time. He too was out.

More realistic options were Henry's former France team-mate Willy Sagnol, in charge of Georgia at the time, and the more unsung figure of Eric Ramsay. He'd had a much less stellar playing career than Henry and Sagnol with Welshpool Town, Loughborough University, and as captain of the Welsh futsal side, but was making a startling rise through the coaching ranks as Manchester United assistant to Ole Gunnar Solskjær, Ralf Rangnick and Erik ten Hag.

The FAW had to do their due diligence by exploring the various options. As such, Ramsay was a credible candidate, but in the end the only person Adams and Mooney felt they needed to interview was Bellamy. Once they had done that, Mooney's mind was made up.

'I told Dave that I couldn't necessarily back any other person as 100 per cent as I could this one,' he says. 'It was Dave's job to make the recommendation, but obviously the CEO needs to be on board as I'm the one answerable to the board. I had zero doubts about Craig. As it happens, we were each totally comfortable with the appointment, just knew it was right.'

Mooney and Adams first met Bellamy in an informal capacity while guests at an Everton versus Burnley Premier League match at Goodison Park towards the end of the 2023–24 season. Burnley played the football that day; Everton luckily won 1–0 thanks to a Dominic Calvert-Lewin smash-and-grab goal. They chatted with him afterwards, discussing the game, Burnley's impressive style of play, promotion to the top flight, the subsequent relegation battle, what it was like to work next to Kompany and, of course, about everything to do with Welsh football. Fair to say, Mooney and Adams were immediately bowled over by Bellamy's deep knowledge of what was happening back home. There was no manager's vacancy at the time, but if one were to arise in the future this guy surely would have to be a leading contender.

As it happens, two months on Page was dismissed. Bellamy's name cropped up straightaway and Mooney and Adams were off on their travels up north again, this time to conduct a formal interview at Burnley's training ground. Bellamy had given that 'Hollywood interview' previously when narrowly overlooked for Giggs in 2018. With six further years of top-level coaching behind him, he was even more impressive this time, flipping from PowerPoint presentation to Burnley's tactics board nearby to outline his vision of what he wanted to happen, which players could implement his plan, the youngsters coming through, how he would play and the dream he had to take Wales towards the top table of world football.

For that to happen, Bellamy explained, Wales would create a new identity, an aggressive, high-tempo game played at pace which would blow the opposition off their feet. He had marvelled at how little South Korea marched to the semi-finals of the 2002 World Cup, beating Italy, Portugal and Spain en route, adopting these high-intensity methods. More than two decades on, Bellamy wanted to mirror that kind of approach, fine tune it and make it even better. Press, close down, pin the opposition back towards their own goal. Everything done at speed. Win the ball back high up the pitch and pounce. Bellamy had obsessively studied the data. Players in the Premier League and Championship ran more than any other footballers in the world, he determined. It was a high-risk strategy, but the current group of Wales stars were of the right age demographic to play exactly the way he wanted. Young, athletic, energetic, and with legs. Within that, Bellamy would fill their heads with what he called 'a library of alternative shapes and systems' they would adopt at different points of the game. Light on their feet, tactical, flexible, but very modern. The Wales he inherited may have lacked the world-class talent of yesteryear, Gareth Bale, Ryan Giggs, Ian Rush, Mark Hughes, even someone as good as Bellamy himself, but this was very much about the whole sum of the team parts usurping any individual genius.

Wow. Mooney and Adams were certainly sold. There was no need to discuss others on the shortlist. Everything was pretty much instantly agreed.

'When we left Burnley I sang the whole way home,' smiles Mooney. 'This was so exciting. We had uncovered something special for Welsh football. Once back, I could barely sleep that night knowing we were going to announce somebody who I felt would transform us. I had not the slightest doubt we had hired the perfect person for Wales.

'On his first day I asked Craig to pop into my office. To his left was our chair Alys Carlton, to his right was our acting president Mike Jones, with Dave Adams also in the room. We just wanted to make him feel welcome. He spoke again about his vision for Welsh football, at every level. After Craig finished talking I said to everyone in that room, "I believe 100 per cent that we've hired a football genius. If that guy does not go on to manage a top club in the world I will be shocked." And I meant it, too.

'I also asked Craig if he would briefly address the full FAW Council for ten minutes. Just to say hello. Little did I know he would talk to them for an hour, telling them his entire game plan for his first match in charge against a strong Turkey team. It was a hugely ambitious new way of playing that he was setting out. He only had the players for a couple of training sessions to work on it, but we dominated the game exactly as Craig had predicted. It may have finished 0–0, but we were so much the superior side.

'I've heard some people say, "Why didn't you make the change earlier?" Well, firstly Rob Page got us to within a penalty kick of Euro 2024. And, secondly, Craig was not going to leave the Premier League. At first I wasn't convinced he was going to come to us. Then Vincent Kompany left Burnley for Bayern Munich. Craig could have gone with him, but chose us. Timing was crucial, it was serendipity, the perfect moment for him, the perfect moment for us.'

So, having left Cardiff at the age of 15 to begin his football journey in East Anglia with Norwich City, Bellamy was coming home just a few days before his 45th birthday to reconnect with Wales. He instantly threw himself into those Q&A forums with fans in towns, villages and cities up and down the land, eagerly taking on board the opportunity to increase his knowledge of historical events in particular areas of the country.

Instead of attending a FIFA Congress of coaches which was being held on 16 September, thus clashing with Owain Glyndŵr Day, Bellamy chose instead to head up to the mid Wales town of Machynlleth to join in the celebrations commemorating the last native Prince of Wales. Bellamy has a tattoo of the legendary freedom fighter depicted on his arm and wanted to learn more about what happened in Machynlleth, where Glyndŵr held his first Welsh Parliament during a Middle Ages revolt he led against English rule.

Perhaps it is what prompts Bellamy to say: 'I'm beyond proud to be Welsh. My identity is so important to me, I hold on to it really personally. Every nation is proud… but we perhaps hold on to it more than most.'

Of course, it's fine telling the FAW – and in due course the Welsh media – about his dynamic plans for the team. Bellamy needed to prove he could walk the walk, as well as talk the talk. Well he certainly started well enough, Wales eclipsing Turkey to top spot in their Nations League group to instantly win promotion among the European elite in Group A.

Much more important challenges were ahead, though. Qualifying for the 2026 World Cup in the United States, Canada and Mexico and then the UK-hosted Euro 2028, which Mooney hopes will see Wales kicking off the tournament at a passion-filled 74,000 Principality Stadium sell-out crowd in Cardiff. Heady days to look forward to, indeed, but the kind of tasks Bellamy and Mooney wanted to meet head-on. Two driven individuals who each intend to leave a legacy for the future in Wales. If Jonathan Ford, the former FAW chief executive, deserves enormous credit for modernising the anciently-old governing body, Mooney is akin to Ford on steroids!

'My nature is to have a we-can-do-anything approach,' he says. 'We believe we are building the best FA in the world; Craig feels Wales can be the best team. His ambition matches ours, but even we had to take a step back and think "Crikey, he's driven". My attitude is always let's try things. Sometimes it won't work and you're left disappointed, but at least aim high.'

Indeed, walk into FAW headquarters a few miles outside Cardiff these days and it is certainly a galaxy away from the organisation I first had dealings with in the 1990s when purse strings were tight, Alun Evans was CEO and had about seven members of staff working under him. Today the employees, numbering 180, scurry around the office, interacting, looking to create, build and enhance upon what is already in place. There is a bustle of noise as various departments, marketing, sponsorship, ticketing, sports science, analytics and data, player registrations, age grade sides and grassroots are catered for. There is also a massive drive by Mooney on women's football. He says proudly: 'In 2025 the men's and women's teams were each in Nations League A. That is an incredible feat for a country of 3.2 million people.'

Bellamy's side are the main attraction, the big money-spinner and the centrepiece of everything, but the manager immediately threw his weight four-square behind the whole structure to ensure foundations were put in place which help ensure Wales do not revert to the cycle of boom-bust which he knows drove Speed mad and which has been detailed so starkly in this book.

To that end, he felt fortunate to have inherited the *TogetherStronger* mantra started under previous regimes. Six Nations or big autumn rugby games were historically the must-attend experience in Welsh sport, but that started to change. As Welsh rugby became more and more of a mess, with a match-day drinking culture leading to the Principality Stadium being dubbed 'the biggest pub in the world', Welsh football was held up as the shining light of how to do things. The pre-game singing of the Welsh-language folk song, *'Yma o Hyd'* (We're still here), ramped up an atmosphere already made special by dimmed lights inside the ground and the playing of Zombie Nation to get everyone in the mood. Then, to cap everything, Wales were first to master the art of background music for the first few lines of the anthem, followed by the most stirring a cappella version of the rest you can possibly imagine, with fans and players in complete harmony. Oh how Gary Speed would have loved to have seen this all unfold.

How can the team not be up for the fight after that? Bellamy used it all to help instil the passion into his players that burns so proudly within his own soul, but at the same time kept a cool head about how to achieve the goals set. Second is nothing to Bellers. When told by Sky Sports presenter Dave Jones that he had taken over a small football nation – which in relative terms Wales is of course – Bellamy was having none of it. 'No, I disagree with that,' he asserted as a guest on their *Monday Night Football* show. 'I don't look to be underdog or second-best to anybody.'

It represented an attitude FAW boss Mooney loved. 'Craig sees things we can't see and has produced an ambition that is making us re-evaluate for the future. He wants everybody to embrace the challenge of aiming for the top,' Mooney explains.

'I recall looking at him when we played Turkey away early on. The ground was full an hour before kick-off, it was an intimidating atmosphere – and there Craig was down on the pitch, gazing around at the Turkish fans with a huge smile on his face. This is brilliant, he told the players, the type of occasion they should love being involved in rather than be fearful of.

'To that end, knowing Craig, he won't just be content with Wales playing the first game at home at Euro 2028 – a dream scenario for everyone else. He'll probably expect to win the tournament! His attitude will be that we may not be the best team in the world, we may not have the best individuals, but we'll be the best prepared side because of the extra thoroughness he has brought with data and analytics. That, combined with the feeling of Welshness and togetherness, will always give us, and Craig, a chance.

'When he leaves Wales, he will not be back. He'll go on a very special journey with a top club, either in the Premier League, or in Spain, Germany or Italy. We'll be proud to have played our part in that journey. But what Craig leaves behind will be a new ambition for Welsh football, that we can never be put down again, we can never accept we're not deserving of a place among the best.'

As outlined earlier in the book, that is exactly what Gary Speed wanted. Welsh football didn't just start in 2016. Maybe, just maybe, the boom-bust ride so many of us have been on is finally over and further golden sands lie ahead.

Let's hope so. On the other hand, if the last 30-plus years have taught me anything, it is to expect the totally unexpected. One of John Toshack's famous sayings was 'The only thing that surprises me in football is that people are surprised'. Well, as the previous 258 pages have amply demonstrated, the truth is Welsh football never ceases to amaze.

More twists and turns are doubtless around the corner, but one way or another, we'll keep enjoying the ride.

Yma o Hyd.

12

Strange phone calls, Prince William's passion and Bruno's barb

WHAT WE'LL CALL 'interesting' conversations are quite commonplace when you hold down the kind of job I've been fortunate to have as head of sport for the major Welsh newspapers. Telephone calls of complaint from managers, players, boardroom officials and fans go with the territory, be that about your own stories or those of your colleagues.

Such are the pressures – and passions – of top-level sport, which can often override the reality of situations. You become accustomed to dealing with it, along with the requests for 'more positive articles'. Not to mention the inevitable contact when a managerial vacancy arises and someone wants their name put forward.

As well as top sports stars you also get to meet royalty, prime ministers and leading figures from the world of showbiz.

Here are a few behind-the-scenes tales I'm able to share.

A Grand Slam like no other

It is 48 hours before the Wales rugby team meet Ireland for the Six Nations Grand Slam in 2005 and a very senior member of the coaching staff telephones out of the blue.

'We need you to write something on the back of the *Western Mail* which helps ease the pressure being put on us,' I'm told. 'Make out Ireland are favourites instead – and I'll ensure a copy of the paper is stuck under the door of every player's hotel room, Wales and Irish, so they read it and feel calmer about things.'

Now it has to be said that while all the subsequent success achieved under Warren Gatland was something to savour, this first Grand Slam in 27 years, spearheaded by coach Mike Ruddock and fans' favourites Shane Williams and Gavin Henson, was the best by a country mile. Not since the days of Gareth Edwards and Phil Bennett in the 1970s had Wales been in a position like this.

More than 150,000 fervent Welsh fans descended into Cardiff city centre that Saturday afternoon to be part of the special 'I was there' moment. Even at the exorbitant prices charged by the Welsh Rugby Union, tickets for this particular Millennium Stadium game were among the hottest in history. The build-up was insane and the highly-placed Wales official ringing me wanted to tone down the fever-pitch sense of expectation.

Personally, I felt I was being asked the impossible. However, as a passionate Welsh newspaper willing to provide our teams with any assistance we could, I noted how Wales hadn't beaten Ireland at home in 22 years. Thus the day before the game we splashed the back of the newspaper with an article stating, 'Why Wales have to buck Cardiff Six Nations trend to beat Ireland', outlining the preceding facts and figures and why excitement levels might need to be dampened down a teeny bit.

It hardly made Ireland favourites in my eyes – no chance of that amid the buzz – but it did point to how they were Wales' bogey team in Cardiff and thus everyone would need to keep a little sense of perspective.

Job done, I received a thank-you call from said member of the Wales team. I have not the slightest idea whether he did indeed put the newspaper under the bedroom door of every Welsh player, hoping to ease the pressure on them a little, and Ireland's, wishing to lull them into a false sense of security. I also doubt it had any bearing whatsoever on the result. But it does demonstrate the kind of mind games that take place in elite sport when the pressures are at their greatest.

Wales won 32–20, by the way. Cue a party that lasted for about a month; whether we had anything to do with it or not!

A rivalry like no other

We can talk up Liverpool versus Everton, Rangers against Celtic, El Clásico between Barcelona and Real Madrid. Obviously much bigger fixtures, but when it comes to derby day there remains something quite unique about Cardiff City versus Swansea City.

It is the only 'bubble game' in British football, with away fans having to travel under severe coach and police restriction. If anything, the rivalry is becoming even more intense.

I learned right from the start the Welsh media can't win with this one. Swans fans accuse you of favouring Cardiff; Bluebirds followers reckon the bias is the other way around. It was best summed up with two emails we received in quick succession when the clubs were battling for Championship play-off top-six spots in 2020.

The first was from Swansea, complaining of what they perceived as 'negative' reporting about the team, which manager Steve Cooper 'wasn't happy about' and contrasting it to what they claimed was 'more favourable Cardiff coverage'.

The second was from a Cardiff supporter. He reckoned we were being far too critical about the Bluebirds' play-off prospects and way too kind to Swansea about theirs.

A microcosm right there of the arguments I've heard many, many times down the decades! As I say, you can't win.

Stick it up your arse

I received a tip-off that Swansea City, hard-up for money, were putting every single player on the transfer list and had circulated a letter to the League's other 91 clubs to let them know.

Our banner headline read: 'Fancy a Swan – because they're all for sale.'

Cue outcry from the manager, who I won't embarrass by naming. He telephoned in a furious rant, demanding to know where I'd got my story from. When I calmly explained I wasn't at liberty to disclose that, he got even angrier, eventually ending our conversation by shouting down the line, 'Well then, don't bother trying to speak to me again... you can stick it up your arse.'

How dignified, I reasoned. Now in football you have fall-outs with managers all the time. It's inevitable when you're reporting things they'd rather keep out of the public domain. The truth can sometimes hurt. Personally, I reckoned the fans had a right to know what was happening with their club.

In any case, a veteran *Western Mail* colleague, far more worldly-wise than me, explained his philosophy whenever threatened by managers. 'I had a blazing row with one and told him, "I've already seen off 14 of you lot at this club – I will see you off too." And I did.'

The pen is mightier than the sword and all that. Anyway, while I wasn't as blunt as that, I did recall those words, as the aforementioned Swansea boss didn't last much longer in the post himself. Funniest thing is this, though, he left our conversation adamant someone at Cardiff had leaked the letter about Swansea's firesale to me. I was happy to let him think that – because it was actually Wrexham who told me!

A City gent

By contrast, Eddie May could hardly have been more cordial as boss of Cardiff City. Standing at 6ft 4in, with more than 300 games at Wrexham and 100 matches as a centre-half with Swansea behind him, he possessed stature. You didn't mess with the big man. But the truth is Eddie was a gentle giant. Mr Popular with the supporters and media of all three Welsh teams.

His three-year spell in charge of Cardiff, when he won promotion with a side dubbed 'The Darling Buds of Eddie May', remains the favourite period of following the club for many Bluebirds fans, even though it was only the old Fourth Division with games against Scunthorpe, Barnet and Rochdale.

After matches Eddie would invite a tiny group of us journos into his cramped office underneath the stairs at Ninian Park. There, fag in one hand, beer bottle in the other, he'd rock back in his chair and regale us with enchanting football stories, past and present. You couldn't help but warm to this guy.

He was replaced by Wolves legend Kenny Hibbitt, another thoroughly decent bloke who followed Eddie's lead by giving us a private post-match debrief inside that tiny room. Mind, we had to smile one day when, after a lower league win over the powerhouse of Rotherham United, Hibbitt declared his captain Dave Penney 'was world class out there today'.

As I recall, we altered 'world class' to something more sensible like 'excellent'. Sometimes you have to protect these managers from themselves!

Keano's Wembley fury

I'm standing in the tunnel at Wembley, minutes after Manchester United have beaten Newcastle to win the FA Cup en route to winning the treble in 1999. A couple of feet away Roy Keane is holding court with 20-plus London-based national reporters gathered around him. In those days it was far less formal, access most areas for us scribes.

Keane is talking about the upcoming Champions League final with Bayern Munich and whether Sir Alex Ferguson will finally get his hands on the big prize. I'm not interested in that, I'm waiting down there in the hope of grabbing a word with Ryan Giggs about the biggest game of his career and, just as importantly for our Welsh audience, Wales' Euro 2000 qualifier against Italy in Bologna the following week.

As Keano finishes up and the other journos depart, he spots match referee Peter Jones from Leicestershire. It's just those two and me now. Keane is hobbling, having been forced out of the Wembley showpiece after just seven minutes by a fierce Gary Speed challenge. He is banned from the Euro final, so limping away from 83 minutes of United's Wembley win doesn't exactly put him in the greatest of moods.

Pointing to his swollen ankle he demands of the referee, 'Why didn't you book him?'

'Who did it?' the smiling, somewhat perplexed official responds.

'*Speed*, that's who,' says Keane, his voice rising thunderously. Many years on, I still recognise that higher pitch whenever Keano rips into a player in his role these days as a must-watch pundit prepared to speak his mind with Sky and ITV.

Having witnessed this exchange first hand, 'Man Utd ace in Wembley Cup final rant over Welsh captain' seemed a decent enough back page line to me for the following day's *Wales on Sunday*.

Before filing my copy, though, I had to wait for Giggs. And wait… and wait. An hour later he still hadn't turned up. Bit like a Wales friendly, I hear you say!

'He's gone straight on the team bus,' one of Giggsy's United team-mates who was going back and forth in the tunnel eventually explained, probably feeling a tad sorry for me. Ah well, Keane's rant over Speed's tackle wasn't a bad consolation story. I'd catch up with Giggs in Bologna. That was the night time caught up with Bobby Gould, too.

The clown princes

Among the players I always enjoyed interviewing the most were Mickey Thomas and Joey Jones, two Wrexham and Welsh football stalwarts. Get them together and your sides were splitting so much you had absolutely zero chance of scribbling down anything they had to say!

If only football threw up characters like those two more often. So sad to learn that Joey left us at the age of 70, shortly before this book came out.

Anyway, in the mid-1980s, these two Clown Princes of the Welsh game were playing for Chelsea in Division One, now the Premier League. Not for them the modern-day trend of train, rest, recovery and sports science. Mickey and Joey were home-birds, so they insisted upon commuting daily from north Wales to training and matches.

Taking turns to share the driving, they would set off at silly o'clock to make the 198-mile journey down to Chelsea's training ground on the outskirts of London in time for a 10am start. Then, once it was over, they'd have a bite to eat and do the reverse trip. Occasionally they'd stay over, kipping on a chair, or under a table somewhere in the offices.

Google maps reckon that trip, one-way, takes a shade under four hours, traffic permitting.

'We'd easily do it in less than three,' Mickey proudly told me when I wrote an article with him reflecting upon those crazy Chelsea years. 'Mind, that was before the days of speed cameras! We'd have no chance now!' he laughed.

Prince charming

The Prince of Wales – or plain old Prince William as he was back then – officially opened our swish new Media Wales offices right next to the Millennium Stadium in the heart of Cardiff city centre in 2008.

Seeing these royal functions first hand is interesting. The prince was surrounded by an army of staff, security, media, courtiers, advisors, and they rushed him from group to group of employees in different parts of the newsroom to have a quick chat about the newspaper business. In no time, he'd be ushered away again. It seemed the accustomed way of doing things.

Members of the sports department, standing by our desks near the exit door, were last in line. Over came the prince – and suddenly the veneer dropped as he talked sport. Momentarily it was just like chatting to a mate in the pub. Who did we think would win between Wales and South Africa the next day, Wills wanted to know. By how many? Which players did we like? Who didn't we rate? The normal conversations you'd have over a beer with the lads.

I was mindful of the strict timetable the prince needed to adhere to, with other functions to attend in Wales that day, but he couldn't get enough of talking Welsh sport, and his staff left him to it, seeing this was now a labour of love.

William's passion came across loud and clear. Very different to David Cameron, another VIP visitor when he became prime minister, who I felt couldn't get away from us on the sports desk quickly enough!

Evidently Welsh football and rugby isn't for everyone.

Katherine the songstress

Katherine Jenkins, the Welsh mezzo-soprano, was one of the many showbiz figures to visit our offices as she looked to promote a new album. She's another who loves Welsh football and rugby, often singing the national anthem before games. In for a penny, in for a pound, I decided to chance my arm by asking her to give us a rendition.

'Of course,' she said straightaway, even though she must

have known us journalists can often be among the most cynical, critical and hard-to-please people in the world. Standing there with no music, in front of this group of complete strangers, she produced the most beautiful a cappella version you can possibly imagine.

Well, how could we not say lovely words about her new album after that!

Standing up for Wales

Nothing used to annoy me more than critics taking what I felt were cheap swipes at Wales after Cardiff – for a wonderful period in the late 1990s and early noughties – became the sporting capital of the UK. In quick succession we had a plethora of world title fights coming to the Welsh capital, plus FA Cup finals, League Cup finals, big play-off games, Rugby World Cup final, Ashes cricket and the Ryder Cup held just up the M4 at the Celtic Manor in Newport.

Lots of public funding helped land these gigantic sporting occasions which put Wales on the world map, but I couldn't help notice some of the sniping from outside. After an epic first FA Cup final at the Millennium Stadium, Michael Owen's Liverpool beating Arsenal 2–1 in 2001, the introduction to a report in one London tabloid was along the lines of, 'Great game, great stadium, great atmosphere – shame it's miles from anywhere.'

I couldn't let that go without a robust response. The Millennium (now Principality) Stadium may be 150 miles from London, but it is smack-bang in the centre of Cardiff, with bars, restaurants and sight-seeing attractions all around, I pointed out. Wembley, by contrast, is stuck in the middle of an industrial estate, I continued.

Yes, there were major M4 Brynglas tunnel traffic issues that day, still are, but these were teething matters which fans would become accustomed to. Indeed, thereafter I only heard hugely positive things about the Cardiff experience from the football followers of Arsenal, Liverpool, Manchester United, Chelsea, West Ham and a host of other clubs. They loved the unique city centre location, the ability to be able to walk out of a nearby pub and straight into their allotted entrance gate.

Personally, I felt there was a little bit of snobbery when the unfashionable Sophia Gardens twice landed the first England versus Australia Ashes Test match, with Manchester's more historic Old Trafford ground missing out. Cue an outcry from one or two. Luckily, that was quickly forgotten when, in front of a raucous and largely Welsh crowd, Jimmy Anderson and Monty Panesar held out for that epic last-wicket stand to secure a last-gasp draw in 2009, then a Joe Root century led England to a 169-run victory in 2015.

One of my favourite moments came in a one-day international game when brilliant opening batsman Derek Hales prevented a boundary with an excellent diving stop in the outfield. 'Hales, Hales, Hales', the Wales fans in the stand behind started singing in unison.

I know you think you're Joe 90

During the 1990s there seemed to be a world title fight held every month in Cardiff, with Steve Robinson, Robbie Regan, Nicky Piper, Floyd Havard, Barry Jones and then the great Joe Calzaghe in action.

I got to know Joe and his dad Enzo well and was there ringside in Sheffield when he beat Chris Eubank to win the world super-middleweight title. A true superstar of boxing had emerged, as Calzaghe's unblemished record of 46 fights, 46 wins, testifies to.

I would head to the humble Calzaghe gym in the Gwent Valleys town of Newbridge, where they were feted, to write articles ahead of one of Joe's upcoming fights. At least, that was always the plan. I tended to leave with nothing in my notebook.

Joe and Enzo loved their football as much as their boxing

and, more often than not, we just ended up talking about the Italian national side, Juventus, Wales or Cardiff City. After half an hour or so of this I'd say, 'Look, we need to speak about the fight.'

'Ah, don't bother about that! Do you think Italy will win the World Cup?' would come the reply.

It never mattered though. In a sport where hype goes into overdrive, Calzaghe did most of his talking inside the ring.

I hadn't seen Joe for a while when our paths crossed again during a glittering Welsh Sports Hall of Fame black-tie ceremony held at Cardiff City Hall. For some reason they gave me an award as Welsh Sports Journalist of the Year (don't ask me why!) and it was Joe who presented me with a beautiful crystal glass bowl.

'You're losing your hair a bit,' were his first words.

'Well, you're not going to argue with *him*, are you?!' laughed my wife.

Ha, nor was I exactly going to have a ruck with the legend that is Frank Bruno when he was unhappy with some of my questioning. The Peoples' Champ had invited me to his Essex training gym ahead of his world heavyweight title showdown with Lennox Lewis at Cardiff Arms Park, and after he'd finished 12 rounds of sparring we sat together in the corner of the ring. I'm not exactly small, but Big Frank towered over me so much I could have auditioned for a supporting part in *Snow White*. Anyway, back then I wore big thick-rimmed spectacles, and after asking Bruno a series of questions he suddenly stopped and gave me a quizzical glare.

'Look, I know you think you're Joe 90 in those glasses, but no need to try to be intelligent,' said Bruno. For younger readers, he was the schoolboy with the large specs in the popular TV sci-fi drama.

It was the humour of an eight year old, yet it was part of Frank's charm and what made him such a loveable personality. I didn't argue with him, either!

The inner Lord's sanctum

Glamorgan cricketers seemed to get a raw deal when it came to England selection, so the Welsh media campaigned for Steve James to earn a Test call-up after he scored a mountain of runs at county level.

Eventually the selectors saw sense, so off I headed to Lord's in the summer of 1998 to watch Jameo against a South African side containing the fearsome Allan Donald and Shaun Pollock as spearheads of their bowling attack. Unfortunately, he fell to the pair of them on the same day, for ten in the first innings as England were all out for 110, and then a duck in the second as they followed on.

After play finished, I approached the England and Wales Cricket Board media chief to see if I could grab a quick word with Steve. 'He won't want to talk,' came the brush-off. Absolutely no chance.

'Could you please at least ask?' I responded.

The official disappeared, never to be seen again I suspected. Yet he re-emerged a few minutes later, saying Steve would see me but it would need to be away from the normal media area. So, instead, I was beckoned towards the England dressing room. In I walked, right inside the Lord's inner sanctum, just Steve and myself sitting on the players' balcony overlooking the home of cricket on a beautiful sunny evening. This was surreal. Sometimes being a Welsh journalist opens doors denied to even the most high profile of national newspaper and TV reporters.

Despite his abject disappointment, Steve didn't wish to hide from scrutiny, spoke about his two innings and how he hoped he would get another chance. As I recall he only had one more Test match before hanging up his whites to become a very decent rugby and cricket journalist with the *Times* and *Telegraph*. I bet flashing his press card wouldn't even get Steve close to the England players' balcony these days!

The greatest... and the greatest

I was fortunate to get to know Gareth Edwards and Barry John well, those peerless half-backs for the Lions and Wales back in the 1970s Welsh rugby heyday. For some shrewd pundits Barry, known as 'The King' or 'The George Best of Rugby', remains the most mercurial talent the oval ball game has known. Gareth, who lasted the test of time, actually has been voted the greatest rugby player of all time in various polls.

I had ghost-written BJ's column for the *Wales on Sunday*, as well as his autobiography for him. However, upon leaving the paper to become head of sport at the *Western Mail*, I'd arranged to write a new column with Gareth. So there I am on Monday morning, having literally just started my new job, when I notice two voice messages on my mobile.

I press 121. The first says: 'Hello Paul, it's Barry here. Just want to say thank-you for your help over the years and to wish you the best in your new role.'

The second says: 'Hello Paul, it's Gareth here. Just want to say good luck in the job and when can we meet up for the first column?'

There's a nice little double for you. The two greatest, unknowingly still in tandem all those years after hanging up their boots. Now I could begin to understand how their telepathic partnership destroyed the greatest defences on the planet!

Welcome Miss World

OK, hands up, this one has nothing whatsoever to do with Welsh sport, but it's a good 'un to tell anyway!

One sunny evening I was asked by the organisers of the Miss Wales contest to collect Miss World herself, an Icelandic lady by the name of Unnur Birna Vilhjálmsdóttir, and chaperone her down to a venue in Cardiff Bay where she had kindly agreed to judge the Welsh pageant.

I was told by the people around Unnur to be at her Cardiff hotel at 6pm. 'How will I know who she is?' I asked.

Silence at the other end of the line. 'You'll know,' came the eventual reply.

Anyway I did know, and I can truthfully say Miss World was a passenger in my car for as long as I could stretch out the two-mile journey down to Cardiff Bay.

Eat your heart out George Best!

13

Dream team
to beat the world

IN TRUE PUB spirit style I'm going to round off by picking my dream XI – la crème de la crème from the stellar cast list of players I have seen pull on the Wales shirt during my time as a football writer. The beauty of this, as with all pub debates, is that everyone has an opinion. While there are one or two shoo-ins, Gareth Bale and Neville Southall, who will by and large have universal approval, my guess is that if 10,000 people tried the same exercise you'd probably end up with 9,999 different line-ups.

So this is how I see the greatest Wales XI from the past 30-plus years. I reckon it's a side that could win the World Cup.

Neville Southhall (goalkeeper)

The first name on the team-sheet, in every sense. Over a 15-year period Big Nev made the No. 1 jersey indisputably his own. For a period he was the best goalkeeper in the world, a commanding presence at the back capable of pulling off truly out of the ordinary stops.

Mark Hughes told me that when Wales won big matches during the 1980s and '90s, it was largely down to Nev's brilliance between the sticks which kept the team in the game, before Ian Rush would pop up with a goal. Then, with Wales invariably under siege once again, Southall would continue to defy the opposition to ensure the lead was preserved.

Between them Southall, Paul Jones (50 caps) and Wayne Hennessey (109 caps) held down the Wales goalkeeping shirt for the best part of 40 years. The other two won't be offended if I say Nev was in a class of his own.

He rarely seems to get mentioned in these lists of the greatest goalkeepers of all time, which invariably feature Southall's peers such as Peter Shilton, Dino Zoff, Peter Schmeichel and Oliver Kahn, among others. Maybe that is because he played for Wales and never got to feature in a major tournament, but Big Nev is right up there in that company.

Mark Delaney (right-back)

OK, 36 caps over a seven-year period pales by comparison to the 109 for Chris Gunter, but Delaney might have won treble his number were he not plagued by injuries.

He was an absolute Rolls-Royce of a full-back in the Mark Hughes era, quick, rangy, athletic, solid in the tackle, decent in the air, comfortable on the ball. Delaney's rampages forward on the overlap were a joy to behold and always gave Wales an extra edge. He oozed class with Cardiff City before joining Aston Villa in the Premier League, but was so unfortunate to be beset by a number of injury issues which eventually spelt the end of his career way too early.

The fact that Gunter played over 100 games for Wales speaks volumes for his longevity and character. I first saw him as a 17 year old in a Cardiff team reduced to nine men against Leeds United after two players were sent off by Mark Clattenburg, yet the Bluebirds dug in to win 1–0. In such adverse circumstances Gunter did not flinch or take a backward step, right there you could see there was a player in the making.

But when fit Delaney was a cut above. In time, Neco Williams will probably eclipse everyone.

Kevin Ratcliffe (centre-back)

His best days were a little behind him when I first began reporting on Wales, but that know-how and ability still shone through. You don't skipper Everton to two League title wins, plus the FA Cup, League Cup and European Cup Winners' Cup, without learning a thing or two.

In the mid-1980s, Ratcliffe had been right up there with the world's greatest centre-backs, strong in the tackle and lightning quick which meant he could put out fires just as opposition strikers were about to pounce. When the pace slowed down during the early 1990s, Ratcliffe was able to compensate because the first few yards were now in his head, meaning he could close down space and still deny the best forwards with Wales.

Danny Gabbidon (centre-back)

'Who cleared that?' we'd ask in the press box. Gabbidon was the answer.

'Who headed that away?' Gabbidon.

'Who put in that last-ditch block to stop a goal?' Gabbidon again.

What a defender he was. Brilliant at the back, allied to blinding pace and calmness personified on the ball. It's not often you're excited to watch defenders, but seeing the young Gabbidon charge forward Alan Hansen-style was a joy to behold. Shame those swashbuckling forays were coached out of him and he was told to stay back and defend!

When he joined West Ham from Cardiff and shone in the claret and blue shirt, Gabbidon even earned comparisons to Bobby Moore – there can be no higher compliment. A further transfer to one of the Premier League's top four appeared inevitable, only for a back injury which had troubled him from an early age to hinder his progress. Without that problem Gabbidon would have won more than 100 caps.

It's harsh to overlook Ashley Williams, captain of the Euro 2016 semi-final side. No-one in the media talked up Ash more than yours truly, particularly during troubling early times when this late developer was plucked from Stockport County and placed into John Toshack's Wales team. For a guy who'd worked at a petrol station and as a waiter at Beefeater, it was some rise, albeit Ash had to do it against a backdrop of scepticism and criticism.

Like Toshack, I could see Ash had something about him and needed to be backed in the press. He improved as he got older, wringing every last drop out of his career. But football just came easier to Gabbs, his talent was more natural. He gets the nod.

Ben Davies (left-back)

'If I were one of the Premier League big guns, I'd be taking a chance on him.'

The words of Mark Bowen, Mark Hughes' former Wales number two, to me when Davies was still in the embryonic stages of his career with Swansea City. Bows had been a decent left-back himself for Wales, knew a thing or two about the position, so I took note. His judgement was spot on. Tottenham subsequently swooped and Davies went on to spend a decade with the London giants.

Davies is one of the more understated players of the modern era, never particularly capturing the headlines in the way some of his team-mates did for Spurs or Wales, but he has been an absolute model of reliability and professionalism. The best Wales defender of the 21st century thus far.

Joe Allen (midfield)

'Every day is Joe Allen day,' Gareth Bale once said, an indication of how highly the likeable man was regarded within the Welsh dressing room as a person and a player.

277

While never in the class of his peers Bale and Aaron Ramsey, Allen was always next choice on Chris Coleman's team-sheet and produced some fine displays of midfield authority for his country that saw him punch above his weight. Despite being small in stature, Joe was thunderous in the tackle and won 50–50 duels with bigger guys more often than he lost them.

In winning 74 caps over a 13-year period, Allen offered a better package than others who have filled the role, like Vinnie Jones, Robbie Savage, Barry Horne and more recently Ethan Ampadu.

Gary Speed (midfield, captain)

Wales' Mr Dependable. Always fit, always turned up, always a minimum of a seven out of ten. Often an eight or nine, too. Whoever the manager, whatever the game, wherever the fixture, Speed could be relied upon. The headlines tended to go to the truly world-class forward aces around him, but Speedo was the player inside the dressing room his team-mates looked up to more than anybody else.

That was certainly how Ryan Giggs once described him, which says everything really.

Speed was the perfect team player. He never shirked when the going got tough, won the tackles and headers, passed the ball with expertise, put in the hard yards, popped up with key goals.

He started as a swashbuckling wide player, evolved into a dominant central midfielder, then unselfishly played left-back under Mark Hughes. I'm not sure I have ever seen someone look so comfortable appearing in defence. Speedo absolutely nailed it.

He was also, of course, a great leader, captaining Wales 44 times during his then record-breaking number of 85 caps for an outfield player. His commitment to the cause was second to none. The fact that Speed would play Tom Jones' iconic track, 'The Green, Green Grass of Home', the moment he crossed the Welsh border while travelling to meet up with the squad, demonstrates what playing for his country meant to him.

Aaron Ramsey (midfield)

The greatest players tend to wear the No. 10 shirt – Pelé, Maradona, Messi, Neymar, Platini. Obviously Ramsey is not of that ilk, but he is the best playmaker we have seen with Wales. It's hard to imagine there will be a better one.

Ramsey overcame a horror injury to score 21 goals in 84 internationals, an excellent ratio for a midfielder. Often they tended to be key ones, too – like the brace bagged in a win-or-bust Euro 2020 qualifier versus Hungary which sent Wales to the finals. I've lost count of the number of goals he also set up for team-mates, possessing the vision for a defence-splitting pass and the rare ability to execute it perfectly.

Ramsey delivered when it mattered most. If only the brilliant Welsh sides under Terry Yorath and Mark Hughes had him controlling the midfield for them, they too would have qualified for a tournament.

Gareth Bale (right-wing)

Do I really have to justify this one?

OK, here goes. Most appearances for his country, 111. Most goals, 41. Most man of the match performances, lost count.

Blinding speed, lethal shot, ability to race past defenders, great passing, footwork, trickery, superb in the air, best free-kick taker we have seen. Plus immense commitment which meant he gave every last drop to the Welsh cause.

Where Gareth the talisman and captain led, his team-mates followed. No need to say any more.

Ian Rush (centre-forward)

The world's greatest striker during his heyday, Rushie was pretty much peerless. His goal record speaks for itself, 28 in

73 Wales games over a 16-year period when the service, at times, was limited. The tally stood for years as Wales' best, before a guy by the name of Bale came along to smash it to smithereens.

Rush is still Liverpool's record scorer, a whopping 346 goals in 660 games for the Anfield giants. It's hard to see how that figure gets broken. For context, Mo Salah has just gone through the 240-goal barrier, Robbie Fowler bagged 183, Kenny Dalglish 172 and Michael Owen 158. They're all miles off. Rushie was a brilliant finisher, whether with right foot, left foot or header.

He was far more than just a supreme goal-scorer, though. He was also the first exponent of the forward press which has become so vogue in the modern era under Pep Guardiola and Jürgen Klopp. Rush would simply prefer the old-fashioned term of defending from the front. He used his speed to close down startled defenders, Liverpool had turnover ball and another goal invariably followed.

He has since gone on to become an ambassador for the FA of Wales and Liverpool FC. The perfect fit.

Ryan Giggs (left-wing)

Giggs never brought his Manchester United club form to Wales, reckoned the critics. I'm not buying that. He was obviously surrounded by better players at Old Trafford, but many was the time he wowed Welsh fans with brilliant performances, his dynamic running, searing pace and trickery getting them on the edge of their seats whenever the ball landed at his magical left foot.

Of course, he should have played more often and scored more for Wales. Twelve goals at international level is a scandalously low return for a player of his talent. Yet even then Giggs actually netted every 5.3 games for Wales, compared to every 5.7 matches for Manchester United. So maybe the club versus country form argument doesn't really stack up?

Yes, he could have performed better in a few key games for his country, but Giggs was a football genius – for Manchester United and Wales.

Substitute: Mark Hughes

Nothing sums up the strength of this dream XI better than the fact that Sparky, an absolute warrior for his country and scorer of truly great goals for Wales, Manchester United, Barcelona and Bayern Munich, cannot get into it.

But he can't. Nor can Craig Bellamy. Neither would be a bad substitute to send on, mind. Hughes gets the nod.

The final word

So to sum up, a brilliant goalkeeper, formidable defence, the class of Speed and Ramsey in the middle – and a front three of blistering pace, skill and goal threat every other country in the world would covet.

I reckon you might have to go all the way back to Brazil 1970, Jairzinho, Pelé, Rivelino, to find a better international forward line than Bale, Rush and Giggs.

England's best three of the last 30 years – maybe John Barnes, Harry Kane, Wayne Rooney? Very special, but not quite of the same quality.

As for my dream team manager, it's such a tough call. Terry Yorath did a splendid job at the beginning of the 1990s, Mark Hughes revived the team at the turn of the century, John Toshack clearly has the greatest managerial gravitas of the lot and courageously pushed through so many of the young guns behind the Euro 2016 fairytale. Gary Speed started something special, so did Ryan Giggs. Chris Coleman led the Euro semi-finals march, Chris Bellamy will hope to eclipse the lot.

They each had strengths, they each had weaknesses. How do you choose between them? I can't. Given I had countless dealings with them all over 30-plus years, respected each and every one, and in differing ways they have each been instrumental in me putting this 30 years in the making book together, I'm going to do something extremely rare here and pass on an opinion.

And, as you will tell by now, not having one of those when it comes to Welsh football is most unlike me!

It's been a truly wonderful ride. Dramatic ups and downs, but always utterly compelling. A football story simply like no other. I hope you've enjoyed it as much as I have, more memories are to come.

Diolch. Grazie.

Acknowledgements

THERE ARE SO many people to thank, inside and outside of football, without whose help I would not have been able to put this 30-years-in-the-making book together.

I'm so grateful for the many, many chats – often over a coffee and bacon sandwich – and the compelling insight you have all given me.

It's impossible to name you all, but you know who you are. I think you enjoyed reminiscing about the good old days – even the bad old days – as much as I did.

Thanks to my sports journalism colleagues and editors for your support over the years and guidance provided for *In the Dragons' Den*. Thanks to Lefi, Eirian and others at Y Lolfa for their invaluable input and book publishing expertise.

Thanks to all the Wales players, managers, coaches and powerbrokers down the decades who have provided the headline-making thrills and spills which provide the backdrop for this project.

Finally, but most important of the lot, thanks to my three children, Ben, Sam and Joe, who are now grown up, love their football… and know more about the beautiful game than their dad!

Grazie all.

Also by the author:

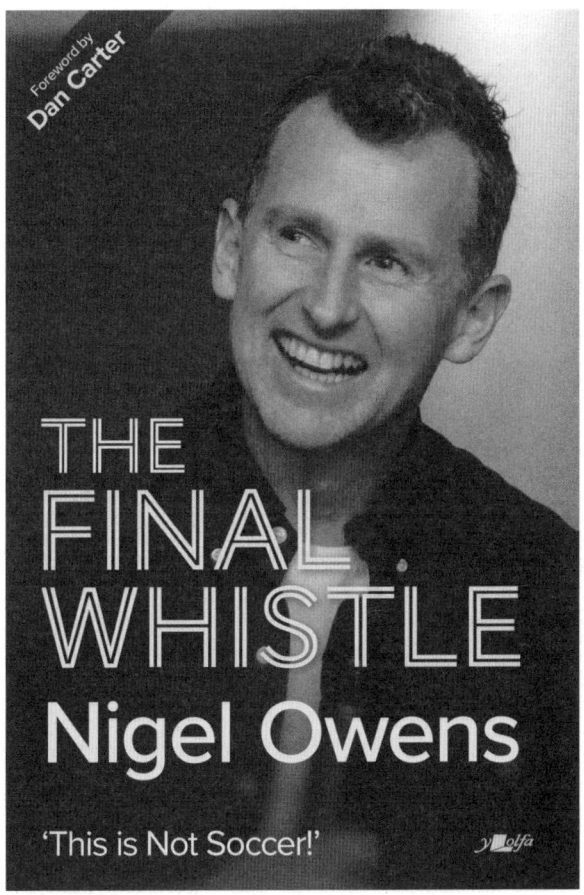

£20
(hardback)

Also from Y Lolfa:

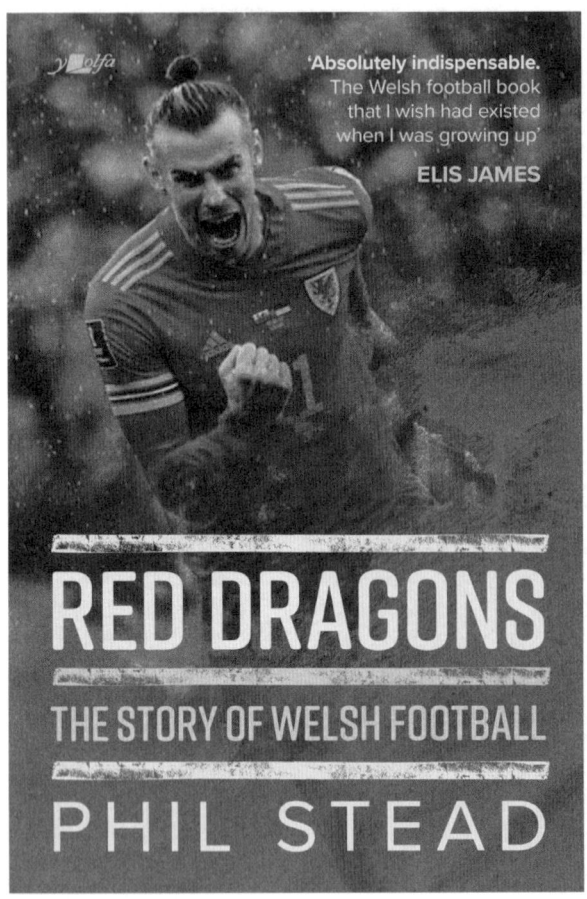

£14.99

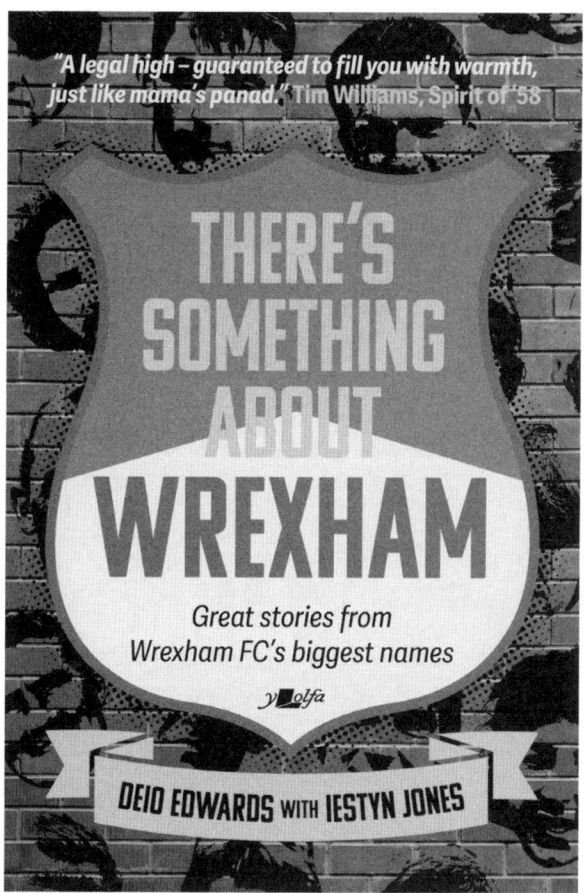

"A legal high – guaranteed to fill you with warmth, just like mama's panad." Tim Williams, Spirit of '58

THERE'S SOMETHING ABOUT WREXHAM

Great stories from
Wrexham FC's biggest names

y olfa

DEIO EDWARDS WITH IESTYN JONES

£12.99